Teaching

MODERN FOREIGN LANGUAGES

A **Handbook** FOR TEACHERS

Carol MORGAN and Peter NEIL

KOGAN PAGE

First published 2001

Apart from any fair dealing for the purposes of research or private study, or criticism or review, as permitted under the Copyright, Designs and Patents Act 1988, this publication may only be reproduced, stored or transmitted, in any form or by any means, with the prior permission in writing of the publishers, or in the case of reprographic reproduction in accordance with the terms and licences issued by the CLA. Enquiries concerning reproduction outside these terms should be sent to the publishers at the undermentioned address:

Kogan Page Limited
120 Pentonville Road
London N1 9JN
UK

Stylus Publishing Inc
22883 Quicksilver Drive
Sterling VA 20166-2012
USA

© Carol Morgan and Peter Neil, 2001

The right of Carol Morgan and Peter Neil and named contributors to be identified as the authors of this work has been asserted by them in accordance with the Copyright, Designs and Patents Act 1988.

British Library Cataloguing in Publication Data

A CIP record for this book is available from the British Library.

ISBN 0 7494 3347 7

Typeset by Saxon Graphics Ltd, Derby
Printed and bound in Great Britain by Bell & Bain Ltd, Glasgow

Contents

Series editor's foreword		v
Preface		vii
Acknowledgements		xi
1	Foreign language teaching past and present	1
2	The modern foreign languages curriculum	22
3	Planning and classroom management	43
4	Physical and human resources	64
5	Using information and communication technologies	85
6	Assessment	107
7	Equal opportunities and special needs	131
8	Using the target language	142
9	Learner strategies	150
10	Teaching foreign languages at primary level	159
11	Future subject developments in modern foreign languages	172
12	Personal and professional development	185
References		201
Index		211

The Kogan Page Teaching Series

Series Editor: Gill Nicholls

Learning to Teach, Gill Nicholls
Teaching Values and Citizenship, Richard Bailey
Teaching Modern Foreign Languages, Carol Morgan and Peter Neil
Teaching Science, Steve Alsop and Keith Hicks
Teaching Physical Education, Richard Bailey

Series editor's foreword

The teaching of Modern Foreign Languages is a key subject at school level, and an area of great debate at national and government level. The development, recruitment and retention of good modern foreign language teachers is ever more challenging, while successfully delivering the national curriculum for modern foreign languages is demanding on the individual teacher, requiring depth, breadth and diversity of knowledge and understanding.

Teachers entering the world of modern language education need to appreciate the complexities of teaching languages as well as understanding that the pupils they will teach will have a broad spectrum of ability and awareness of language based issues. Developing successfully as a teacher of modern foreign languages requires an acknowledgement and appreciation of these issues, in addition to the practical skills and personal direction that will assist in career development. This book aims to help teachers achieve all of these aims by giving authoritative guidance backed up by practical tasks and theoretical perspectives. These will help readers engage with ideas and concepts of modern foreign languages and language education across the curriculum.

Carol Morgan and Peter Neil have written a rich and valuable book that will help to develop an awareness of the broad academic, social, political and cultural contexts in which the challenges of teaching and learning about languages are addressed. The chapters reflect both pragmatic and theoretical issues that are of relevance to the delivery of the MFL national curriculum. All chapters have a commitment to providing a high quality learning experience and reflect not only on teaching in this subject area itself, but also on the learning outcomes from engaging with the concepts and issues related to languages education.

The key elements of this book are its combination of generic and specific teaching ideas, its wide ranging and expert perspective, its regard for the future and its coverage of the requirements of being a languages teacher today. These significant elements are presented to help experienced, newly qualified and trainee teachers alike. By addressing issues across phases, this book will be uniquely helpful for all teaching professionals.

Professor Gill Nicholls
King's College, University of London

Preface

The current climate for teachers of modern foreign languages (MFL) is a challenging one. Not only must trainees achieve standards set out in the circular 04/98 *Requirements for Courses of Initial Teacher Training* but there are considerable difficulties in schools and classrooms with a decline in popularity of MFL as a subject. On the other hand there are also new and exciting initiatives intended to support MFL.

Circular 04/98 provides clear categories and standards under which trainees have to demonstrate their abilities. These include:

- knowledge and understanding;
- planning, teaching and class management;
- monitoring, assessment, reporting and accountability;
- other professional requirements.

This book aims to guide trainees through each category – with help from their mentor. In each chapter or chapter section there are references to specific standards in 04/98 that should help with this guidance. In addition, tasks are set specifically to aid trainees' development.

There are three main strands in the book:

- guidance in dealing with current demands from the Teacher Training Agency (TTA), Department for Education and Employment (DfEE), the Qualifications and Curriculum Authority (QCA), and so forth;
- a practical focus on classroom teaching;
- a discussion of the wider context of MFL teaching, both in terms of the subject and of the teacher's own professional development.

Current research findings are discussed and related to classroom practice. Insights from the rest of Europe are included, both in terms of support available from different European bodies and new initiatives and developments taking place across Europe.

STRUCTURE OF THE BOOK

The twelve chapters in the book are grouped in sequence covering the following four key areas:

- the context of MFL teaching;
- the content of MFL teaching;
- key issues relating to MFL teaching
- future developments in MFL teaching.

The context

Chapters 1 and 2 describe the history of language teaching and the current situation in terms of both provision and curriculum. These chapters should help trainees to contextualize their experience in schools; to understand the constraints that are in place, to appreciate what may happen in other schools; and to recognize previous contexts that will have shaped and contributed to current situations.

The content

Chapters 3, 4, 5 and 6 focus on classroom practice – what trainees need to learn in terms of planning their lessons, managing classrooms, exploiting resources and assessing students following different programmes of study. Tasks set in these chapters should help to develop trainees' classroom expertise.

Key issues

Chapters 7, 8, 9 and 10 discuss key issues in MFL where there has been research, debate and controversy. These are:

- equal opportunities and special needs;
- the use of target language;
- learner strategies and grammar;
- teaching MFL at primary level.

Different perspectives are offered on all of these areas and trainees will need to consider their own stance on these issues in the light of their experience and pedagogical aims.

Future developments

Chapter 11 describes two key documents that are likely to have repercussions for MFL teaching in the future: the Nuffield Inquiry final report and the Council of Europe framework for teaching. A teaching methodology (CLIL) is also described that has become very popular in other European countries and that may develop further in the future in the UK. Chapter 12 considers the future professional development of the trainee.

The different facets of this book allow for different insights, although all focus on key developments and issues that need to be addressed in order to gain qualified teacher status (QTS). The book may thus be used as a whole, working through from start to finish, or as a reference resource that can be used according to the trainee's learning and development needs.

Acknowledgements

The authors would like to acknowledge the support and advice of those without whom the book would have been less well informed. Wendy Phipps, for permission to integrate her PGCE material on SEN; Isobel Moore for her invaluable advice and suggestions; and Jo Peach, Fiona Cameron and Claire Braham for their suggestions. Our thanks also go to Sally Williamson for her prompt and efficient secretarial support.

1 Foreign language teaching past and present

In the first two chapters an introduction is provided to the *context* of MFL teaching. This chapter introduces the history of different MFL teaching approaches and considers the current situation in terms of language provision, the current status of MFL as a subject and attitudes towards foreign language learning.

Objectives

By the end of this chapter the trainee should have an understanding of:

- the history of different teaching approaches;
- the history and current state of diversification;
- the current government requirements for teachers;
- the current status of MFL.

The history of different MFL teaching approaches

The aim of this section is to present the context of teaching modern foreign languages in terms of teaching methods, choice of language, current attitudes and new institutional opportunities, all of which will affect the situation in the classroom. It is important for a teacher of any subject to know the background to current teaching methods. The teacher of modern languages needs to understand the place of the subject within the curriculum and to be aware of specific initiatives.

Since the introduction of modern foreign languages into the school curriculum, the subject has undergone several changes in aim and emphasis. Over the decades methods were introduced that were designed to equip learners with the perceived skills and proficiency required for the time. In the following paragraphs, some of the methods are described and critiqued. A more detailed critique of each of the methods can be found in the works of Richards and Rodgers (1986), Stern (1992), Brown (1994), Rowlinson (1994) and Mitchell and Myles (1998).

Grammar/translation method

The grammar/translation method was reminiscent of classical education in Latin and Greek from which modern language teaching in schools emerged; this was the prevalent method in language teaching from the end of the 19th century until the end of the 1940s, according to Richards and Rodgers (1986). They list the following as the principal characteristics of this method:

- the aim of learning a foreign language was to read the literature of the language or to develop the mind from the intellectual pursuit of studying a language;
- reading and writing were the main skills taught;
- vocabulary was based on the appearance of words in the texts read;
- lessons were based on translation exercises from the text;
- accuracy was paramount;
- grammar was taught deductively by presentation of the rules followed by practice;
- teaching of the foreign language was done through English. (From Richards and Rodgers, 1986: 3ff.)

This method was not based on any theory of language, however, and oral and aural skills were almost totally avoided. Towards the end of the 19th century this method was rejected in parts of Europe as the need for students of languages to be proficient orally became more marked, although assessment techniques over the years have used this model. The traditional advanced and ordinary level examinations included extensive translations in and out of the modern language.

Direct method

As a reaction against this neglect of oral performance a method was introduced known generally as the direct method (see Hawkins, 1987). Richards and Rodgers (1986: 9ff) list the following features of this method:

- lessons were entirely in the target language;
- vocabulary taught was based on relevant topics;
- vocabulary was taught by demonstration and visual elements;
- oral skills were built up systematically through question and answer sessions;
- grammar was taught inductively;
- oral and aural skills were emphasized.

Although there was extensive provision of foreign language by the teacher, the learner was not able to assimilate the language well (Guthrie, 1987). Furthermore, the method in general was not based on any sound theory of language or language learning. Many of today's technological aids were also not available.

Audio-lingual/visual methods

The audiolingual method that emerged during the 1960s and, with the development of technological aids, the audiovisual method that complemented it, were largely based on behaviourist learning theory. The behaviourist view of language prevalent in the 1950s and early 1960s regarded language learning as primarily a process of habit formation, in which the role of the linguistic environment or 'input' was all important. Language acquisition was thought to result from imitation so that the learner imitated structures modelled by the teacher. Feedback was designed to act as the reinforcer, which imprinted the desired language behaviour on the learner. The main barrier to effective assimilation of the target structures was presumed to be interference from the mother tongue. It was presumed that if the main areas of difference from the native language could be highlighted and practised, the problems would be eradicated.

The features of language lessons in the audio-lingual/visual method were:

- language structures were presented to students;
- students imitated structure;
- feedback was given in the form of the correct utterance spoken by the teacher;
- students repeated corrected utterance;
- structures were presented in hierarchy of difficulty.

This method of teaching resulted in many schools buying language laboratories, although later they were considered to be non-effective (Green, 1975). The main criticism of these methods was theoretical and concerned the nature of language. It was thought that language was more than imitation and habit formation and that the learner should have a creative role in the process. Another criticism was that drills taught only structured-language chunks and that learners who performed well in the language laboratory were incapable of flexible language use in a real-life situation. This kind of approach has been much enhanced by current advances in technology, which allow for use of video, interactive computers, the Internet and so forth. These are explored in greater detail in Chapter 5.

Communicative language teaching

Over a relatively long period, several factors emerged that changed ideas in language teaching. With the rise of the European Community and an increase in European awareness, improved travel, improved communications, developments in research into language and egalitarian principles affecting education in general, the climate was ripe for change. Das (1985) comments:

TEACHING MODERN FOREIGN LANGUAGES

> Communicative Language Teaching is perhaps the latest in a long succession of revolutions in language teaching: to its advocates, it represents a fundamental 'paradigm shift' – a radically new approach to the teaching-learning process. Communicative Language Teaching, it is claimed, involves the making of new and different assumptions about the two fundamental questions: what is learnt and how it is learnt. (Das, 1985: x)

Communicative language teaching was influenced by developments in linguistics, sociolinguistics, psycholinguistics and syllabus design. The following diagram illustrates how communicative language teaching incorporates all elements:

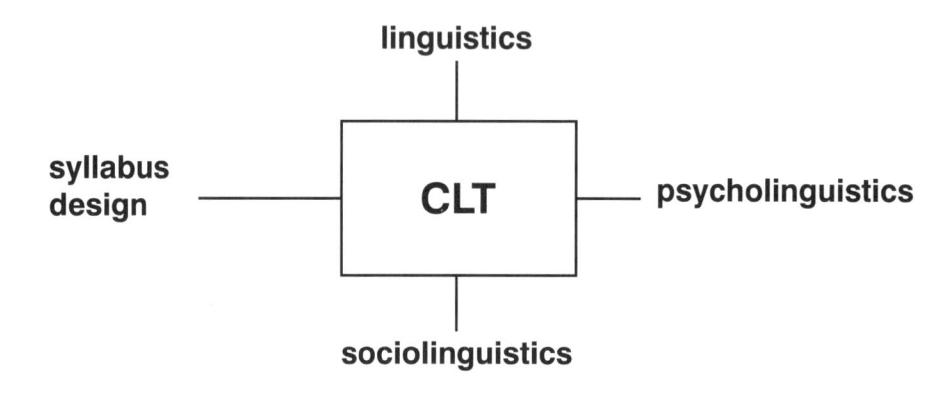

Figure 1.1 Communicative language teaching

Developments in linguistics

In the late 1950s a revolution took place in the area of linguistics with the work of Chomsky, who introduced the notions of 'competence' and 'performance' (Chomsky, 1957). The former describes the native speaker's implicit knowledge of the grammatical system of his/her language. Performance, on the other hand, is language use. When learners perform, they may make errors because of memory lapses or because they are nervous. They may therefore not be able to demonstrate their underlying competence. Chomsky believed that children acquire the rules of a language using an innate *language acquisition device* (LAD). His idea was that children already possessed this programming device and therefore learnt their mother tongue automatically. Chomsky's ideas were the basis of Krashen's theory, which is dealt with in the section on psycholinguistics.

Sociolinguistic developments

Sociolinguistics also developed theories that were to have wide-ranging effects on the way languages were taught. Chomsky's definition of 'competence' was seen as failing to take into account the sociocultural dimension and the difference between speakers. Hymes (1972) introduced the notion of 'communicative competence', which, in addition to referring to the knowledge of the grammatical system, included a sociolinguistic dimension that relates to the knowledge of the rules of language use. The idea of communicative competence was developed further by Canale and Swain (1980) and later by Canale (1983) who defined four interconnected components of communicative competence: grammatical competence, discourse competence, sociolinguistic competence and strategic competence:

- *Grammatical competence* indicated knowledge of language rules governing vocabulary, spelling and grammar in general.
- *Discourse competence* indicated knowing how to put together forms and meaning in a spoken or written text.
- *Sociolinguistic competence* indicated knowing the appropriateness of language both in terms of meaning and form in the relevant social context.
- *Strategic competence* indicated knowing how to use verbal or non-verbal strategies either to compensate for breakdowns in communication or to enhance communication. (Canale, 1983: 7ff.)

Psycholinguistic developments

The main theorist of importance was Krashen with his monitor theory or input hypothesis. Krashen's theories have been widely criticized (for example see Brumfit, 1983; Gregg, 1984, 1986; McLaughlin, 1987) but nevertheless, his influence on communicative language teaching has been very significant. His five main ideas related to 'acquisition'/'learning', the natural order, the monitor, the affective filter and the input hypothesis.

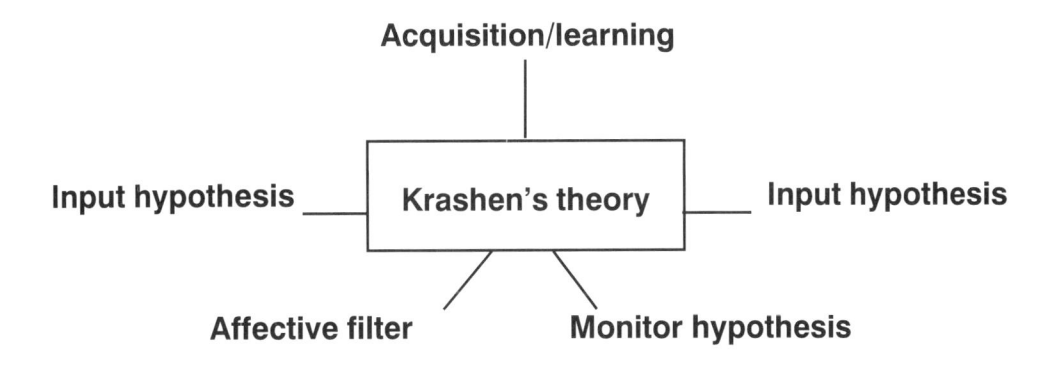

Figure 1.2 Krashen's Input Hypothesis

Krashen made an important distinction between 'acquisition' and 'learning'. 'Acquisition' was like the subconscious process by which children acquire their mother tongue, whereby learners internalize incoming data and generate the rules of the foreign language by means of a device. It was similar to Chomsky's LAD. 'Learning', on the other hand, was the construction of conscious knowledge of a language. Krashen's now much-disputed claim was that conscious learning prevented natural acquisition. He thought that learning policed acquisition by using what was termed a 'monitor', bringing about changes in utterances, either written or spoken, before or after performance. In order for the monitor to operate you need:

- sufficient time in order to think about the rules;
- focus on form and thinking about correctness;
- knowledge of the rule. (Krashen, 1982: 16)

Krashen also believed in a natural order in which second language acquisition takes place and he based this on research into first language acquisition.

One of the main reasons, according to Krashen, for the variation in performance of learners is what he called the 'affective filter'. He believed it was necessary to create a learning environment that is comfortable (he called this 'lowering the affective filter'). Thus students should not be corrected when errors are made.

Krashen's input hypothesis claims that in order for 'acquisition' to take place, learners have to be exposed to 'comprehensible input'. This input should be gauged at just above the learners' present state of competence, what Krashen called (i + 1) where i represents the learner's competence at that time.

Developments in syllabus design

The desire for a more communicative approach to language teaching led to developments in syllabus design. Traditional language syllabuses had followed a grammar-based framework, graded according to difficulty and frequency of language used, where learners progressed in a systematic fashion through the structures that were practised, with limited, often obscure vocabulary used to illustrate the individual grammar points.

Since the mid-1970s many different syllabuses emerged (functional, notional, interactional, situational, topic-based, for example) – see Wilkins (1974a, 1974b, 1976) and Yalden (1983). Particularly relevant is the work of the Council of Europe. In the early 1970s the Council of Europe set up a committee to produce a syllabus appropriate for adult language learners, the result of which was the unit/credit scheme for adult learners. This was followed by Van Ek who drew up a 'threshold' level, which described language according to functions (for example asking, negotiating), notions (for example space, quantity) and topic-related behaviour divided into specific settings.

At about the same time as the Council of Europe initiatives the graded objectives (GOML) movement in the UK became popular (Downes, 1978). This specified language according to lists of functions and notions and expressed objectives in behavioural terms with a 'situational' syllabus. The graded objectives approach has been criticized because topic-based syllabuses are not based on grammatical progression and students will simply learn set phrases and not progress in their learning of the language. Current GCSE syllabuses are loosely based on functional/notional aspects of language, which hark back to these two initiatives.

Communicative language teaching in the classroom

So what is communicative language teaching and how is it manifested in the classroom? Communicative language teaching has moved on from the early days when there appeared to be an overemphasis on oral communication to the exclusion of the other skills. There was a time also when teachers were told not to correct errors in case they undermined learners' confidence and where there was an emphasis on fluency at the expense of accuracy.

The main developments that have taken place within the communicative classroom can be summarized as follows:

- an increase in the amount of foreign language in the classroom;
- the introduction of functions in addition to grammar, vocabulary and situations;
- a move beyond coursebooks towards the use of authentic texts;
- a variety of learning strategies to supplement whole-class teaching;
- information-exchange activities and games. (Johnstone, 1988: 12)

The main practical aspects of teaching language according to a communicative approach have been condensed into a 10-point summary by the Centre for Information on Language Teaching and Research (CILT):

- there should be a purposeful use of language;
- these should be an information gap (related to purposeful use of language);
- pupil ownership of the language; it should be personalized for them;
- there should be more emphasis on dealing with the unexpected;
- tasks and activities should be genuine and more motivating;
- the target language should be used as the main medium of instruction;
- there should be an emphasis on positive marking;
- the language used should be authentic, with authentic materials used from the target culture;
- the distinction between spoken and written language should be made clear and the distinction between registers should be taught;
- there should be a distinction made between practice and real language and pupils should be encouraged to move to the real language phase. (Adapted from CILT, 1985.)

It should be emphasized that grammar now plays more of a part in communicative language teaching as can be seen in Chapter 6 where particular syllabuses are discussed. One of the major challenges for teachers of modern languages is this final point, the moving away from language that is used for practice to the real-life situation in which real language is required. Learners will need to have confidence in using language in a controlled situation before they are able to transfer their learning to a real-life situation. Littlewood (1981) divides classroom activities into pre-communicative and communicative activities. Pre-communicative activities are those that focus on the linguistic structures or vocabulary items but where students are not required to use them for a genuine communicative purpose (activities here might be drills or question-and-answer sessions). Communicative activities, on the other hand, require learners to put into use the structures and vocabulary they have been practising for communication. In the foreign language classroom it can be difficult to create a genuine communicative situation and sometimes the activities can remain at a pre-communicative stage. It is, therefore, important to think of ways of making activities that are genuinely communicative.

Autonomous language learning

At around the same time as the introduction of the communicative approach to language teaching, there was emerging a movement towards autonomous language learning, defined by Holec (1981) as 'the ability to take charge of one's learning' (p 3). This entails a change from a focus on teaching to a focus on learning: the roles of the teacher and the learner are different from the traditionally held notions that the teacher is the one who holds the information and the learner the one who needs to be taught. Autonomous learning requires the learner to set the objectives, to define the content, to select the methods and to evaluate their progress (Holec, 1981). It requires the following changes to be made to the role of the teacher, who will:

- focus on learning rather than teaching;
- be engaged in the learner's learning process;
- be open to learners' ideas and suggestions;
- support learners' initiatives;
- initiate or encourage further activities;
- observe and analyse learning behaviour for later evaluation with learners;
- map out working methods and ways of evaluating progress in collaboration with the learners;
- be a consultant as well as a participant and a co-learner in the learning process. (Dam, 1995: 5)

This change in orientation for the teacher means that the learner:

- focuses on the learning process;
- takes responsibility for his/her learning;
- develops strategies to learn how to learn;
- can use resources independently;
- regards the teacher as a resource rather than the fount of all knowledge;
- evaluates progress and seeks to progress.

Such a change of emphasis complements the communicative language teaching objectives and enables learners to identify their language needs and to develop strategies to meet these needs.

Eclecticism

There is still no one way or one method which is 'the right and only way to teach languages' and one cannot be dogmatic about what should and should not be done. It is important, therefore, that practising teachers develop an eclectic approach to their teaching and use techniques and strategies which:

- take account of their own teaching style and personality;
- acknowledge that learners have different learning styles;

- motivate learners;
- incorporate variety;
- encourage progression.

Above all teachers should continue to examine their practice critically, be flexible, keep up to date with developments based on research into learning and teaching and remember: 'if it works, use it'.

> **Task 1.1**
> Consider how you learned a modern language. Which skills were emphasized? Can you identify which methods were used?

Diversification

This section presents the research evidence for and against the offering of languages other than French in the school curriculum.

Which language?

The National Curriculum (DfEE/QCA, 1999) states that schools must offer one or more of the official working languages of the European Union. Schools therefore have no obligation to continue offering French, which has been the main modern foreign language offered in secondary schools.

Background to diversification

Before the introduction of the National Curriculum, in the 1980s, there was a move towards the introduction of teaching languages other than French as a first foreign language. The term 'diversification' has become synonymous with the offering of languages other than French to children in their first year of post-primary education. For an overview of the history of diversification, see Phillips and Filmer-Sankey (1993) and Neil and Mallon (1998). This idea that French is not the only foreign language which could serve as the first language to learn is not new, however.

Reports since 1918 noted the value of studying languages other than French. Inspectors' reports had been indicating a need for diversification, as this policy became known, for some time. There are many reasons why languages other than French might be more appropriate as a first foreign language: many children would have holiday destinations such as Spain and Italy; industry might prefer German or Japanese; Italian would be regarded by some as an easier introduction to languages. Cases in favour of different languages are presented in the book *Which Language* by David Phillips (1989).

Since the 1980s several reports and studies have been carried out into the languages being offered in post-primary schools in all parts of the UK, the most influential of which was the group of OXPROD studies (Phillips, 1987; Clarke, 1989; Filmer-Sankey, 1989, 1991, 1993; Phillips and Filmer-Sankey, 1989, 1993). These identified the models of language provision offered in schools and highlighted a number of issues specific to the offering of languages other than French in year seven. Other projects have focused on aspects of diversification (Marshall, 1988; Calvert, 1989; Dickson and Lee, 1990; McCrory, 1990; Kenning, 1992, 1994; Neil, 1993; Chambers, 1995; McLagan, 1996; Neil and Mallon 1998; Neil *et al*, 1999).

Factors influencing choice of language

A number of factors might influence the language(s) offered as first foreign languages in schools:

- size of language department;
- language qualification of teachers;
- school timetable;
- languages taught in feeder primary schools (where languages are taught at KS2).

In a department where only one teacher is qualified in a language, problems are created should this teacher leave the school. In smaller departments it may not be possible to include languages other than French because no teacher is qualified in more than one language. In a recent survey of language departments in Northern Ireland, heads of department mentioned various reasons that they felt militated against the introduction of alternative languages (Neil *et al*, 1999). The main ones were:

- timetabling difficulties;
- tradition;
- difficulties for second modern language;
- lack of qualified staff;
- departmental preference;
- size of school;
- lack of funding;
- lack of resources;
- ability range of students;
- requirements of the curriculum.

Models of languages on offer

In schools where languages other than French are offered to students in year seven, or where they are offered in combination with French, one of a number of models of diversification will be in operation. The main ones are:

- *sole foreign language* – one foreign language is offered to all students in the year group;
- *wave model* – all students in a year-group do one language (the following year group does another language);
- *split provision* – 50 per cent of the year group take one language, 50 per cent take another;
- *dual provision* – all students do two languages (either for the whole year or one language for half the year);
- *modular provision* or *carousel model* – all students are given a sample of a variety of languages.

Advantages and disadvantages of the models

In both the sole and wave model there is no choice for students. In the wave model, the language offered depends on the year in which a child enters a school. On the other hand, both these models are easy to organize in terms of staff. Students who transfer into the school may be at a disadvantage, in the wave model, if they happen not to have learned the language on offer in the secondary school when they arrive.

In the split provision model the question of choice arises: who chooses the language? In some schools students are allocated randomly to classes, in others students and their parents are given the choice, but some would have no experience on which to base their choices. Where students are given choice, the problem of class size may arise; if 90 per cent of the year intake should choose one language and 10 per cent the other, the department would have problems offering the second language.

In both dual provision and the modular/carousel approaches, the question of depth of content arises. Particularly in schools where four languages are taught to year seven students, some have problems differentiating between languages and they become confused with the structures for the very basic topics studied.

The second modern language

There is an increasing unease amongst language teachers, principals of schools and inspectors that additional languages, and dual linguists, are becoming rarer (Dobson, 1998; Nuffield Foundation, 2000). This is having a knock-on effect in higher education, which, in turn, filters back into the system with far more teachers trained in a single language seeking employment in schools. The model offered varies from school to school; offering of additional languages may be:

- compulsory for all students;
- optional for all students;
- compulsory for high attainers;
- optional for high attainers;
- optional for students showing interest and enthusiasm.

Again it will depend on the staffing level of the department and on timetabling constraints. Pressure on the curriculum from other subject areas is also causing difficulty. Students who want to take both languages and sciences, for example, are being forced in some schools to have to choose an either/or option. In some departments the only way the second language is being kept alive is by the devotion of staff and students giving up free time after school.

The alternative second language is unique to Northern Ireland because the Northern Ireland Common Curriculum (DENI, 1992) makes provision for a change of language at the end of key stage three for students who had reached a plateau by that stage. As yet, this option has not been adopted by many schools in Northern Ireland (Neil *et al*, 1999).

Conclusion

The above sections have presented some of the issues relating to the offering of languages other than French to students in year seven and the implications this may have for the second modern language. The model of languages provided will depend on the school in which you are based, on school policies, language department, local environment etc. This chapter should have provided you with some awareness of the issues so that you may be in a position to make informed decisions about the languages offered.

Links to teaching standards

Under *Subject Knowledge and Understanding* trainees are asked to demonstrate that they are aware of and know how to access recent inspection evidence, classroom-relevant research, evidence on teaching secondary students in their specialist subject(s) and know how to use this to inform and improve their teaching. Understanding the history of diversification and the issues related to diversification should help trainees towards achieving this standard.

Government requirements

As a trainee teacher or as a newly qualified teacher (NQT), your development will have been measured against national standards. In Northern Ireland's integrated 'three "I"s' (initial teacher education, induction and in-service) beginning teachers (BT) are required to continue developing competences into the first three years of taking up post. This section sets out the criteria listed in the documentation published by the Department for Education and Employment (DfEE), the Teacher Training Agency (TTA) and the departments in Scotland (SEED) and Northern Ireland (DENI).

In order to obtain qualified teacher status in England, trainees must meet the National Standards set out in DfEE Circular 04/98 (DfEE, 1998). The standards are set out in four broad areas:

A. Knowledge and understanding.
B. Planning, teaching and class management.
C. Monitoring, assessment, recording, reporting and accountability.
D. Other professional requirements.

A – knowledge and understanding

Under this heading, the standards relate to the trainee's knowledge of the specialist subjects that he or she wants to teach, the knowledge of the structure of qualification routes, including vocational qualifications, the knowledge of the curricular requirements for the subject at key stages three and four and post-16 and a knowledge of key skills as they can be incorporated into subject teaching. The standards also relate to more generic issues, such as a knowledge of the programme of study for ICT in subject teaching and health and safety aspects where appropriate. One of the standards requires trainees to be confident in accessing and using evidence from inspection documentation and current research.

B – planning, teaching and class management

In these areas the trainee must be able to plan lessons to ensure that learning takes place, that progression is achieved and that all students' needs are catered for. This incorporates differentiation, a knowledge of special educational needs, the use of variety of task, skill and classroom management strategies. Trainees need to have a good working knowledge of resources, including ICT, and to be able to use them effectively in their teaching. In short, this section details all the requirements of good lesson planning and delivery.

C – monitoring, assessment, recording, reporting and accountability

This section relates to all aspects of evaluating lesson success and student progression. It involves setting of tasks, assessing student performance, providing feedback, reporting performance and using the results to inform future lesson planning. Being able to meet these requirements demands a knowledge of the documentation relating to the assessment procedures, such as the Programme of Study, the GCSE and other syllabuses and any other related documents published by the DfEE.

D – other professional requirements

This final section of standards requires trainees to have a knowledge of the statutory documents on race relations, sex discrimination, health and safety at work, appropriate physical contact and restraint of students and detention.

In addition there are standards that relate to professional conduct within the school context and ongoing professional development on completion of induction. It also requires teachers to be concerned with pastoral issues and to be aware of the need for liaison with external agencies for the welfare of students.

Full details of these standards can be found at the Web site of the DfEE (www.dfee.gov.uk). At the end of most of the sections in the different chapters in this book, we have linked the section content to particular standards.

In Northern Ireland, where teacher education is a competence-based model, teachers must have attained an acceptable standard in the competence areas, which are also listed in five broad headings:

- Understanding the curriculum, and professional knowledge.
- Subject knowledge and subject application.
- Teaching strategies and techniques and classroom management.
- Assessment and recording of students' progress.
- Foundation for further professional development.

These competences mirror very closely the standards set out above. The full list of competences listed under these headings is printed in the *Teacher Education Handbook*, published by the Department of Education (DENI, 1998) and can also be found at its Web sites (www.deni.gov.uk; www.nine.org.uk).

In Scotland, teacher education is governed by regulations for partnership set down by the General Teaching Council (GTC, 1997) and the courses are competence based. Trainees in Scottish institutions are required to acquire competences under the following headings:

1. Subject and content of teaching.
2.1. Communication and approaches to teaching and learning.
2.2. Class organization and management.
2.3 Assessment.
3. The school and the education system.
4. The values, attributes and abilities integral to professionalism.

The full list of competences and the guidelines for ITE (Initial Teacher Education) in Scotland can be found at the Web site of the Scottish Office: www.scotland.gov.uk/documents.

The other main difference in the courses in the different parts of the UK relates to the time spent in schools. All PGCE courses are of 36 weeks duration, 24 of which, in England and Northern Ireland, must be spent in the school context; in Scotland 18 weeks are spent in schools. All courses are run in partnership with schools.

Trainees will, of course, be working with the documents containing the standards and competences as they will be judged against the indicators at the end of the training year and into the professional development years. In addition to these standards, trainees are required to meet criteria on ICT (Information and Communication Technology) in subject teaching. Details of these requirements will be set out in Chapter 5.

At the end of the training year, newly qualified teachers will complete a Career Entry Profile, which will contain details of progress on the various standards. This document will accompany the new teacher into the second phase of professional development, induction. The CEP may be written by the subject tutor but in negotiation with the student teacher. The evidence for the CEP will be lesson observations from school, reports from the mentor and self-evaluation from the student. Areas in which the trainee has little or no experience can be remedied during the next phase. Aspects such as pastoral care or assessment, which may not have been major features during the school experience part of the course, can be highlighted as areas of priority in the induction year.

Conclusion

The regulations for the curriculum and those for initial teacher education form the backbone of the training year. Much time will be spent during the PGCE year familiarizing you with the relevant documentation so that by the end of your training you will be able to situate your teaching and your own professional development in the context of the regulations set out by the various departments of education and the Teacher Training Agency.

The current status of MFL

Two conflicting modern foreign language scenarios seem to be in place. On the one hand positive initiatives by the government are evident (for example, support for primary initiatives and expansion of the language college programme) plus an independent national enquiry into languages (the Nuffield Inquiry) and individual initiatives at the school level.

On the other hand there is a large body of evidence to confirm a rapidly deteriorating situation for foreign languages (low uptake at all levels and negative attitudes). It will be useful here to consider the situation on both a macro institutional and policy level and also on the micro level of the classroom, teacher and pupil.

The positive indicators

On an institutional level and governmental level there have been several initiatives in England to support languages. The most notable of these is the 'Language College Initiative', launched in 1993, following on from the setting up of Community Technology Colleges. To date, this initiative has resulted in 99 colleges with a wide range of languages and enhanced multi-media provision and other resources. There is clearly also support for primary initiatives with the launch of Government initiatives to study feasibility and to provide materials and models of good practice (discussed more fully in Chapter 10). Another government incentive to encourage contact has been Dialogue 2000, funding month-long visits to France.

In the 1999 National Curriculum documentation a positive gloss on foreign languages is also presented (pp 14–15) with a stress on the importance of languages, and quotations from celebrities reaffirming the usefulness of foreign language learning. In terms of institutional support it is encouraging that the Nuffield Foundation funded an enquiry into the future foreign language needs of the UK (the Nuffield Languages Inquiry 1998–2000). The Centre for Information on Language Teaching and Research and its partner bodies in Scotland, Northern Ireland and Wales also offer excellent support and facilities to language teachers with their centres and conferences (explored in more detail in Chapter 12).

Other institutional initiatives include a thriving language-teaching network in the shape of the Association for Language Learning, which runs a large-scale annual conference and many local seminars and workshops; and guidance from the School Curriculum and Assessment Authority (SCAA) and its successor the Qualifications and Curriculum

Authority (QCA) in such documents as *Keeping the Curriculum under Review* (1997) and *KS4 Curriculum in Action* (1998). The ASDAN (Award Scheme Development and Accreditation Network) *International Challenge Award* scheme with accreditation for European projects also encourages inter-European activity (Neumark, 1997). The Languages National Training Organization (LNTO) was accredited in April 1998 to promote vocational aspects of language. The Subject Centre for Languages, Linguistics and Area Studies has been established at the University of Southampton to disseminate information on MFL (particularly in the area of higher education). The year 2001 has been designated European Year of Languages and various initiatives for this have been organized by the Centre for Information on Language Teaching and Research (CILT).

At the school level there has been a revolution in teaching methodology with students now able to express themselves orally much more fluently than before and with new textbooks and technologies providing a dynamic environment. There is also research evidence that students in Britain 'learn as fast if not faster than learners elsewhere' (Milton and Meara, 1998). Recent research for QCA (Morgan and Freedman, 1999) has shown that there is good provision of languages at key stages three and four and that several schools have set up internal school initiatives to promote languages which have been successful.

Evidence of exciting and interesting initiatives in modern foreign language training also comes from reports in various publications from CILT (*Links, CILT Information Bulletins, Comenius News, Pathfinders* etc.); from articles in *The Times Educational Supplement* and in the *Language Learning Journal* and its subsidiary publications; and from information from many other publications and informal contacts. Initiatives in modern foreign language teaching include videoconferencing; Internet connections; letters to French officials; interviews with foreign footballers; games for children with special educational needs; poetry competitions; storytelling; 'language and industry' days; 'shoe box' projects; learning through raps and representation at the European Youth Parliament. All these examples provide evidence of high commitment from teachers and high levels of enthusiasm from pupils. In an article based on research into year 10 student attitudes to the German language and culture, Thornton and Cajkler were able to report that 'attitudes ... were generally positive' (1996: 38). Research by Lee *et al* (1998) also identified positive pupil attitudes.

Another area of success that has been identified by the Nuffield Languages Inquiry is that of Welsh medium schools, showing that negative attitudes can be turned around by an ambitious and energetic language policy (Nuffield Foundation, 2000, 34–35).

On a European scale pupils and students may take advantage of Brussels-funded schemes including: the SOCRATES programme, in particular the COMENIUS (school) and LINGUA (language) actions; and the LEONARDO programme, which is more vocationally focused. Many pupils and teachers take advantage of the funding offered in these ways. The Central Bureau mediates this funding process and in addition offers its own service of organizing exchanges.

In sum, then, there are many activities and situations in the field of modern foreign language teaching and learning that present an extremely positive profile, both in terms of what happens in the classroom and in what is made available on an institutional level both in this country and Europe-wide.

The negative indicators

The downside of the modern foreign language scene, however, seems equally powerful. Research by Stables and Wikeley on students' perceptions of subject option choices (involving a questionnaire survey of 1600 year nine students, 127 year nine student interviews and 110 year 10 student interviews) revealed a low level of popularity for modern foreign languages. Interview data in particular showed that not only were foreign languages unpopular but also that they were seen as unimportant, with just 7 per cent of respondents placing a modern foreign language among the top three subjects for importance in year 10 (Stables and Wikeley, 1999). Liking for French and German amongst 13/14 year olds was placed in equal bottom place for both boys and girls.

In terms of subject take-up, the General Certificate of Secondary Education (GCSE) results for 1998 did show that overall numbers had increased from 1997, reflecting the statutory required take-up (328,299 to 335,698 for French; 132,615 to 133,638 for German and 43,826 to 47,269 for Spanish). However, reports from OFSTED inspectors have indicated that the numbers of *dual linguists* have been dropping steadily (from 12 per cent to an estimated 5 per cent). Data from *The Times Educational Supplement* TES/CILT survey in 1996, based on 1140 questionnaire responses, also indicated that although 34.2 per cent of secondary schools had made two foreign languages compulsory at some stage, in only 6.4 per cent of these schools did more than half the students go on to sit GCSE examinations in two languages. Nearly all of these students came from independent or grant-maintained secondary schools (O'Malley, 1996a). The TES/CILT survey results also showed that key stage three programmes did not include extensive dual language provision, with 54.7 per cent of schools offering French only, 30 per cent offering French and German and 8.2 per cent offering French and Spanish.

The low number of dual linguists at GCSE level was also confirmed by the 1999 QCA research. Out of the 229 institutions giving data for GCSE students only four had sizeable numbers of dual linguists, two schools already being language colleges and the other two being in the process of bidding for specialist college status.

General Certificate of Education (GCE) 'Advanced' level figures for 1998 also present a picture that is not encouraging. The lack of dual linguists at key stage four is clearly crucial in the poor take-up of two languages after the age of 16.

Milton and Meara's research comparing Greek, German and British foreign language learners show that at pre-16 level, British learners perform badly in comparison with the two other European countries. The UK learners' vocabulary knowledge is one-third to one-half of the foreign language knowledge of the other European learners and the GCSE syllabus much less demanding than the equivalent counterparts. This can be attributed to the reduced amount of time available to British learners because their actual rate of learning *is* comparable.

A picture of negative attitudes towards foreign cultures (and languages) can further be gleaned from statistics, which provide comparative European data. *Eurobarometer,* which collects information Europe-wide provides data, for example, on perceptions of national identity. In a 1996 survey of the 15 European Union countries, the UK scored second highest in terms of perceptions of national identity over European identity (60 per cent compared to 26 per cent of Luxembourg and 33 per cent for France). The picture overall then appears currently unfavourable for foreign languages, with low takeup of two languages and some discernible antipathy, although clearly in some areas there are positive and motivating activities also taking place.

Possible reasons

Three different zones of inference can be identified that contribute to the negative attitudes currently dogging foreign languages:

- the teaching/learning process;
- the school context;
- the national context.

The teaching/learning process

Currently, one of the most discussed aspects of teaching and learning is the disaffection and under-achievement amongst boys, and this gains a particularly sharp focus in the field of modern foreign languages because languages are often regarded as a 'girls' subject' (Graham 1997). Not surprisingly, then, there are several suggestions as to why boys might not warm to foreign languages. (The problems associated with boys are discussed at greater length in Chapter 7).

Another factor that is seen as important is the perception of foreign languages as 'difficult'. This was one of the three main student perceptions identified in Stables and Wikeley's research, the other two attributes given by students being 'not useful' and 'not enjoyable' (Stables and Wikeley, 1999). An interesting rider is added in their research report (p 30):

> While science and mathematics may also be considered difficult, the effort is deemed necessary because of the importance of the qualification ... (but) the difficulty ... with modern foreign languages ... is not offset in many cases by the belief that the effort is really worth-while.

'Difficulty' on its own may thus not be sufficient to result in antipathy.

A further factor that is identified in the Stables and Wikeley research is the potential problem of target language use in teaching, already noted above as problematic for some boys. In their view: 'the normal power differential between teacher and pupil may be exacerbated when communication is limited to a language in which the pupil (p 30) is a novice'. With the advent of target language assessment at key stage 4, many views have been advanced both for and against target language use (Chambers, 1991; Atkinson, 1993; Clarke, 1994 and Clark, 1998). This issue is explored further in Chapter 8.

The two other student perceptions ('lack of relevance' and 'lack of enjoyment') from the Stables and Wikeley research also provide food for thought. The 'lack of relevance' derived according to several interviewees in the research from students' views that they were unlikely to work in France and Germany. This view echoes Clark and Trafford's concern (1996) that students from less privileged backgrounds may find it hard to see much point in modern language learning. Stables and Wikeley also suggest that 'lack of enjoyment' of foreign languages may be the result of English being a dominant world language (see also Jones, 1998; King, 1998; Johnstone, 2000) but other factors identified elsewhere may also be contributory. Callaghan for example points to 'perhaps the biggest problem … that … topics are visited and revisited year after year' (1998: 6), a problem also identified by Clark and Trafford who highlighted the 'frustration about the repetitive nature of their [pupils'] learning experience' (1996: 43; see also Clark, 1998) and by Coyle (1999) who comments on the pedestrian and anodyne nature of topics.

An important factor identified by the Nuffield Languages Inquiry is that grades achieved in GCSE are lower for languages than for other subjects. At key stage three, lower achievement is partly due to the shorter period of time available to achieve different levels with no MFL at key stage two. Headteachers looking to boost their school's results may discriminate against languages (Nuffield Foundation, 2000).

The school context

Further reasons for disaffection at the school level may be the language background of teaching staff, and the integration of foreign languages into the school timetable. Information from two surveys has pointed to the difficulties schools are experiencing with catering for languages other than French. In a 1992 school staffing survey it was found that 13 per cent of German teaching was being conducted by staff with qualifications no higher than A-level, while for other languages such as Russian and Spanish the figure was 19 per cent (Passmore, 1995). The TES/CILT survey in 1996 identified a particularly large number of schools that were unable to find staff qualified in two or more languages. More than half of all schools looking for staff in the previous five years had encountered this problem, and in 70 per cent of cases the desired combination had been French and German (O'Malley, 1996a). The problem here not only has an immediate short-term effect on schools, limiting what can be made available to pupils, but there are equally damaging knock-on effects: in the medium term teacher trainers may be unable to find placements for those wishing to teach languages other than French (O'Malley, 1996b), and in the long term, as noted in the section on diversification above, the pupils from these schools will not be forming part of an available pool for teachers of these languages in the future (O'Malley, 1996b). The 1999 QCA research and the Nuffield Inquiry also both confirm concern over teacher supply.

One further reason for problems in accommodating more than one language within the curriculum may be timetable constraints. In comments from the TES/CILT survey reported in 1996, a headteacher of a large comprehensive suggested that 'it's not really an option to do languages at the expense of say, technology. It's a question of available curriculum time' (O'Malley, 1996a). If schools are large they may have more flexibility. They may then have the capacity to provide the 'smaller classes at KS3 and 4', 'more teachers of Spanish' and 'more teachers of German', which Marshall suggests in his research could result in better take-up at 'A-level' and beyond (Marshall, 2000: 67). Responses in the 1999 QCA research also pointed to the crippling effects of compulsory subjects for GCSE. Subsequent to this research the government has eased restrictions so that the previous effects of constraints may now be lifted with the possibility of more pupils opting for a second foreign language.

The national context

The two major influences in the school context, relating to teacher background and timetabling constraints, also relate to the national picture of nationwide trends in university options and to the stipulations of the National Curriculum, which apply to all schools. The profile of influences on a national scale can thus be seen to mirror on a wider canvas the trends that have already been identified at the micro level.

The lack of staff qualified in several languages can be linked to the decline of traditional 'pure' subjects in university course options and to the rise in vocational degree courses identified in the recent UCAS (Universities and Colleges Admissions Service) data in *A Statistical Bulletin of Subject Trends,* 1997, and also by the Nuffield Inquiry (2000). The higher level of dual language provision in independent schools, identified in the 1996 TES/CILT survey (O'Malley, 1996c) is sharpened by the further nationwide perspective that fee-paying schools outperform their state sector counterparts, producing 33.5 per cent at grade A compared to the national average of 16.8 per cent (Dean, 1998). Recent initiatives where state and independent schools work as partners can create a more collaborative environment (Johnston, 1998) but are unlikely to remove the significant differentials. It was noted earlier that the government diversification initiative was strongly supported by local education authority (LEA) advisers. The fall in LEA advisory support for language teaching on a national scale was identified in the TES/CILT survey as one of the reasons why schools were no longer able to diversify. In all of these cases, then, the broader national picture tends to exacerbate or reinforce the picture in schools.

One final dimension on a national scale that can be said to provide further negative reinforcement is the area of attitudes to foreign languages and cultures. This can be viewed at both a general and a particular level. It was noted earlier that attitudes in the UK reaffirm a national rather than a European identity. This can also be identified with stereotypical and dismissive portrayals of foreigners in the media, both in television and situation comedies (*'Allo, 'Allo*) and advertising (the Renault 'Clio' advertisements for example), and in xenophobic comments in the popular press (see Byram and Morgan, 1994); other Europeans may be seen as figures of fun or as threatening our national stability (articles in *The Sun*, November 1998, for example). Running alongside these negative attitudes there may also be a lack of explicit emphasis on the usefulness of foreign languages for career purposes. As Thomas indicates (1997:76), the language option in GNVQ (General National Vocational Qualifications) had only optional status and a minor servicing role. In an extra supplement entitled 'Business Links' in *The Times Educational Supplement* there was no mention at all of foreign languages (*TES*, 26 June, 1998; see also Clark, 1998 and King, 1998), and Blunkett (1999) in his mission statement on the National Curriculum also failed to mention MFL. These negative influences were also noted by the Nuffield Languages Inquiry (Nuffield Foundation, 2000).

Conclusion

For the trainee teacher, then, there may be some difficulties to be overcome in terms of negative attitudes towards foreign languages amongst some students. However, these problems have been recognized nationwide and initiatives are under way to promote a more positive profile – not least the 121 recommendations of the Nuffield Languages Inquiry, (Nuffield Foundation, 2000), and the government response in January 2001 suggesting that language colleges would spearhead new developments and that they would work closely with the LNTO.

Task 1.2

Talk with your mentor about the initiatives in your school for promoting foreign languages.

Links to teaching standards

Under *subject knowledge and understanding*, trainees are asked to 'demonstrate that they … are aware of and know how to access recent inspection evidence and classroom-relevant research evidence on teaching secondary pupils in their specialist subject(s) and know how to use this to inform and improve their teaching' and also to 'demonstrate that they understand how pupils' learning is affected by their physical, intellectual, emotional and social development'.

A deeper understanding of the context in which foreign language learning takes place should help to contribute towards these standards.

2 The modern foreign languages curriculum

The aim of this second chapter on *context* is to introduce the trainee to both statutory and recommended aspects of the National Curriculum. Teachers need to be aware of both those elements, which will be assessed at GCSE, and also of the dimensions of the curriculum that are considered to contribute to pupils' learning.

Objectives

By the end of the chapter the trainee will have an understanding of:

- the aims and objectives of the National Curriculum;
- required standards from different government agencies;
- teaching cultural awareness;
- incorporating creativity;
- incorporating literacy and numeracy and other key and cross-curricular skills.

The current National Curriculum

In the previous chapter the history of modern language teaching was outlined and the issue of diversification discussed. The current context of language teaching is changing as we write. From the time when the National Curriculum was introduced (DES/WO, 1990), it was compulsory for all students, including those with special needs, up to the age of 16 to study a modern language. It was also compulsory for all students to be entered for a qualification in the language. The introduction of GCSE was intended to provide some qualification for all students. It became quite clear, however, that even the most basic tasks were beyond the capability of some students. Other courses were introduced such as the Certificate in

Modern Language Competence by the Welsh Examination Authority (WJEC), which catered for those at the lower attainment end. Short courses, which were in content half a GCSE, were introduced by most examination boards in England and Wales; these however were not easier but required students to cover the same content in a shorter time. With the review of the curriculum in 2000 (DfEE, 2000), the term 'disapplication' was introduced, which in effect overturned the policy of languages for all. Schools can now exempt a student from a course of study, including modern languages, if they can present a case that they will be involved in other aspects of the curriculum. Anecdotal evidence would suggest that the main subjects affected by this change in policy are almost exclusively modern languages.

Some teachers have been questioning the value of forcing students to continue with language study far beyond their ability and interest and perhaps now will welcome this development. By contrast, the publication of the Nuffield Inquiry (Nuffield Foundation, 2000) and the realization that our country still lags far behind our European counterparts in relation to proficiency in languages, suggests that there is an even greater need for languages to be taught as part of the compulsory curriculum.

Scotland, by contrast, introduced an innovative policy of languages in primary school and since 1989 there has been a programme of development of languages at primary level. Nevertheless a recent research report suggests that languages in the upper stages of post-primary schools are in crisis; drop-out rates seem to suggest that early introduction to a language does not lead to more students opting for languages at the Scottish 'Higher' level (McPake *et al*, 1999).

The following section gives details of the Programme of Study for Modern Foreign Languages as part of the National Curriculum.

The National Curriculum

In 1990 the government introduced what has become known as the National Curriculum (DES/WO, 1990) for students at key stages one, two, three and four; these represented the stages for the age groups 7, 11, 14 and 16. The curriculum in other parts of the UK is governed by similar documents; for example the Northern Ireland or Common curriculum was introduced in 1992 (DENI, 1992) and in Scotland the 5–14 Guidelines in 1991 (SOED, 1991). Although not identical in content, these documents sought to provide a framework for the teaching of modern foreign languages across the country.

In 1999 the curriculum for England was revised and a new programme of study produced. References in this chapter will be to that document (DfEE/QCA, 1999), which can be found at the following Web site www.nc.uk.net. Unlike other subjects on the curriculum, statutory MFL guidelines exist for key stages three and four only, although this revised document presents some non-statutory advice on including languages at KS 2.

There are two main parts to the National Curriculum document for modern foreign languages: the programme of study (PoS) and attainment targets (ATs) with level descriptors. The PoS defines the content and the ATs define the assessment.

The programme of study

The revised programme of study presents the content, skills and processes that should be taught in MFL. It is set out under two subheadings: 'knowledge, skills and understanding' and 'breadth of study'.

In the first section, the general aims of language learning are listed – that students should be taught the relationship of sounds and writing in the target language (TL), grammar and how to express themselves using a range of vocabulary and structures.

It then lists the specific skills, strategies and techniques with which students should become familiar in the course of their language learning. These are subdivided into language skills, language-learning skills and cultural awareness.

Language skills include:

- listening for gist and for detail;
- pronunciation;
- responding to questions;
- initiating and developing conversations;
- adapting the language to context and audience;
- dealing with the unpredictable;
- reading strategies such as skimming and scanning;
- summarizing, note taking;
- redrafting work, including using ICT.

In addition to these skills, the students should be given practice in language learning skills, including:

- memorizing;
- interpreting meaning;
- using knowledge of English in learning the TL;
- using reference material;
- developing independence in learning and using the TL.

Fleming and Walls (1998) note that the division between these two groups of skills is rather arbitrary and they do not conform to the distinction between metacognitive and cognitive skills made by O'Malley *et al* (1985).

In order to develop a cultural awareness, the students should be given access to authentic texts, including ICT materials, and to native speakers. They should compare and contrast their own culture with that of the target country.

The section on breadth of study indicates how students should be taught knowledge, skills and understanding, namely by:

- communicating in pairs, groups and with the teacher;
- using everyday classroom events as opportunities for spontaneous speech;
- discussing personal feelings and opinions;
- producing and responding to different types of spoken and written language;

- using a range of resources;
- using the TL creatively and imaginatively and for real purposes;
- using the five areas of experience.

When planning in the longer term it is necessary to ensure that students are given access to the full range of learning experiences throughout the key stages, although it is not necessary that every lesson or every unit of work covers every aspect.

The five areas of experience for learning are:

- everyday activities;
- personal and social life;
- the world around us;
- the world of work;
- the international world.

These contexts should form the basis of the schemes of work for both key stages. Key stage three represents the first three years of the post-primary sector (years seven to nine) and KS4 are the two years leading up to GCSE (years 10 and 11). The difference between key stages three and four is, however, that there should be progression in terms of the language to which the learners are exposed and the range of contexts in which the language is used. In terms of the learner, they should be producing more complex utterances, using a wider range of vocabulary and structure and should be more independent in producing creative sentences. There should also be greater accuracy in pronunciation and in written language.

In addition to the skills required of language learning in particular, there are other aspects to which students need to be given access through the language learning classes, namely the permeating elements that are common to all subjects across the National Curriculum. These fall under three headings:

- spiritual, moral, social and cultural development;
- key skills (communication, application of number, IT, working with others, improving own learning and performance and problem solving);
- other aspects of the curriculum (thinking skills, financial capability and work-related learning).

Some of these elements will be more easily integrated into lessons than others but modern languages can contribute to many of the strands of the curriculum such as communication, interpersonal collaboration, problem solving and information technology. The integration of the key skills is discussed later in this chapter.

Attainment targets

At the end of the programme of study, each subject in the National Curriculum is divided into so-called attainment targets, which represent the areas in which students will require to perform throughout and at the end of the key stage. In modern foreign languages there are four ATs, as follows:

- listening and responding (AT1);
- speaking (AT2);
- reading and responding (AT3);
- writing (AT4).

The terms used throughout the National Curriculum are designed to ensure that there is consistency across subject areas. For modern languages it would probably be more accurate to refer to the attainment targets as skills because they are not actually 'attained'. Although the ATs are presented as discrete skill areas, the teaching should be multi-skill, which is indicated by the addition of 'responding' to ATs 1 and 3. A listening passage, for example, may require students to write a letter in the TL (AT4) or to prepare an oral response (AT2). The writing of an article (AT4) may require prior reading of information (AT3). The skill areas are still assessed separately.

Each of the four ATs is graded according to eight level descriptors. Since modern languages are not statutory at KS2, the lower levels (1–3) should be attainable fairly rapidly so that students will perform as well as in other subjects that have been studied at earlier key stages, although experience and perceptions in schools suggest that MFL is a subject where levels are lower (Morgan and Freedman, 1999). At the lower levels, for example levels one to three, the same words are used to describe the language which features in all four ATs, such as 'simple', 'short', 'familiar', and 'modified' language. As the levels progress, there is increase in length of text, less modification of texts, increase in the type of tasks and cognitive demands on the learner and less support provided; more accuracy in terms of pronunciation, intonation and language use is also expected as the learners progress through the levels. From level four they are expected to have an increasing awareness of the grammar of the language and at level six (AT4) they are expected to apply grammar in new contexts. At the highest levels the students are expected to respond to unfamiliar texts from unadapted authentic sources and are expected to recognize different registers of language. They should be able to recognize the attitude of writers/speakers of the language and respond at a high level to unpredicted language. Above level eight there is one further level, 'exceptional performance', which caters for students who perform at an outstanding level at the end of KS3.

An average learner of a language might be expected to have the following profile:

- year seven – levels one to three;
- year eight – levels four to five;
- year nine – levels five to seven.

It must be emphasized, however, that learners develop at different rates and some might not get beyond levels 2 or 3. It is also possible that some learners may perform better in some ATs than in others and it is quite possible that someone could attain level five for speaking but only level two for writing. The integrated skills approach to teaching, however, will ensure that learners are not given exposure to only one or two ATs.

Cross-curricular themes

As with the key skills, cross-curricular themes were identified in earlier documentation and these should be integrated into lesson planning across all subject areas. The cross-curricular themes are: economic and industrial understanding, careers education and guidance, health education, education for citizenship and environmental education. These will be dealt with in Chapter 3.

Links with other subjects and cross curricular themes

These links are designed to create more coherence across individual subjects. More details of these will be given in Chapter 3.

Key stage four

Although the teaching of languages at key stage four is also governed by the programme of study, most teaching will be aimed at one of the many external examinations provided by the examination boards. The GCSE, Standard Grade (in Scotland), Graded Objectives (in Northern Ireland), Certificate of Language Competence (in Wales) and vocational qualifications all publish detailed syllabuses or subject specifications, together with guidance for teaching which inform the process of teaching at this level. More details will be given on these examinations in Chapter 6.

Links to teaching standards

Under *subject knowledge and understanding* trainees are asked to demonstrate that they 'have for their specialized subject ... a detailed knowledge and understanding of the National Curriculum, programmes of study, level descriptions, or end of key stage descriptions for KS3 and ... National Curriculum programmes of Study for KS4'. By considering factors relating to KS3 and 4, this should contribute to trainees' achievement of this standard.

Task 2.1

Take one of the ATs and trace the steps of progression from levels one to eight. Take one topic area and find ways of teaching the same topic gauged at different levels.

Teaching cultural awareness

Three major questions can be posed regarding the teaching of cultural awareness in the context of the National Curriculum:

- What are the official recommendations?
- What might be desirable to support MFL teaching?
- How can you teach cultural awareness?

Official recommendations

'Developing cultural awareness' has been included in all the National Curriculum documentation during the decade or so of proposals and reviews (DES/LSO, 1990: 36 and 37; DES, 1991: 25 and 26; DFE, 1995: 3; DfFE/QCA 1999: 8 and 17). There is a recognition generally, then, in official recommendations that language teaching needs to include a cultural context.

The detail of the recommendations has altered a little during the various reviews. Two elements have remained constant: working with authentic materials, and communicating with native speakers (DES, 1999:17). In earlier documentation the second recommendation reads 'coming into contact' with native speakers, so the communicative, socializing aspect is emphasized more in the 1999 version.

This emphasis on social-cultural competence, being able to communicate with others and to appreciate their point of view, is also the underlying message in the other changes that have been made leading up to the 1999 document. At all stages the government document suggests that learners both *compare* their own culture with the target culture and try to *understand* what the target culture is in its own right. In 1990 pupils were asked to 'appreciate' similarities and differences (p 36); and in 1991 to 'consider and discuss' them (p 26). In 1999 this has become 'consider' (p 17). The intellectual focus then might be said here to have become narrower.

This is further confirmed by the narrowing of suggestions as to how pupils should use the experience of comparison. In 1990 pupils were asked 'to use this knowledge to develop a more objective view of their own customs and ways of thinking' (p 36), in other words to see the values of their own culture as relative. In 1991 there is an emphasis on discussion 'consider and discuss … similarities and differences'; 'investigate, discuss and report on aspects of the language and culture of these countries and communities' (p 26). There is also a much more developed emphasis on the link between language and culture in the 1991 provisions: 'learn the use of social conventions … and become increasingly aware of cultural attitudes as expressed in language' (p 26).

In the 1999 document then the 'opportunity to relativize is played down, with pupils being asked just to 'consider' differences and similarities. The area that *is* emphasized is using these insights to become a better communicator. Thus in the section on 'spiritual, moral, social and cultural development' (which is new in the 1999 booklet) there is considerable emphasis on language and communication: '*Spiritual development*, through stimulating pupils' interest and fascination in the phenomenon of language and the meanings and feelings it can transmit' (although the emphasis here seems intellectual and aesthetic rather than spiritual), and:

> *social development*, through exploring different social conventions …, through developing pupils' ability to communicate with others, particularly speakers of foreign languages, in an appropriate, sympathetic and tolerant manner and through fostering the spirit of co-operation when using a foreign language to communicate. (p18)

There is then a strong linking of language and culture and a particular emphasis on using cultural insights to inform linguistic and social behaviour. Although there appears to be general agreement as to the value of cultural insights, there is no assessment of this at key stages three and four. It is the four linguistic skills that are assessed.

Cultural awareness as part of MFL teaching

There is also general agreement in literature at large that language and culture go hand in hand; we learn cultural meanings as we learn our own language. We thus need to know something of the foreign culture when we learn the language, particularly as has been indicated in the government guidelines, when communicating with native speakers.

What is not clear is what should be taught and how teachers should react in terms of attitudes to target cultures (and languages).

In terms of content this could be represented as two different sorts of progression (Morgan, 1995; Byram and Morgan, 1994). At first there is a progression from knowledge to understanding values, to comparing cultures, to understanding otherness, to relativizing cultures. Here pupils could convert a knowledge and understanding base to an ability to be more objective about their own culture and the target culture (in the spirit of the 1990 proposals).

Another way of describing cultural content progression is to link it to a language. Here the progression is from 'survival language' with little cultural content, to understanding cultural behaviour and then, to understanding cultural values.

Here then the functional language common in many textbooks is recognized as not contributing very much to cultural understanding, but pupils could augment this by learning about cultural behaviour (the 'social conventions' mentioned in government documentation) and the cultural values that underpin every aspect of life.

The question of fostering particular attitudes may be more problematic. In Chapter 1 it has already been suggested that attitudes to foreign languages and cultures in the UK can be negative because of outside factors. You may feel that you are neither in a position to foster positive attitudes, nor may this be a desirable thing from an ethical standpoint.

However, if we move away from a straight positive/negative choice to a more extended range of possibilities, then these problematic areas may be less difficult. One could suggest a set of stages in terms of appreciating a target culture. Here the progression would be from ignorance to understanding with a negative attitude, to neutral understanding, to tolerant understanding and finally, to positive endorsement.

It may be helpful to think of a cultural curriculum leading to an understanding of the foreign culture, which is either neutral or tolerant, thus avoiding the pitfalls of negative rejection or positive euphoria.

If we suggest 'tolerance' then as an acceptable attitude to foster, the question of a progression of cultural understanding still remains. Linguistic progression is familiar: textbooks build on knowledge and encourage pupils to consolidate what has been learnt. However, cultural information in textbooks usually occurs in an ad hoc fashion (Morgan, 1995). It can be sensible, then, to plan progression in pupils' cultural learning in the same way as progression in language learning is catered for.

TEACHING MODERN FOREIGN LANGUAGES

How to teach cultural awareness

If we consider a possible progression framework for teaching cultural awareness, then it will be useful to see how activities that have already been tried or suggested fit into this framework (see below).

A series of four steps towards cultural competence can be suggested (this links in as well to the new Council of Europe framework described in Chapter 12):

- knowledge of cultural facts;
- decoding cultural 'symbols';
- relativizing cultures through comparison;
- linking language and culture.

Knowledge of cultural facts

This level of cultural awareness teaching is already fairly well catered for. Information is included in most textbooks on the target culture, including recognizing diverse cultures within a country and the different countries where the target language may be spoken. One interesting cultural awareness project that sharpened knowledge of a country is described by Jones (1995). This is his Council of Europe 'shoe-box project' where 13–14 year old pupils exchanged shoe boxes containing cultural artefacts that they believed represented their own country and where they wrote a brief explanation of their choices. This project was run in the context of the 32 European Union counties and included countries such as Turkey, Poland and Malta. Here, then, there was a gathering of cultural information about Europe in general, not necessarily linked to the learning of a foreign language.

It may also be useful when dealing with 'knowledge' to do work on stereotypes linking this to facts or sources of cultural information such as native speakers in a school; and how they fit in with a stereotypical picture (see also Steele and Suozzi, 1994).

Decoding cultural symbols

If pupils are to become more culturally aware then they will need to be able to decode the outward signs of another culture, and these may not immediately be transparent. It is one thing to be given facts about a country but quite another to confront something from another country and be able to decipher it culturally as well as linguistically.

Tomalin and Stempelski suggest an interesting 'stamp detectives' exercise (1993: 52) where pupils are encouraged to analyse stamps from the target country in order to identify cultural priorities. (This activity has the added advantage of providing a different 'text' for each pupil to work on.) One could undertake a similar kind of exercise by looking at the street names in a capital city to see what (or who) was considered famous enough to qualify.

Another example of decoding can be found in an intercultural project set up between a French classroom and an English classroom in 1995, which involved pupils creating their own materials in their own language on a shared cultural topic (Morgan and Cain, 2000). To help decode these materials, help sheets were also prepared explaining possible cultural (and linguistic) difficulties. This is a task for the teacher that can specifically help pupils to become aware of how to decode 'texts' from the target culture.

A further example is the intercultural Anglo-French project run in Durham (1990–3) where pupils were helped, amongst other things, to decode literary texts to understand how descriptions of cultural practices could lead to a greater understanding of life in France. Thus, in a unit on the family, different texts on weddings were taken from contemporary literature to give a flavour of cultural expectations during this kind of family festival. (Other aspects of this project are described in Byram and Morgan 1994.)

Here, then, pupils move from straight absorption of facts to a more interactive approach working as cultural detectives.

Relativizing cultures through comparison

The 1995 Anglo-French project mentioned earlier (Morgan and Cain, 2000) also helped pupils to consider their own culture in a new light. Pupils were asked to produce texts in their own language that represented 'law and order' in their own country. The French pupils produced cartoons (from magazines) and a caricature depicting the roles of the police and traffic chaos. The English pupils, with a large number participating, produced eight texts (one video, two cassettes and five written texts) relating to the police and to law and order in school (school rules, prefects and so forth). Pupils were thus able to see different attitudes to law and order and different preferred ways of representing things in their partner schools and countries. Interviews with the pupils, both at the time and later, showed that they became particularly aware of their own culture by taking part in this project.

Work at Thames Valley University (Byram and Morgan, 1994) also encouraged the students to analyse an aspect of their own environment anthropologically or ethnographically. The students were asked to choose a social situation in their own country and then try to view it as though they were a complete stranger to it, noting aspects such as the way in which people behaved and what they said. This activity defamiliarized their own culture as a first step to understanding another one. Although this activity was used for the students preparing for their year abroad, it could also be adapted for younger age groups.

At this stage more demands are made of the learners. They must think themselves into someone else's shoes.

Linking language and culture

In a helpful article (1997) Byram outlines several cultural awareness activities that could alert learners to the links between language and culture: using sets of monolingual dictionaries or computer data to identify associations of words; interviewing native speakers and identifying the associations they make with different words and using ethnographic texts that describe aspects of daily life in the author's own culture. This stage is likely to come later in a 'cultural programme', as it requires considerable linguistic sophistication.

It can be helpful to consider leading pupils through the various stages identified here. The later stages are likely to be difficult if learners do not already have a good knowledge and some expertise in decoding a foreign culture.

Task 2.2

Ask a group of year nine pupils to become 'cultural detectives' investigating an aspect of social life in this country and in the target country. Information could be pooled and displayed in diagrammatic or shortened form on posters.

Task 2.3

Try the stamp exercise with a class of year 10 pupils. Ask pupils to bring a collection of English stamps and stamps from the target country. Divide pupils into pairs, each with a few stamps from one country. Pupils should try to list what is featured on the stamps and group the ideas together. Lists can be compared to see if there are any common cultural priorities.

A final issue

Two issues are often raised when discussing cultural matters: how stable/durable or unified cultural values are (Jones, 1995 usefully distinguishes between 'provisional' and 'permanent'). Thus we can alert pupils to the dangers of stereotyping; and the language of discussion. It may be difficult for pupils to explore issues in full if there is an insistence on target language. This may be an occasion when cultural understanding may take precedence over language practice.

Links to teaching standards

- Under *subject knowledge and understanding* trainees are asked to 'understand how pupils' learning in the subject is affected by their physical, intellectual, emotional and social development'.
- Under *planning* they are asked to 'plan opportunities to contribute to pupils' spiritual, moral, personal, social and cultural development'.
- Under *teaching and class management* trainees are asked to keep all pupils engaged through 'exploring opportunities to contribute to the pupils' wider educational development including their spiritual, moral, personal, social and cultural development'.

Including 'cultural awareness' activities should help to contribute to all these areas.

Incorporating creativity

'Creativity' can be used quite loosely as a term. It may just mean 'getting the most out of something' so that 'creative use of texts' may mean thinking of lots of different ways of working with texts; or it may mean providing opportunities for contributions that are original to an individual and that require using imagination. Activities may be set up that are entirely 'creative' or there may be a 'creative' component to what is otherwise a structured and predictable task. There is also the complication of whether it is the teacher who is seen as being creative or the learner.

In the section below, creativity is considered from the point of view of the student, since an imaginative and wide ranging approach to preparing learning materials and activities by teachers is already likely to be a part of their planning.

Advantages of incorporating creativity

Giving students the opportunity to contribute something from their own experience and imagination can be seen to have three main advantages:

- encouraging motivation;
- extending learning skills;
- mirroring learning processes.

Encouraging motivation

Williams and Burden (1997) identify several factors that can help to motivate second or foreign language learners. These include:

- choice;
- challenge;
- curiosity;
- involvement.

Providing opportunities for creative activities can be seen to cater for all these factors.

With regard to *choice*, if some areas of an activity are left open then students can exercise their own choice and preferences. It may even be that students can choose their own order of tasks, for example, in a carousel programme of varied autonomous activities. Jones (1992: 4) comments on creativity from this aspect as 'making language communicate what a learner needs or wants, sometimes as chosen by the learner rather than the teacher'. Williams and Burden confirm the value of personal contribution, seeing 'choice' as the main factor in a cognitive view of motivation: 'A cognitive view of motivation centres around individuals making decisions about their own actions as opposed to being at the mercy of external forces over which they have no control' (1997: 119).

As far as *challenge* is concerned, using creative activities may be more challenging than following predictable and familiar patterns. If students feel confident of their creative skills then they may welcome challenges which stretch those skills, what Williams and Burden (1997: 127) describe as part of a 'flow experience'.

With regard to *curiosity,* creative activities can often involve guessing, using one's imagination to fill in a gap or to predict something. Lack of imagination or a space to be filled can often induce curiosity, a key factor seen to contribute to students' engagement or 'arousal' (Williams and Burden, 1997: 126).

As for *involvement,* allowing students a forum where a contribution from their own store of knowledge and ideas is welcomed also gives pupils some sense of ownership (Morgan, 1996). In this way they can become more involved and thus motivated.

Perhaps one word of warning is needed here. The motivational factors mentioned above depend on students' own internal disposition and their view of themselves, the school, their foreign language lessons and so forth. It may be that some students do not have a learning style or do not believe they have a learning style that is in tune with 'creative' activities. This may also be true of a teacher who may favour more controlled and structured activities. In these cases it may be helpful to think of including creativity only as a small part of any teaching programme.

Extending learning skills

Using creative activities can be seen to extend learning skills in two main ways: by encouraging empathy, and by promoting flexibility.

With regard to *empathy,* where creative activities require pupils to put themselves in someone else's shoes, to imagine situations, then this can contribute to cultural awareness learning (see previous section in this chapter).

As for *flexibility,* creative activities can be helpful in familiarizing students with the unpredictable and promoting flexibility. Level eight of attainment targets 1 and 2 and levels seven and eight of attainment target 3 all mention students' ability to cope with the unfamiliar. Encouraging creativity can thus be seen as helping students towards those higher levels of achievement.

Mirroring learning processes

Part of any learning process is likely to involve trial and error (heuristic learning). Creative approaches that invent and try out new ways of doing something can be seen then as an integral part of a learning process. Guessing can also be part of a creative activity and, again, this can be seen as a key stage of advancing learning.

Creativity and the national curriculum

In early proposals for the National Curriculum (DES,1990; DES,1991), creativity had a relatively high profile because it featured specifically as one of the seven *areas of experience (Area G: Imagination and Creativity).* In later reviews when the number of areas was reduced to five, Area G was dropped and 'creativity' incorporated into the general rubrics. Thus in the 1999 document we find 'creativity' mentioned in two places. First, it is mentioned as one of the nine dimensions of *breadth of study:* where pupils should be taught 'knowledge skills and understanding through ... using the target language creatively and imaginatively'. Second, it is mentioned as one feature of 'promoting other aspects of the curriculum', namely as part of helping *'thinking skills ...* through developing pupils' creative use of language and expression of their own ideas, attitudes and opinions' (1999a: 9).

'Creativity' is thus seen as a useful cross-curricular and transferable skill in government documentation and may anyway be seen as a useful dimension in teaching MFL.

Creative activities

Two very useful source books for incorporating creativity across all the four skills are *Being Creative* (Jones, 1992) and *Creativity* (Miller, 1995). Articles that focus specifically on creative writing may also be useful (Morgan, 1996; Hartmann, 1996).

Three activities that can be useful for encouraging creativity are:

- guessing;
- drama;
- creative writing.

Guessing

Students' curiosity and involvement can be called on by using guessing activities and asking for creative responses. Good activities could include guessing the contents of a bag with different objects in it; guessing individual items that are 'blocked out' by an outline on an overhead projector (for example a square box representing a 'present' laid over different items); filling in blanked out speech bubbles; guessing the identity of someone from specific clues; or guessing what might happen next in a sequence of events. Jones suggests an engaging activity where a drawing on an overhead transparency (he gives the example of a kangaroo) is revealed only bit by bit with students having the opportunity to guess the identity of the object in a structured and progressive way (1992: 11–12).

Guessing can be seen as a *structured* form of creativity because there is likely to be a 'right answer'. In the two further activities described below there is no 'correct version', although the teacher is likely to want to encourage correct language use.

Drama

Role plays are a frequent feature of textbooks and also part of the GCSE key stage 4 examination (see the first section of this chapter). Often though the dialogues are fairly predictable with the dramatization activity serving as a consolidation for structures learnt previously. It may be helpful to extend this kind of role-play for two reasons: to provide a more personalized creative opportunity for students, and to stimulate the unpredictability of dialogues which may take place in the target country.

Miller provides some excellent suggestions and also comments on the value of drama activities for improving pupils' fluency and self-confidence (1995: 17). Particularly useful suggestions are scenarios based on TV shows where students are already likely to know the format and feel comfortable about the activity. She suggests: *The Price is Right*; *Blind Date*; *The Antiques Roadshow*; and *Husbands and Wives*, with the added suggestion that 'the performance will be improved if you can persuade a pupil to record the theme music from the real programme, (1995: 19).

While one could object to the cultural format representing Anglo-American cultural values, nevertheless the familiarity of the game show format is likely to be of real benefit.

Creative writing

The idea of using a familiar format is one also often pursued in creative writing projects: taking a model and making your own version, or using a prescribed outline. It may provide more of a creative challenge however to allow pupils to choose their own format as well. Morgan's (1996) article provides examples of creative writing in different contexts and emphasizes the freedom allowed in their production: 'students were free to choose the subjects of their poems, free to choose the form and free to work alone or with a partner' (p 47).

Hartmann (1996) describes an interesting creative writing project that involved the use of e-mail. Two 'chains' of English schools (10 in each chain) joined in the writing of a story. The first chapter (written by Sten Nadolyny of the Deutsche Schule in London) was sent to the first school of both groups where an A level German group then wrote the next chapter and passed the story on to the next school for a further chapter to be written, and so on.

One important aspect of creative writing in general is allowing enough time for there to be production trial and error. Miller talks of the need for tolerance by the teacher: 'you will have to accept that there will be some mistakes made, and, as in all creative work, some floundering around before inspiration arrives' (1995: 18). Another important aspect is the opportunity for display. Morgan's pupils displayed their poems within the school and Hartmann's pupils produced an 11-chapter novel.

Other prompts for creative writing could be music and art, perhaps playing a piece of music (the 'storm' sequence from Beethoven's *Pastoral Symphony* is an appropriate example) or using a dramatic painting and asking pupils to provide an accompanying story.

Task 2.4

Provide a creative dimension. Consider one of the activities that you have planned already as part of your teaching and consider how you might add a creative component.

Task 2:5

Set up a creative activity. Consult one of the source books mentioned, choose a creative activity and then discuss with your mentor how this might be set up within one of your teaching groups.

A final issue

If some of the more creative activities are attempted, it may be that students then feel able to reveal their innermost thoughts. Care will need to be taken in handling this situation, should it occur.

Links to teaching standards

Trainees are asked as part of their *planning* to 'plan their teaching to advance progression in pupils' learning through setting tasks … which challenge pupils and ensure high levels of interest'. They are also asked to 'plan opportunities to contribute to pupils' spiritual, moral, personal, social and cultural development'.

Under *teaching and class management* they are asked to use teaching methods that sustain the momentum of pupils' work and keep all pupils engaged through maintaining their motivation.

Using creative activities in the classroom should help to contribute towards achieving these standards.

Literacy and key skills

The relationship between foreign languages and key skills in the curriculum is complicated. One can see it operating in two directions: on the one hand foreign language skills are not directly identifiable in the six key skills outlined in government documentation, or in the National Literacy Strategy. On the other hand government guidelines urge us to make links with key skills in the teaching of foreign languages (DfEE/QCA, 1999).

The six key skills identified in government documentation (DfEE/QCA, 1999: 8) are:

- communication;
- application of number;
- information and communication technology;
- working with others;
- improving own learning and performance;
- problem solving.

The skills outlined for *communication* overlap considerably with those required in the National Literacy Strategy (DfEE, 1998).

It is also worth noting that an earlier emphasis on cross-curricularity in terms of topics evident in the late 1980s and early 1990s (DES, 1990) appears now to have refocused on transferable skills across subject – 'key skills'.

It is helpful to think about the relationship of MFL to the key skills and literacy in four different ways:

- the possible contribution of MFL to literacy and the key skill of communication;
- links between literacy work and MFL;
- modern foreign language activities building on literacy work;
- the relationship between MFL and key skills other than communication.

Contribution of MFL to literacy and communication

Clearly the key skill of communication and the skills of literacy at primary level are the areas most closely connected to MFL because of the common focus on language.

The closeness of 'literacy' and 'communication' can be seen by examining the outlined focus of each. In the National Literacy Strategy (DfEE, 1998: 3), 11 different skills are named that constitute literacy:

- reading and writing with confidence, fluency and understanding;
- using reading cues;
- understanding spelling and sound systems;
- having fluent and legible handwriting;
- having an interest in vocabulary;
- understanding literacy genres;
- understanding non-fiction texts;
- being able to plan, redraft and edit writing;
- knowing a metalanguage (or technical vocabulary) for describing language systems;
- being interested in books;
- developing imagination.

Communication in the MFL National Curriculum (DfEE/QCA, 1999: 8) documentation is described as:

> Developing ... awareness of the way language is structured and how it can be manipulated to meet range of needs, and ... reinforcing learning in specific areas such as listening, reading for gist, and detail and using grammar correctly.

Although the focus in 'literacy' operates on a macro level with general familiarity with texts, while 'communication' concentrates more specifically on language skills, there are nevertheless considerable areas of overlap.

The Nuffield Inquiry, which investigated the foreign language context of the late 1990s identified some areas where the inquiry team felt MFL could add to 'literacy' and 'communication' skills.

The team suggests that language awareness programmes that 'improve a planned exploration of how different languages look, sound and relate to their cultures' (Nuffield Foundation, 2000: 42) could usefully be included in the National Literacy Strategy. They suggest that 'for pupils who have not yet started another language, it can generate enthusiasm and curiosity and help "train the ear"'.

This echoes views voiced by others. For example, Driscoll and Frost (1999: 3) suggest in the introduction to their edited collection of articles on primary first language teaching that 'one of the most effective ways of understanding the structure of a language is to compare it with the structures of another language'. Hawkins (1996: 21), in his review of 30 years of language teaching, suggests that we should consider a new definition of literacy for the new millennium which would be *'a fundamental literacy including mastery of another language'*.

There is a suggestion here than that literacy skills should include both awareness of other languages and mastery of a foreign language and that this would be operative at primary level.

The Nuffield Inquiry also suggests that the key skill of *communication*, identified in secondary curricula, could be enhanced by considering MFL dimensions. They outline two possible developments: including knowledge of another language, and considering effective use of English when dealing with speakers of another language.

The latter skill is considered particularly important in the context of business and tourism. The team regrets particularly that students 'are not taught the skills and techniques of adjusting their own use of English in order to overcome barriers of understanding with the large numbers of visitors (to the UK) who have only a partial knowledge of the language' (2000: 24).

There appear, then, to be several ways that MFL could contribute to literacy and communication in general in the curriculum.

Links between literacy teaching and MFL

There has been some interest at primary and secondary level in English and MFL collaboration, linking literacy work with foreign language learning. It should be remembered that there are government plans to extend the National Literacy Strategy (introduced in 1998) into secondary schools by September 2001 with 200 schools piloting the initiative from September 2000 (initial difficulties with this pilot are described by Cassidy, 2000e).

In the National Curriculum for MFL there are specific references to the English programme of study in the areas of grammar, drafting written work and knowing the technical vocabulary of a language (DfEE/QCA, 1999: 16–17).

One example of linking literacy with MFL is a project in Bedfordshire middle schools (where French is taught to most year five pupils). Activities here have included comparing idioms in French and English, looking at the sentence position of the imperative and comparing introductory phrases in five languages (Gill, 2000).

Another project, *Language for Life* in Liverpool has involved a local computer firm, the government's north-west regional office and the LEA. Video conferencing has linked 20 primary schools for live tuition from language specialists in French, Spanish and Italian; this will lead on to a project in 2001 with a creative English course combined with either French or Spanish (Neumark, 2000).

At secondary level a recognition of coherence between subjects on the language front can be useful. Staff in all subjects are being asked to teach spelling (Cassidy, 2000a). A useful 'language for learning' component is built into the schemes of work for key stage four, prepared by the Qualifications and Curriculum Authority (QCA) and to match with the new 'use of language' requirement in the revised National Curriculum (Horner, 2000). The use of language requirements in the National Curriculum (DfEE/QCA, 1999: 29) relate to accurate handling of languages across the four skills. This includes spelling, interactive skills, summarizing and discourse competence (constructing sentences and paragraphs).

One area where there can be helpful complementarity between work in the English and MFL departments is in the area of special needs. Learning a foreign language can be particularly useful for students with learning difficulties in that they have an extra chance to improve their understanding of language in general (Deane, 1992).

Building on literacy work

As well as working side by side with English departments at secondary level, it will also now be the case that teachers of year seven classes can expect a certain level of language understanding that students will have acquired in primary school.

In the National Literacy Strategy students should have learnt the meaning of adjective, conjunction, noun, pronoun, verb, tense, first, second and third persons (year three); adverb, clause, connectives, possessive apostrophe (year four); imperative, preposition, reported speech, subject (year five); and active and passive voice (year six). Given that the revised criteria for marking GCSE will now include 20 per cent allocation for accurate and appropriate use of grammar, it will be useful to be able to draw on students' existing knowledge of the metalanguage of grammar and its technical vocabulary. Year seven students should also be familiar with particular kinds of language teaching. Eleven teaching strategies are included in the National Literacy Strategy:

- drawing attention;
- demonstrating;
- modelling;
- scaffolding (for example, providing writing frames);
- explanation;
- questioning;
- guiding exploration;
- investigating ideas;
- discussing and arguing;
- listening to and responding.

Year seven MFL teachers can use these approaches in their discussions of language and grammar.

Links to other key skills

There are five other key skills: application of number, IT, working with others, improving learning and performance and problem solving. Integrating MFL work with ICT is dealt with in more detail in Chapter 5.

Application of number

The focus on numeracy has been sharpened by the requirement enforced in 1999–2000 for all PGCE trainees to take a numeracy test. In the National Curriculum MFL booklet (DfEE/QCA, 1999: 8) links with numeracy are described as follows:

> MFL provides the opportunities for pupils to develop the key skills of ... *application of number* through talking and writing about the time and measures in the target language, and carrying out conversations about distances and currency. It can be particularly beneficial for students with learning difficulties to have an extra opportunity to practise telling the time and measuring.

Systems of constructing numbers are different in different languages: the digit which comes last in English numeration comes first in German: 76 = *sechsundsiebzig* (six-and-seventy); in French numbers are grouped in twenties after 60: 76 = *soixante-dix-sept* (60 and 17). This could be an interesting conceptual area to explore with students (particularly given the French tendency to give marks out of 20).

Examining key skills post-16

Kilmartin (2000) points out that the skills which are most needed in the workplace are those that will not be examined: working with others, improving our own learning and performance and problem solving. Nevertheless it should be possible to integrate these into a modern language post-16 syllabus and to build on work that has been done lower down in the school.

Task 2.6
Examine the content of one of your year seven lessons and consider how this could link in to work done in primary schools in the literacy hour.

Task 2.7
Take one of the other key skills and consider how this could be covered in one of your lessons.

Links with teaching standards

Under *subject knowledge and understanding,* trainees are asked: to demonstrate that they … have for their specialist subject(s) … a detailed knowledge and understanding of the National Curriculum programmes of study … [that they] know and can teach the key skills required for current qualifications relevant to their specialist subject(s), for pupils aged 14–19, and understand the contribution that their specialist subject(s) makes to the development of the key skills.

Under *planning* they are asked to 'demonstrate that they … where applicable, ensure coverage of the relevant … National Curriculum programmes of study'. Under *teaching and class management* they are asked to 'demonstrate that they … use teaching methods which sustain the momentum of pupils' work and keep all pupils engaged through … exploiting opportunities to improve pupils' basic skills in literacy, numeracy and ICT'.

Focusing on the links between MFL and the key skills should contribute to achieving these standards.

3 Planning and classroom management

This chapter is the first of four chapters that describe and analyse the *content* of MFL teaching.

Objectives

By the end of this chapter you should be able to:

- construct schemes of work;
- make detailed units of work;
- write lesson plans;
- evaluate lessons.

Planning and class management

Planning and preparation are vital components of the teaching process. You will be involved in planning at various levels. The previous chapter has dealt with the content of the programme of study that must form the basis of your teaching at key stages three and four. In addition to the PoS, school policies and departmental policies will need to be considered in planning at all levels. The hierarchy of planning might look something like:

1. statutory requirements (PoS);
2. school policies – department policies;
3. scheme of work;
4. units of work;
5. lesson plans;
6. personal development plans.

The programme of study has been dealt with in the previous chapter. In this section each of the other elements will be discussed in turn.

School policies

Every school will have its own policies on the major elements of the teaching/learning process, such as policies on homework, discipline, literacy/numeracy, assessment, and special educational needs. In the early years of teaching you may not have much input into formulating the school policies but in some schools you may be a member of working parties that make recommendations to be adopted as whole school policy. All of the policies at school level will take account of statutory requirements, such as the programme of study and other regulations that are laid down by the departments of education.

Departmental policies

At departmental level there will also be policies on the main issues and these will be in accordance with the school policies. In many modern language departments, all staff have a role to play in formulating policies. These will depend on the nature of the school and the department. The main aspects of departmental policy relevant to key stages three and four will be incorporated into the department's scheme of work.

Scheme of work

Based on the content of the PoS and, taking into account any school-specific issues, a scheme of work will contain details of elements such as:

- the role of modern languages in the curriculum;
- content to be taught at both key stages;
- learning experiences of students;
- guidance on teaching the four ATs;
- assessment and level descriptors;
- using the target language;
- homework;
- resources;
- outline of programme for year divided into units of work;
- timing of units.

The details in the scheme must be reflected in the units of work and in the lesson plans.

Units of work

Each unit of work (which will be summarized in the scheme of work) will need to be much more detailed in presentation than the outline contained in the scheme of work. In some schools, new members of staff are sometimes given sole responsibility to devise new units of work either for new topics, a new course book or, in fewer cases, a new language that is being introduced into the school. A unit will contain work that will cover a topic or subtopic and it could range from 3 to 10 lessons, depending on the nature of the topic. Some coursebooks have very short subunits that take only two or three lessons; others have long chapters as units, which have to be subdivided by the teacher. Although many of the coursebooks on the market for some languages contain detailed units of work the curriculum has changed and you would need to ensure that the units adhere to the most recent statutory guidelines. The detailed units of work should contain the following:

- aims;
- objectives for the unit;
- resources (including extra resources);
- attainment targets;
- level descriptors;
- activities and tasks;
- language items to be taught (vocabulary and grammar);
- language/language learning/personal and social skills;
- links with other topics/subjects;
- information and communication technology (ICT) skills;
- differentiation;
- target language/mother tongue;
- cross-curricular themes;
- homework;
- assessment plan.

Cross-curricular themes and links with other subjects

In order to ensure that students are given a coherent learning experience across subject areas there are two linking elements in the curriculum, namely the cross-curricular themes that have to be covered in all subject areas and also links with other subjects on the curriculum. Although still in existence, these cross-curricular themes (CCTs) have assumed a less significant role in the programme of study. The cross-curricular themes are: economic and industrial understanding, careers education and guidance, health education, education for citizenship and environmental education. In Northern Ireland these themes are similar but not identical and will be changing with the revised curriculum. At the moment they are: education for mutual understanding; cultural heritage; health education; career education; economic awareness; information technology. In addition the curriculum should focus on European awareness and environmental education. Modern languages will be able to contribute to some areas better than to others. The main thing of which to be aware is that, where appropriate, the CCTs are highlighted in schemes and units of work and in lesson plans.

Examples of such links might be:

Topic	Subject link	Cross-curricular link
food/drink	home economics	health education
money	mathematics	economic awareness
travel	geography	European awareness
festivals	history	cultural heritage
weather	geography/science	environmental education
home/family	English	health
holidays	English/geography	European awareness
ICT theme	computing	ICT
self	English	citizenship
professions	various	career awareness

At times this might seem contrived and lessons should not be artificially constructed in order to highlight a particular theme or subject. Where the topic does lend itself to another subject or theme, this should be noted in the units of work and lesson plans. Some useful techniques on how to teach languages with a cross-curricular approach are contained in Brown and Brown (1996).

Progression

The main element that has to be included in lessons and in units of work is that of progression. At the end of each lesson, students should have moved another step along the road of language learning. Progression can refer to different aspects:

- new vocabulary;
- new language structures;
- familiar language in an unfamiliar context;
- increased range of topics;
- moving from concrete to abstract notions.

Although there might not be new material in any given lesson, students should be required to show some progression. This might also involve progression in other skill areas. For example they might be required to work in groups using familiar vocabulary and structures learnt in previous lessons.

Task 3.1

Plan a sequence of three lessons, incorporating progression. Describe what you learnt from this planning activity.

In the guidelines on schemes of work issued by the DfEE (QCA/DfEE, 2000), planning for progression is dealt with at length. In terms of each of the four ATs, progression is outlined as being characterized by the following:

AT1

- Increased speed of response and greater depth of understanding.
- Growing competence in dealing with complex texts, tasks and unpredictable elements.
- Increased confidence in deducing meaning from the grammatical context.

AT2

- Improved pronunciation and intonation.
- Increased speed and fluency of response.
- Increased readiness and ability to use TL routinely in the classroom.
- Greater confidence when dealing with unpredictable elements.
- Increased ability to vary language, using a range of suitable structures and vocabulary in different contexts.
- Greater understanding and correct application of language rules.
- Increased readiness to use complex language when appropriate.

AT3

- Increased speed of response and greater depth of understanding.
- Growing competence and confidence in dealing with a range of texts and tasks.
- Increased confidence in deducing meaning from the grammatical context.
- Developing independence in language learning and use.

AT4

- Increased speed and fluency of response.
- Improved accuracy and precision in the use of the TL.
- Readiness to experiment with the language.
- Increased ability to vary and adapt language to suit the purpose.
- Greater understanding and application of language rules.
- Increased use of a range of structures and vocabulary in different contexts.
- Increased readiness to use complex language when appropriate. (From QCA/DfEE, 2000: 8.)

In your scheme of work and in the individual units of work, you would need to ensure that there is progression in all the four attainment targets in various ways, to take account of the different types of progression outlined in the documentation.

Individual topics may be touched upon at various stages at both key stage three and key stage four, it is necessary to have progress within a topic area. Such progressions could include the following:

- concrete to abstract ideas;
- simple to complex ideas;
- specific to general themes;
- factual – imaginative topics;
- classroom – outside class experiences;
- straightforward – controversial aspects (adapted from NICC, 1992).

The DfEE document (QCA/DfEE, 2000) also divides progression into four elements and suggests ways in which progression fits into the categories:

- learning, understanding and applying grammar:
    - teaching grammar and structures within a planned programme, such as a scheme of work;
    - showing students how new language can be incorporated into previously learnt language, and in a growing range of contexts;
- listening, speaking, reading and writing skills:
    - encouraging accurate pronunciation and intonation;
    - increasing the range of contexts, speakers and range of tasks;
    - widening the range of language uses and audiences;
    - increasing the complexity of the TL which students encounter;
    - encouraging use of more complex and accurate language;
    - helping students to perform with an increasing degree of confidence and fluency, reducing the need for repetition and reliance on non-verbal support.
- language and language-learning skills:
    - training students to memorize effectively and to learn and apply rules;
    - teaching students how to use grammatical and other clues to help understanding;
    - showing them how knowledge of English or another language can help with learning the TL;
    - helping them to learn independently, and to use reference materials as support.
- awareness of different countries, cultures and people:
    - an increasing variety of authentic materials, including materials using ICT;
    - opportunities to learn about and come into contact with a growing range of native speakers in different contexts. (From QCA/DfEE, 2000: 7.)

It is necessary to ensure, therefore, that progression is not confined to the individual attainment targets but that, in the broader sense, there is progression in the students' overall language learning experience, which will accompany them once they have left the language classroom.

Differentiation

Within the mixed-ability classroom, it is important to ensure that there is progression for everyone and that lessons do not simply meet the needs of the middle group of students. It is vital that the students at the top end of the ability range are pushed to do even better whereas those at the lower end are given work with which they can cope but which is challenging for them.

Differentiation is the provision of different levels of activities for students of varying ability and interest levels. It can take several forms:

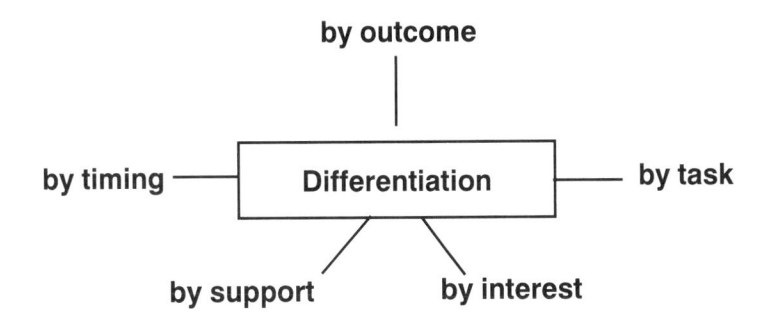

```
                    by outcome
                        |
   by timing ——[ Differentiation ]—— by task
                    /       \
              by support   by interest
```

Differentiated tasks should be written into the units of work and into lesson plans. In providing differentiation it is not practically possible to differentiate every activity. In the course of a series of lessons, however, there should be occasions when differentiated activities are provided, either in individual work, pair work or group work.

Lesson plans

Detailed lesson plans form the basis for your day-to-day teaching. They should be based on the units of work and should specify the content of individual lessons, taking account of what has gone before and what the longer term aims are. Lesson plans will differ in format but they should contain the following elements:

- details of the class;
- objectives;
- resources;
- linguistic items;
- possible difficulties;
- phases of lesson (sequence of activities);
- activities – integrated skills;
- TL/MT;
- differentiation;
- timing of activities;

TEACHING MODERN FOREIGN LANGUAGES

- questions;
- assessment;
- homework;
- evaluation.

Individual lessons must take account of various factors such as:

- class size;
- class composition;
- level of ability;
- previous knowledge of class;
- previous lessons (based on evaluation);
- time of day;
- length of lesson;
- time of year;
- resources available;
- syllabus constraints.

Objectives

Objectives are short term and are stepping stones along the way to achieving the aims mentioned in the units of work. Objectives are usually stated in the form of verbs. Examples of verbs to be used in objectives from the teaching point of view might be: to introduce, to revise, to consolidate, to demonstrate, to highlight. From the learning point of view they might be: to practise, to learn, to collaborate, to listen, to respond.

When devising objectives, it is necessary to make sure that they are clear, achievable and measurable by the end of the lesson. In a sequence of lessons, there should be progression in the objectives. For example if in lesson one the objective is to introduce eight items of vocabulary about the topic of 'town', lesson two should start with the objective 'to revise vocabulary introduced', followed by 'to enable students to practise using the vocabulary'. By following a series of lessons through, the students should be led systematically to be able to use the vocabulary and structures that have been introduced, practised, highlighted and consolidated. The objectives contained in each lesson must be in accordance with the objectives set out for the unit.

Linguistic items

The linguistic items represent the new vocabulary, structures or functions/notions that are to be introduced in a lesson. These can be stated in grammatical terms ('to introduce the students to the perfect tense') or in communicative terms ('to introduce the students to talking about their weekend activities in the past'). They may also contain details of the functions or notions that are to feature in the lesson. A function is a speech act that involves interaction between two people. Examples of functions would be: asking for, apologising, greeting. A notion, on the other hand, is a concept or idea, such as: time, size, space, movement. Any good course book will contain details of the functions and notions covered within individual units. In terms of progression, however, it should be noted that functions/notions do not progress but rather it is the language used to express them that progresses. For example: 'to state facts about something' is a function. In order to make this function progress, it is the language structure used that will indicate progression. It is possible 'to state facts about something' in the present, the past or the future tenses. In order to have progression within this function, therefore, it is necessary to introduce different tenses. It is necessary, therefore, when constructing your units of work and lesson plans, that you not only cover a variety of functions and notions but that you also consider the language structures covered.

Possible difficulties

In each lesson you should be aware of the possible difficulties students might have with the language. These should be highlighted in your lesson plans so that you can identify strategies for dealing with them. For example in a lesson on the perfect tense, the students may have forgotten the auxiliary verbs, which would require additional revision. There could also be confusion with the mother tongue and the different use of the tenses. With some average to less able students, there will be the added difficulty that they have no concept of tense in English on which to build.

Activities – integrated skills

In this section you should note the types of activities you intend the students to do. Although the programme of study sets out the skills according to the four individual attainment targets, it is envisaged that the teaching and learning should bridge the ATs. For example, a lesson that starts with a reading text (AT3) might require students to make an oral (AT2) response, followed by a written letter (AT4). It is important that you attempt to cover at least two ATs for each activity, so that the students can develop more than one skill at a time, as is required by GCSE and A-level examinations.

Phases of lesson

Each lesson should be sequenced to ensure that students are led step-by-step in the learning process to acquiring the new structures or to working with familiar structures in unfamiliar contexts. There is no one correct sequence for each lesson, as it depends on the objectives of the lesson and what went before. The following stages, however, provide a general outline:

- *Introduction.* In this phase the learners are introduced to the objectives of the lesson – to what they will be learning, why and how. In this phase it is possible to involve the learners in stating what they think they will need to learn by the end of a particular topic. This part of the lesson could be done in the target language but it is also possible to allow the students to use English, especially at the beginning of a new topic. Also in the introduction it is possible to have a warm-up session, using vocabulary and structures with which students are very familiar, such as their names, ages, family. This should be a short activity with quickfire questions to get the class used to hearing and using the language again.

TEACHING MODERN FOREIGN LANGUAGES

- *Revision of previous work.* Following the introduction, it is useful to set the lesson in context, mentioning what was done in previous lessons, checking that students have remembered what was covered, reminding them of key words and phrases that will be used in the lesson.
- *Presentation of new vocabulary/structures.* When you are sure that the students are confident with what they should know by now and what prerequisite knowledge they need for this lesson, it is time to introduce the new vocabulary and linguistic items. Where a new structure is being introduced at this stage, it is important to use familiar vocabulary with which to practise it. For example if the previous lesson had introduced buildings in a town and this lesson is on directions, it is important to use the buildings that have been revised in the earlier lesson. In this phase it is important that the language is modelled and used by the teacher first and that the students listen to the structure before they are required to use it.
- *Imitation/repetition.* A distinction is made between these two phases by Buckby *et al* (1992). Imitation is where students are required to say the word/phrase immediately following the teacher's model. Repetition, on the other hand, is when there is a gap between their hearing of the structure and producing it. In order to avoid boredom in this phase, it is important to have a variety of ways of getting the class to repeat:
    - whole class;
    - groups;
    - one-half of the class/the other half;
    - boys/girls;
    - quietly/loudly;
    - fast/slowly;
    - individuals.

    It is quite possible that the students do not always hear what the teachers think they are modelling. In the repetition phase, therefore, the teacher has to be aware of the pronunciation of students, because if certain groups are getting it wrong at this formative stage, it is possible that they will not unlearn their misconception. Notice that individual repetition should come after there has been variety in the class repetition strategies. This gives students confidence and those who have grasped it early on can be asked to repeat before those who are slower. If the majority of the class is still having problems after the imitation/repetition phase, it may be necessary to go back to the presentation phase and devise ways of making it clearer.
- *Practice.* When the teacher is sure that the students have mastered the new pronunciation, vocabulary, structure, it is time to move on to let them practise the new material in a structured context. This may be by getting them to work in pairs or groups to use the language in a very defined way. Continuing with the topic of town, in this phase the students could be given a worksheet with buildings on it; one student has the question: How do I get to the church? The other student has the answer: Turn left … etc.
- *Pairwork.* This is one of the most successful techniques to get students to use the language independently of the teacher. There are a few words of warning before embarking on pairwork, however:
    - the language practised in pairs must have been modelled and revised in class;
    - if questions and answers are used, the students must have been given sufficient practice with the questions as well as the answers;

- examples should be given before students are told to work in their pairs: the teacher should ask the question and get one student to answer (T-S); one student should ask the question and the teacher provide the answer (S-T); finally one student should ask another student in class the question (S-S);
- only when the teacher is confident that the whole class is clear, should they be left to work in pairs;
- during the pairwork phase the teacher should circulate, checking that each group is working and that there are no misunderstandings. If there are major difficulties either in pronunciation or in using the linguistic items the paired activity should not be allowed to continue;
- the activity should be followed up by examples given by various pairs in the class.

At the end of this stage, students should be confident about using the set vocabulary/structures in a very controlled context. The Pathfinder by Phipps (1999) gives helpful suggestions for pairwork.

- *Explanation*. After the students have interacted with the structures, it is time to spend some time analysing the structures and encouraging them to find patterns or rules in the language they have been working with. In the initial stages of learning the language, students will have little knowledge of how the modern language works, but they will have a bank of perhaps unconscious rules from their mother tongue. It is important to give them the opportunity to apply what they know to the new language, but it is equally important to point out where the languages differ from one another. A basic example is in gender of nouns, which does not exist in English. Once they have mastered that difference it is possible for them to use this knowledge in new contexts (for example, in pronouns, plurals, verb endings etc). The teacher has to find the balance between letting the students explore the language and giving them new information with which to build their knowledge of the language. Rules learned in the course of lessons could be illustrated on a chart, which is added to whenever new material comes to light. One example of this for genders in German is a picture of the coloured flumes that are found at swimming pools:
  - blue: masculine;
  - red: feminine;
  - yellow: neuter;
  - pool at the bottom: plurals.

  When new concepts, such as pronouns or direct objects, have been learned, these are written into the diagram. The systematic presentation of the linguistic structures is vital to enable the students to grasp the language, to develop some metalinguistic awareness that, in turn, will give them confidence in taking risks with new language on their own, which is the ultimate aim of language teaching.
- *Production*. When the students have a grasp of the structures and when they have used them in a confined context, it is possible to let them move to a more independent phase. During this production phase they can use the material in a more communicative setting or they can be involved in carrying out a more cognitively demanding task, but with quite simple language. An example of this from the topic of town would be designing a town and deciding where to put various buildings. As with pairwork, however, the students must be confident with the structures that they are being required to use. In this example the language required could be:

TEACHING MODERN FOREIGN LANGUAGES

- Is there a leisure centre?
- Where is the hospital?
- How do we get to the station from the square?
- How far is the post office from the town centre?

This type of activity could be done well in groups.

- *Groupwork*. The secret of groupwork is in the planning and organizing that goes on beforehand. There are different types of groupwork, different types of activity and various purposes for having students working in groups. It is important above all to ensure that there is a genuine reason for students working in groups, not just for the sake of it. Having students simply sitting at grouped desks does not constitute 'groupwork'. There must be an underlying purpose. This might be the following:
  - to encourage the class to work collaboratively;
  - to foster differentiation;
  - to widen the range of tasks students can attempt.

There are various formats groups can take:
- mixed ability;
- different abilities;
- separate groups working on same task but different activities;
- separate groups working on different skills;
- rotating groups (carousel);
- static groups (activities move).

It must be emphasized again that planning, careful preparation and students being well informed of the purpose of the activities and procedures to be followed during the class are all essential elements of groupwork. The students should be as independent as possible and the role of the teacher should be that of facilitator. Students should be aware of:
- what they have to do;
- how long they have to work on a task;
- what the specific roles are;
- how to move on from one activity to another;
- what resources are needed;
- where to locate the resources;
- where the self-check sheets are;
- what to do when they have finished a particular task.

Groupwork that is integrated and designed to have the class working in groups but with an end product is termed jigsaw groupwork. This is extremely time-consuming to set up but ultimately rewarding for the students who are all working towards a goal. An example of this would be:
- Topic: arranging a holiday.
- Objective: to decide which place would be most suitable for a class trip.
- Group 1: reads brochures of various destinations.
- Group 2: watches video programmes on various destinations.
- Group 3: explores transport possibilities.
- Group 4: designs a questionnaire to find out the interests of others in the class.
- Group 5: finds out about accommodation in the various locations.

Within each group, there could be tasks of different levels for individual students. Differentiated worksheets either by outcome or by task could be designed for each of the tasks, so that a weaker student could fill in blanks whilst the more able has to produce a piece of prose. On the basis of the research each group has to decide which place would be most suitable and the reasons why. At the end of the activity a representative from each group has to present the decision to the class. This could be in different formats for each group: Group 1 produces a travel agent advertising poster for a destination; Group 2 presents a radio announcement; Group 3 does an advertisement for particular modes of transport; Group 4 presents a documentary based on their findings; Group 5 designs a brochure for their choice of accommodation. The most vital element here is that every group member has had some input into the final product, so that it is owned by the whole class. The work will have been varied, stimulating, differentiated and purposeful. As well as the language skills, the transferable skills of working together and problem solving will have been in evidence.

Task 3.2

Plan a lesson that incorporates group work. Involve a variety of skills and ensure that differentiation is built into the activities. Try teaching the lesson and evaluate the success of what has taken place.

- *Assessment.* At certain stages in the unit of work, there will be lessons that directly aim to obtain some sort of measure of what the students can do. You need to have an assessment plan that targets specific skills or combinations of skills. The assessment need not be an addition to the lesson, but particular tasks and activities done in the lesson can be graded and used as evidence of students' performance. These can then be linked to the levels of attainment or the GCSE criteria as appropriate. Remember that each skill need not be assessed at the end of each lesson or unit of work.
- *Concluding phase.* At the end of lessons there should be some summing up or some final plenary session during which the main aspects of the work are restated. This can be by having a feedback session when the students report back on their participation in the individual work, the pairwork or groupwork. If some time is left, a quick revision of the new material can be done, possibly using a game such as 'blockbusters', 'Simon says' or 'Kim's game'. At this stage new material should not normally be introduced. The teacher should check whether students have mastered the information, which is a guide as to the success of the objectives that feature in the evaluation of the lesson.
- *Evaluation.* Evaluation of your lessons is a vital part of lesson planning. At the end of each lesson, it is important to check what has taken place during the lesson, concentrating on what the students have learned. The following set of questions will provide a guide as to the type of areas you should focus on:
  – Were the objectives achieved?
  – Were objectives appropriate?

- What have the students learnt?
- How have they progressed?
- Were the pitch, timing, pace appropriate?
- Was there variety of task or of skill?
- How much target language have I used? Could I improve?
- What areas was the TL used in? Could this be extended?
- How much TL did the students use? Could they use more?
- What strategies need to be in place to encourage greater TL use?
- Is my TL reflecting increased learning on the students' part?
- What did the students have to do in the lesson?
- What grammar have I taught/revised/consolidated/recycled?
- How have I helped students to manipulate the language?
- What went well? What would I do again?
- What did not go well? Why?
- What would I not do again? Why?
- What would I do differently?
- Am I exploring a wide range of teaching resources?
- What use was made of information and communication technology (ICT)?

It is not possible, or appropriate, to focus on all questions after every lesson, nor indeed is the list above exhaustive. It may be that you have set yourself some targets that you wish to evaluate more specifically, such as strategies for developing student use of the target language. In this case you might want to highlight the TL as an area of comment. From the results of your own evaluation, you should be able to identify areas of strength and areas of weakness. By keeping a record of the type of activities your lessons are covering and the skills you are enabling the students to acquire, you should build up a picture of the extent to which your class is gaining exposure to the skills and topics contained in the programme of study. You must ensure that, over a period of time, they do have access to the complete range, otherwise you will be disadvantaging them. Clearly planned units of work should reveal whether the whole range is being covered.

Target setting

From the evaluations on your lessons, aspects of your performance as a teacher and of the students' progress as learners will become evident.

Student targets

In terms of the students in the class, it is important that they get a sense of progression. This can be facilitated by setting targets for them as a class and as individual students. It would even be better to get the students to identify targets for themselves. At the beginning of a topic the students could set their own objectives (see above) and review their progress at the end of each week. They could then set targets for the following week. The following shows a student progress sheet with targets.

> Name
> Class
> Language
> Unit Title
> At the end of this unit I will be able to:
>
> - book into a hotel;
> - express my opinion about accommodation;
> - seek help with problems about accommodation;
> - ask for information about facilities.
>
> Targets
> I am able to:
> By the end of next week I hope to be able to:
>
> - telephone a hotel to book a room;
> - ask for a type of room;
> - give information about myself;
> - understand details of facilities;
> - write a letter confirming a booking.

There could be a slot at the end of each week when the students review their own progress and comment on their work so far. It could be extended to group targets where individuals working together set corporate targets, which encourages collaboration and learning from each other. Again, points could be used to reward the individuals and groups who achieved their own targets and for those who exceeded their own estimates. This would ensure that the students set realistic targets but would also encourage an element of competition. There would also be inbuilt differentiation into the target-setting process.

Personal targets

It may be that you want to focus on specific aspects of your own teaching which you hope to improve, such as:

- setting more attainable objectives;
- adjusting the pitch of lessons;
- using more of the TL;
- using the TL more strategically;
- providing more differentiation;
- creating more variety of activity;
- using more ATs;
- assessing students' performance more systematically;
- being more assertive regarding discipline.

At a more formal level, particularly during your trainee year and the first year of teaching, you will have to measure your performance against the teaching standards criteria set out in the official documentation. Based on a series of lessons you should be in a position to chart your progress as a teacher and produce an individual action plan self-evaluation profile which you can discuss with your mentor in schools or your higher education institution (HEI) tutors. Your own identified needs might include, for example, creating more variety of activity – ensuring effective teaching of whole classes, and of groups and individuals within the whole class setting, so that teaching objectives are met, and best use is made of available teaching time. They might include being more assertive regarding discipline – establishing and maintaining a purposeful working atmosphere. These relate to the standards.

During the course of your development as a trainee teacher, it will be necessary to chart your own progress across all the standards. In Northern Ireland schools, where an integrated structure exists between initial teacher education and induction and between induction and early professional development, the beginning teachers must keep a record of their development as they move through the stages, taking a series of modules over a period of four years.

Task 3.3

Plan to teach the same content to two different classes. Use different approaches, resources and activities. Evaluate the lesson, asking the pupils for their views. Discuss with your mentor what you learnt from the outcomes of these lessons.

Behaviour management

The previous section looked at aspects of planning, preparation, resources, and classroom organization – all with the focus on learning. This section looks at an aspect of classroom management that is one of the major concerns of trainees as they embark on their first period of school experience or of the NQT who takes up a first post in an unknown school – discipline, now euphemistically called behaviour management. All that was said in the previous section is vital for behaviour management. In order for learning to take place within the classroom the conditions must be correct – the environment must be conducive to productive learning. If you are in a classroom where there is inattention, boredom, bad behaviour and disrespect for both teacher and other students it is highly unlikely that successful learning will take place. It is the job of the teacher to ensure that the atmosphere in the classroom is safe, secure and ordered. This is not to say that there must always be silence or that everyone must be sitting in rows; there are times when the language classroom is an interactive place, with students engaged in independent or group learning activities that involve researching information in other parts of the school, such as the library or the computer suite. There do, however, have to be rules and regulations with which students are familiar and that are imposed fairly and consistently by the teacher, for the benefit of all the students in the class.

Indiscipline is better avoided than dealt with – that is to say that the circumstances in the classroom should be such that they do not encourage bad behaviour. Some of the principles of good classroom management are set out below, although this list is not exhaustive.

Personality

The main weapon a teacher has for classroom control is personality. Some teachers are extrovert, loud and eccentric; others are quiet, more introverted and traditional. Whatever your personality, you have to make it work for you. Successful teaching is not about shouting and stamping authority on students. It is about interpersonal relationships between teachers and students. It is not possible, therefore, to present a series of events that might arise in class and provide an answer to what the correct course of action would be. Each teacher will react to a situation differently. Part of the reaction will be determined by the context in which the event takes place, but the other part will be determined by the personality of the teacher. Work on your strengths and act in accordance with your personality. Remember that you are an individual and the students will recognize when you are being genuine.

Smiling and Christmas

It used to be said to student teachers that, when they took up their first post, they should not smile until Christmas. You may or may not agree with the statement but it is necessary to establish your authority on your classes, particularly at the beginning of your time in a school. When you have been there some time your reputation will precede you and you will find it easier.

Preparation

Good lesson planning and preparation are vital for an ordered class. You, as the teacher, need to be sure of what you are going to do in the lesson, which materials you are going to use, the structure of activities, and the difficulties the students might have, in order to give the class confidence. If you hesitate and the students get the impression that you are not sure what you are going to do next, they will take advantage of the hiatus in the lesson.

Entry to class

Make sure that you are in the classroom before the class arrives. This is sometimes not possible if, for example, you do not have your own classroom; in this case be outside the classroom before they arrive. Every school has its own policy on entry into class. If possible, get the students together outside the door before letting them in. This establishes your authority over them and shows them that it is your classroom and you expect them to behave according to your rules. If they arrive from different parts of the school it may be more manageable to let them come into the room when they arrive. In this case, give those who come into the class something to do such as getting their books organized. Do not at this stage overreact to their casual chatting to each other. If you keep telling them to keep quiet and sit in silence you will antagonize them. Wait until most of the class is in and then start the lesson with authority, so that there is a clear break between the settling down phase and the beginning of the actual lesson.

Seating arrangements

You are in control of the seating arrangements in the class. You may decide to seat them in rows, groups, alphabetically, by ability or you may let them choose where to sit. If you allow the students to choose, this should be on the understanding that if they are not able to work in that seat, you will have to move them.

Rules

When you meet a class for the first time, it is necessary to lay down some ground rules. Some teachers prefer to lay down the law, others prefer to establish class rules that are negotiated and agreed by all participants in the class. If you use the latter method, when students break any of the rules, you can point out that these were agreed by everyone in the class, therefore the misbehaviour is not directed at the teacher but at the class in general. Some rules might be:

- have respect for the teacher and for other members of the class;
- no talking when someone else is addressing the class;
- bring equipment to class;
- bring homework in on time;
- do not disrupt the learning of others.

These rules should be kept to a minimum, be simple and understood by the class and there should be clear guidance as to what happens when the rules are broken. If the teacher respects the students and students respect the teacher and each other, the environment should be conducive to learning. It may even be helpful to display the rules (in the TL, if possible) in the classroom.

Causes of indiscipline

It would be naïve to say that if you establish rules, if you are prepared and organized, that the students will not misbehave. You can expect to encounter challenges to your authority. It is important, however, when a whole class becomes consistently unruly, to reflect on what might be the underlying causes. If the individuals in the class are well behaved in other colleagues' classes, what is it about your class that makes them act as they do? Some possible causes might be:

- *Content* – there may be too much or too little material, or there may be too much repetition.
- *Pitch* – the content of the lesson is pitched either too high or too low.
- *Pace* – you may be going either too fast or too slow.
- *Lack of variety* – there may be too much of the one activity or skill being practised.
- *Lack of motivation* – it may be that the students do not like either the subject or the teacher.
- *Previous classes* – if they come to languages from certain other subjects, they may be restless.

The first four reasons are easily remedied by the teacher. You have to be aware of what is happening in your classroom and you must be prepared to adjust the content, the pace, the pitch or the variety. If the causes are lack of motivation or the students' previous class, you need to develop strategies for dealing with this – namely finding ways of motivating the unmotivated. Sometimes the way to do this is not to continue threatening the classes with writing as opposed to other interesting activities, but experimenting with new activities, giving them more independence for their learning, providing rewards instead of sanctions. Halliwell (1991) provides a useful model of 'stir' and 'settle' activities, depending on the mood of the class.

Rewards

If you can focus on the positive elements of language learning and can reward the students for good behaviour as opposed to punishing them for bad, the lessons will be all the more successful. Some teachers use a points system, where the students are given points for good behaviour, for using the target language for genuine communication, for creative work or for achieving specific targets for specific students.

Sanctions

If, after you have done all the above, students misbehave and rules are broken, you need to apply a sanction. It is necessary to make sure that you are aware of the school policy on discipline and the complementary departmental policy. You must be aware of the procedures laid down by the school and department for dealing with misdemeanours and you must apply these consistently and fairly. You can be sure that the students in the class will be aware of the rules, so that you cannot tell a class to stay behind after the final bell if it is not school policy. In some schools, because of transport difficulties, students are kept in at lunchtime instead of after school. Make sure you know the hierarchy of sanctions and do not overreact to a small offence.

Support will be available from the senior staff in each school. Usually the structure would be: head of department, year head, senior teacher, deputy head, head teacher. Make sure that you know who should be your first support. Do not, for example, threaten to take a child to the headteacher for talking in class.

TEACHING MODERN FOREIGN LANGUAGES

Task 3.4

Develop a discipline plan, outlining a series of offences and noting how you think you might react appropriately. Start with minor offences and move to more serious misdemeanours.

Flexibility

This word could be described as the most important term covering both teaching as well as classroom and behaviour management. You have to be well prepared, both in terms of content, activities and in terms of your discipline plan. It is more important, however, to be flexible. Be prepared to adapt your lesson, to skip a planned activity if things are not going well, to recap and reintroduce something if the students are having difficulty. Be flexible enough to adjust your objectives if it is evident that what you are planning is too ambitious and react spontaneously to a discipline situation if it is more appropriate than your planned response. Flexibility requires confidence, however, and confidence comes with practice and experience. Do not lose heart. You will make mistakes, there will be times when you know you have got it wrong, but be resilient. Adapt your strategies and try again.

Observing lessons

During your time as a student in schools you may be observed by various other colleagues, both from within the school itself and from the HEI. The list of people may include: another student, class teacher, head of department, mentor, deputy head, tutor from university/college. The purpose of the observation is not to intimidate you but to give you a different perspective on your lessons. When you have built up trust with a colleague these observed lessons can be a positive learning experience when you can enter into a dialogue not only about teaching but, much more importantly, about the learning which is taking place during your lessons.

If you are fortunate enough to be in a school where there are other student teachers or newly qualified teachers, it might be worth while arranging to sit in on each other's lessons. In order to give you some idea as to the aspects on which to focus, the following list might be helpful:

- student participation (number of learners involved in answering);
- questioning techniques;
- student motivation;
- student use of TL;
- variety of activities;
- attainment targets practised;
- differentiation;

- pace of lesson;
- pitch of material;
- classroom management strategies.

The list could be endless. A set of questions similar to those asked above under the heading 'evaluation' could also be used by peer observers. The advantage of peer observation is that it should be less threatening than the presence of an experienced colleague, in that there should be a level playing field. It is also the case that sitting at the back of the classroom provides a different perspective on the students in the class. If it is not possible to have peer observation you could ask to be videorecorded, but the presence of the video camera may interfere with the classroom dynamics.

Task 3.5

List the main problems you have encountered in your classroom. Note down strategies you could use to deal with such problems. Discuss these difficulties with your mentor.

Conclusion

Good planning and preparation are vital to the success of lessons. Lessons should be planned in a sequence and targets set regularly to ensure that the programme of study is being covered, both in terms of the language skills and the cross-curricular and transferable learning strategies.

Links to teaching standards

Most of the standards mentioned under *teaching and class management* have been covered in this chapter. Focusing on the various aspects of the chapter should help trainees to achieve the standards.

4 Physical and human resources

This second chapter on *content* introduces the trainee to a range of possible physical and human resources that can be drawn on for classroom teaching; and identifies major issues related to using these resources.

Objectives

By the end of this chapter the trainee will have an understanding of:

- issues relating to textbooks;
- ways of using visuals and realia;
- issues connected to visits and exchanges;
- working with a foreign language assistant.

Using textbooks

A wide variety of textbooks for teaching different foreign languages is available and this wide range may at first be bewildering. Inevitably, with the pre-eminence of French noted in Chapter 1, the number of textbooks and resources for French far outweighs those of other languages. However the quality of textbooks does not necessarily relate to their quantity.

It can be helpful to view textbooks in two different ways. First, on a *practical* level, considering:

- locating textbooks;
- departmental practice;
- user friendliness;
- syllabus appropriacy.

PHYSICAL AND HUMAN RESOURCES

Second, on a deeper *ideological* level, considering:

- professed aims and content;
- language learning demands;
- teaching demands;
- cultural representations.

Ur (1996), in her useful guide to teaching (English) foreign language divides these levels into two quite separate discussions on 'course book' and topic content 'hidden messages', but it may be more useful to run them together since there are several areas of overlap.

Locating textbooks

On a practical level you may ask how to access all the different textbooks that are available and how to evaluate them. There is likely to be a range of textbooks available in your training institution and some at your school. Some schools favour buying a set of textbooks, with different graded sets for different year groups, whereas others prefer to use photocopied or self-made materials from a variety of textbooks. In some schools students have their own books; in others there are sets of books shared between classes.

Besides these two immediate sources, there are other helpful locations:

- the Centre for Information on Language Teaching and Research (CILT) in London has an excellent library open every weekday where all the latest teaching materials are available for perusal;
- the Scottish, Welsh and Northern Irish centres, also have libraries of teaching materials as do the 13 Comenius Centres linked to CILT;
- publishers' representatives often contact schools and will send information on their latest publications and come to the school to talk about them;
- at language conferences (for example those run by the Association of Language Learning (ALL) and CILT) there are usually materials exhibitions where publishers display recent textbooks and resources;
- at the ALL annual conference there are usually several presentations from publishers about their most recent publications;
- the *Times Education Supplement* has twice-yearly curriculum supplements on modern languages and new textbooks are often reviewed in these;
- new textbooks are regularly reviewed in the Association of Language Learning journal *(Language Learning Journal)*.

The reviews and publishers' information will give some gloss on the different textbooks, but of course it is only in actually using them in the context of your own teaching and classes that decisions can be made about suitability. However, some suggestions for ways of evaluating textbooks are given later in this section.

TEACHING MODERN FOREIGN LANGUAGES

Departmental practice

As well as deciding whether to use a single textbook or work from several foreign language books, departments in schools are also likely to have a view on how to use textbooks. The teachers in a department may all wish to cover more or less the same ground in a textbook (and this can be useful where students from different classes compare notes) or there may be more flexibility with overall learning aims specified but freedom given to the teacher in terms of what is actually covered.

It will be very important when joining a school to establish the departmental policy regarding textbooks.

User friendliness

It is useful to remember that students have a context outside school that is rich in visuals and language. Advertising, television, computer games and the Internet all provide interesting and often fast-changing images. It is likely, then, that students will bring a discriminating eye to the foreign language textbook.

In order to match students' relatively sophisticated media tastes it will be helpful then if textbooks are colourful, varied and focus on topics of relevance and interest to students. Remembering comments about gender in Chapter 1, it may also be useful for there to be topics and activities likely to appeal to both genders. These factors then can be important to note when evaluating a textbook.

Syllabus relevance

There are clear guidelines in National Curriculum documentation about what is expected (although there are no lists of vocabulary as previously for GCSE) and it will be helpful if this is included in a textbook.

Grammar, target language and authentic texts are also elements that relate to new National Curriculum specifications and which will be important elements to identify in assessing a textbook. There is increased emphasis on pupils achieving proficiency in terms of grammatical accuracy in the National Curriculum, thus signalling a move away from accepting language performance that was fluent and communicative, if not accurate, which characterized earlier GCSE criteria. Grammar then has a higher profile (fitting in with literacy drives and with current language learning theories that emphasize the importance of attention to language forms). In two surveys in the 1980s (O'Sullivan, 1991 and Kay, 1996) students were asked about their preferences in textbooks. In both surveys students revealed that they preferred a summary of all relevant grammar in English at the relevant junctures in the book, rather than separate grammar sections to consult or grammar explanations in the target language. Arrangements for target language examinations rubrics were only put in place at the end of the 1990s so the antipathy also expressed by these two groups may be symptomatic of attitudes earlier in the decade.

The question of 'authentic texts' is somewhat problematic because there are different options here. For those who believed in the 'language-learning bath' theories espoused by Krashen and his followers, exposing learners to texts where not everything was understood was part of the learning experience. In these cases a text taken directly from the target context should not be adapted. Other language-learning theories that view learning as an aided process with specific language patterns being plentiful would identify a useful authentic text as one produced by a native speaker, but probably adapted from an original source. Making judgements then about authentic texts in course books is still a matter of some debate.

An extended list of practical features by which to judge a textbook is provided by Sheldon in his article on evaluating ELT textbooks and material (1988: 242–45). In the 17 factors he identifies he also includes easy availability, clearly stated objectives, overall text organization, progression, physical aspects (space to write in and weight), optional accompanying extras, and teacher guidance. These are all aspects also worth noting.

Professed aims and contents

A more searching framework of analysis is offered by Breen and Candlin (1987) in their 'consumer's and designer's guide' to materials, which they formulate as a series of eight questions:

1. What do ... materials aim to do and what do they contain?
2. What do ... materials make your learners do while they are learning?
3. How do ... materials expect you to teach your learners in the classroom?
4. Are the materials the only resource in classroom language learning?
5. Are the materials appropriate to your learners' needs and interests?
6. Are the materials appropriate to your learners' own approaches to language learning?
7. Are the materials appropriate to the classroom teaching/learning process?
8. Can the materials encourage the classroom group to evaluate learning through the materials?

Although it might appear that questions 4 and 5 replicate two of Sheldon's factors, there is a much deeper engagement because pupils themselves are considered as a resource, and 'needs and interests' are interpreted as long-term objectives and as learning habits acquired already.

In terms of analysing the aims and intent of a textbook it will be useful to track whether the objectives identified by authors are realized in the content of the book (recent research on a textbook for French found that this was quite definitely not the case, Door, 1999).

Language learning demands

It will be helpful to identify what is demanded of the learners by the different tasks in a textbook and consider whether the level of difficulty and challenge is appropriate. In

O'Sullivan's survey, pupils professed a dislike for repetitive exercises (1991: 13), an attitude identified elsewhere by research (as mentioned in Chapter 1). Breen and Candlin also mention the importance of opportunities for pupils' own contributions to be valued, for their own learning styles to be accommodated and for them to evaluate their own learning.

Where these elements are missing it can be useful to plan extra activities to provide these dimensions.

Teaching demands

Underlying any set of tasks in a textbook will be assumptions regarding the teacher's role. This may be reinforced by particular guidance in an accompanying teacher's book.

While there is no requirement to follow to the letter what is suggested in a teacher's book, it may nevertheless be helpful to reflect on any discrepancies with your own preferred teaching style. Breen and Candlin suggest that teachers pose themselves the question: 'What can I do as a teacher which can best help my learners to learn a new language?' and then compare this answer with the kind of role that underpins the activities in the class textbook (1987: 16). This then could be a useful exercise to consider in evaluating a textbook.

Cultural representations

Any textbook will be conveying images of the target culture(s) at the same time as it provides a forum for learning languages. It will be useful to examine the images in a textbook to see how much of a stereotypical picture they provide (and then, if necessary, provide complementary material to counteract this). Diversity is usually a strong factor here. Are different countries represented where the target language is spoken ? Are different cultural and ethnic groups represented? Are different registers of language given? Is a range of situations portrayed: conflict and complaint as well as co-operation and consensus ? Ur identifies sexism and ageism as areas where there may be underrepresentation (1996).

Conclusion

Although there may be little opportunity for a trainee to choose a school textbook, it will be useful to evaluate the textbooks that are being used and to consider how any deficits might be remedied.

Task 4.1

Take a unit from the textbook you are using and apply two or three questions from Breen and Candlin's list to it. Consider then what you might need to provide as a supplement.

PHYSICAL AND HUMAN RESOURCES

Task 4.2
Carry out a small-scale evaluation of a task in a textbook with one of your teaching groups. Consider how the results of this coincide (or do not coincide) with the ideas set out in this chapter.

Links to teaching standards

Under *teaching and class management,* trainees are asked to 'demonstrate that they ... use teaching methods which sustain the momentum of pupils' work and keep all pupils engaged through ... selecting and making good use of textbooks'. The suggestions made in this section should help to contribute towards achieving this standard.

Visuals

The visuals aspect of texts has increasingly become an area of real importance. Foreign language textbooks are now highly colourful with plenty of photos and drawings and the layout of pages carefully planned. Kress and van Leeuwen (1996) in their fascinating study of 'the grammar of visual design' show for example, in an analysis of two scientific textbooks from different eras (1938 and 1978), how the relationship between words and pictures has changed. In the early text the diagrams accompany and illustrate the words; in the later text the diagram carries the meaning with the written text backing it up. This emphasis on the visual within the classroom only mirrors what is happening in the world beyond. Students will be very used to a plethora of visual images, advertisements, cartoons, pictures on food packaging, computer games. In fact it is common for everyday texts (as opposed to fiction and academic texts) to be accompanied by visual support of some kind. There is, then, likely to be an expectation on the part of the students of visual support for learning and in turn they themselves are likely to have some expertise in visual literacy, in decoding visual messages.

In O'Sullivan's survey of pupils' views of textbooks (mentioned earlier), he speaks of 'abundance of illustrations' as the first favoured aspect in his summary of students' views (1991: 12).

Location of visual information

Locations for visual stimuli include:

- the walls of the classroom;
- the blackboard/whiteboard;
- the textbook;

- overhead transparencies;
- flashcards;
- worksheets;
- real objects.

In other words the classroom environment will be providing visual information for the learner on a macro and micro level, not forgetting, of course, visual information which a teacher is able to convey through the use of mime, gesture, facial expressions and so forth.

The classroom walls

It is a good idea to use the walls of the classroom as a passive source of information, learners can be spending some time (not too much we hope !) looking at their surroundings, and changing these visual stimuli may be much appreciated. Reminders of grammar rules can be displayed in a diagrammatic way; pictures of different aspects of the target country or countries may stimulate interest and displayed examples of students' work can encourage an appreciation of the creation of aesthetically pleasing materials and show the teacher's valuing of students' work. It is worth considering not only changing wall displays, but also their individual and overall layout (mounting items on coloured card, considering the size of different items, and so forth). Wright and Haleem (1991) have some useful suggestions on the practical aspects of display in their book on classroom visuals.

The blackboard/whiteboard

The board in a classroom is also an area of visual focus for students and it is worth considering as part of a lesson plan what the board will look like at the end of the lesson and how this area can be used to provide visual support for the learning taking place. As well as drawing on the board (diagrams and stick people illustrations can be useful), items can be stuck on to the board with Blu-Tack or magnets so that they can be visible for the whole lesson.

The board also offers a dynamic site for visuals (as opposed to the more static locations of the classroom wall and the textbook); items can be erased and moved around (if they are stuck on) or added to or obscured. There can be potential interference if the whiteboard is also used for projecting overhead transparencies so this needs to be taken into account when planning a lesson. With using the board, overhead transparencies and flashcards, it is also important not to obscure the visuals unintentionally.

Much of the visual material in current textbooks provides real pleasure: interesting photographs of the target culture(s) and native speakers, maps locating where the target language is spoken and useful illustrations. It is useful to remember that visuals can be the main carriers of meaning and to then use these as a primary focus for teaching.

Overhead transparencies

Overhead transparencies (OHTs) can also provide another dynamic location for visual information. Information can be obscured or added to or moved around (if small pieces of acetate are used). In addition OHTs offer a *permanent* visual resource that can be used year after year. It can also be that the same OHTs can double up for lessons in different foreign languages if the context is culture free (pictures of pets or parts of the body for example). It is worth considering how to store OHTs effectively so that they do not become damaged. Tierney and Humphrey's (1992) helpful Pathfinder book on using the overhead projector has many suggestions for working with OHTs.

Flashcards

Many course books will include sets of flashcards to use, although it may be desirable to replace these. Laminating facilities and clipart software mean that attractive and durable flashcards can be made relatively easily, although students may still prefer the personal touch in home-made cards. For both board work and flashcards it is worth considering the excellent section on drawing stick people in Wright and Haleem's 1991 book on visuals (pp 110–13).

Flashcards can also be used more dynamically than some other sources of visual information; cards can for example be hidden from view; they can be 'flashed' at high speed in front of students; they can be shared out amongst students; and they can be ordered and ranked.

As with OHTs it is worth considering questions of storage and manufacture if home-made flashcards are used. Cards can double up in different language lessons and can be used year after year, so it is worth thinking about durability from the outset.

Worksheets

Many worksheets consist of only written text, although visuals may be included for labelling exercises or matching exercises for example. However, even if the worksheet exercises or information are only written texts it is worth considering including some illustrations (however little) as:

- students are used to visual support;
- students can be oriented into the topic context of the worksheet;
- the general aesthetic appeal of the worksheet is enhanced.

Real objects

Bringing real objects (realia) into the classroom can make language learning come alive for students. For those students who like a hands-on (kinaesthetic) experience, they will be able to touch the objects. The visual information is not mediated by drawing which could be misunderstood. There is also some part of the physical experience of being in another culture (handling rail timetables, menus, brochures, stamps and so forth). Purcell (1994), for example, suggests ways of using a holiday brochure.

Using visuals

As well as considering the location of visual information it is also worth thinking about how to use visuals. It is clear that they offer support and information but it can also be useful to think about function in some more detail as this can affect choice. Two useful books to look at here are *Pictures in Action* (Gerngross and Puchta, 1992), which provides 62 different visually based activities, and the Pathfinder on cross-curricular approaches (Brown and Brown, 1996), which provides good examples of visual support in action.

Five main categories of activity can be linked to visuals:

- acting as an agent in skills-based activity;
- acting as a prompt;
- carrying meaning;
- providing cultural information;
- illustrating texts.

Visuals as agents

Visuals can operate as part of skill-based tasks. For example, students may be asked to match pictures to words in a reading exercise; they may be asked to draw in response to a picture dictation or identify correct visuals in listening exercises; they can converse in pairs to spot differences in two slightly different visual texts or identify missing objects from a group ('Kim's game') or they can be asked to label diagrams or write in speech bubbles. One of the advantages of using visuals in this kind of activity, as with many of the other activities, is that the student obtains clear information about the task without the teacher using English.

Visuals as prompts

As well as simple speech prompts such as using flashcards, visuals can also act as prompts for spoken discussions and creative writing. Thus students could discuss a photograph and imagine what a particular situation might be or how it has come about. They might suggest what happens next. They could suggest different interpretations of doodles. A story could be provided in picture form, which students then write out. Again, the visual is acting as non-verbal partner in the activity but this time with a much wider variety of options available to the student than in the more structured activities where the visual operates as agent.

One point worth considering is whether to choose a culturally less well-defined visual (which might then be viable across a range of languages). If visuals are chosen from the target culture, on the other hand, different information will be provided for the student.

Visuals as meaning carriers

Visual support (flashcards, OHTs, real objects) can be very helpful when introducing new vocabulary, because the meaning of words can be made explicit without recourse to English. Students can also learn words and visual images together, which may help in memorizing that vocabulary.

It is also possible to use visual information to clarify grammatical information. Thus genders and endings may be colour coded to make patterns of use visible and comprehensible. Rules such as those for pronouns taking both accusative and dative case in German can be demonstrated visually: an arrow for Accusative and a dot for Dative.

Visuals as cultural objects

Visual information from the target culture can provide useful information for the student: for example, photos of particular kinds of street sign and of types of housing; maps of countries where the target language is spoken and even using cartoons from children's magazines from the target culture.

One way of providing a deeper cultural experience for students is to use paintings from the target culture (postcards, slides or OHTs, although copyright laws will need to be observed). So for example, in teaching the weather, you could use Renoir's *Les Parapluies* (1982) Van Gogh's *Sower with Setting Sun* (1888) and Monet's *Arm of the Seine near Giverny in the Fog* (1897), instead of the usual weather symbols.

Visuals as illustrations

In textbooks or on worksheets, visuals may appear just to enhance the appearance of the text in general and/or to give some extra information. It is worth encouraging students to think about the visual aspect of their own work and to plan for this when they are creating their own texts, either electronically generated or produced by hand.

Obtaining/creating visuals

Most sources and kinds of visuals have already been mentioned, namely:

- photographs;
- diagrams;
- drawings;
- cartoons;
- clipart;
- real objects.

TEACHING MODERN FOREIGN LANGUAGES

Video of course is also another useful source of visual information (this is discussed in more detail in Chapter 5). There is no need to feel daunted about producing visuals because the advent of clipart software provides an ample range of images for those who feel uncertain about their own drawing skills. Wilson (1999) provides some examples of his own resources generated from three different sources:

- IMSI Master Clips, Premier Collection, 303,000.
- Broderbond Software Clickart 125,000 De Luxe Image Pack.
- Corel Maga Gallery, RJH Enterprises French Clip Art Discs 1–3.

Visuals then constitute an invaluable resource for teachers and it is useful to spend the first few years in teaching building up a bank of materials that can then be added to over the years.

Task 4.3

Evaluate the visuals in a lesson that you observe and consider what role they are playing.

Task 4.4

Identify a particular grammar problem and consider how you might present the relevant information visually to help students' learning. Try this out and evaluate the lesson.

Links to teaching standards

Under *teaching and class management,* trainee teachers are asked to 'demonstrate that they ... use teaching methods which sustain the momentum of pupils' work and keep all pupils engaged through ... clear presentation of content ... using well-chosen illustrations [and through] providing opportunities to develop pupils' wider understanding by relating their learning to real examples'.

Careful planning and choice of visuals should be able to help trainees to achieve these standards.

Visits and exchanges

The experiences offered by visits and exchanges are spending time in another country and meeting people from another country with all the emotional and cognitive adjustments

PHYSICAL AND HUMAN RESOURCES

that become necessary and the levels of understanding that are demanded. It is helpful when planning such activities to consider students' experience in these areas already. It may be that students have no other opportunity to meet native speakers of the target language (although they are likely to have contact in general with people from different cultural backgrounds); they may or may not have had holidays in other countries, but this will have been a different experience to that of a visit or an exchange.

Potentially the visit or exchange can offer huge benefits to the language learner:

- there is direct access to the language and culture without the mediation of teacher, textbook or other media;
- students can orient themselves in a target country: know what things look and feel like;
- a foreign language can be seen in action as the norm for communication for an extended period of time;
- students have the opportunity to practise speaking the target language in real and unpredictable contexts;
- there is the opportunity to investigate the target culture first hand.

With all these possible benefits it would seem that the visit or exchange should be both popular and frequent. However, this is not the case. The Nuffield Inquiry (2000: 46) comments that: 'Schools are finding it difficult to run foreign exchanges, mainly because of pupils' increasing unwillingness to participate.'

However, despite declining interest there are still plenty of initiatives taking place. The Central Bureau in 1998/1999 enabled 3500 students to participate in international activity, facilitated 40,000 school-based partnerships using ICT and linked 3183 schools (Central Bureau, Spring 2000: 3).

Types of possible contact

Possible kinds of contact with the target country or countries include:

- a family-to-family exchange;
- a visit with accompanying teachers;
- work placement;
- contact *sans voyages*.

Family-to-family exchange

This was traditionally the format for students' contact with the foreign country and it is also the area of activity that has declined. There may be many reasons for this: the financial implications; lack of suitable accommodation; difficulty in finding suitable partner schools or perhaps also the declining interest in foreign languages in general noted in Chapter 1.

School-organized visits

Schools may organize day trips (if sufficiently near the channel ports), or visits for longer periods of time. Visits can be organized for modern language groups or can have some other purpose (geography or history fieldwork or for sporting activities). It may be language teachers or other teachers who accompany students.

Work placement

Students following vocational courses may have arrangements with another institution or town in a European country where students can be placed in local businesses for periods of time. This will then link into language work tied to those courses.

Contact *sans voyages*

There can be all kinds of contact with other students and schools in target countries without physical displacement taking place. Some of the intercultural projects described in Chapter 2 incorporate just this kind of project. E-mail and videoconferencing facilitate virtual contact (see Chapter 5). It is interesting to note that the Central Bureau figures quoted include very large numbers for ICT-based contact, suggesting, perhaps, that this may be one of the main ways forward in the future.

For all these kinds of contact there are some important factors and caveats to note:

- any kind of contact will need some kind of preparation, considering, in particular, the purpose and outcome(s) of the contact;
- different kinds of support are likely to be necessary for different aspects and kinds of contact:
  - students will need to be alerted to the difference between the foreign language in the classroom and the foreign language in actual use;
  - students on family exchanges will need particular help with cultural orientation;
  - students on exchanges will need to be given structured guidelines for activities;
- it may well be worth considering the different kinds of contact in a schematic, hierarchical way; in other words contact *sans voyages* could take place as a precursor to other kinds of visit or exchange; study visits could precede family-to-family exchanges;
- students' attitudes may not be improved by contact with the target country or countries. Chambers' (1997: 62) research over a two-year period (1992–4) with students on German exchanges found that: 'little evidence is provided by these data, however, of substantial experience on the exchange which may be regarded as significantly influencing pupils' views of Germans and their culture'.
- Good preparation and follow-up activities, however, should be able to maximize the potential that is offered by visits and exchanges.

Organizing visits and exchanges

There are several levels of organization involved when planning a visit or exchange. These include:

PHYSICAL AND HUMAN RESOURCES

- the practical aspects of the activity;
- preparing the language elements;
- preparing the cultural elements;
- planning suitable follow-up activities.

Practical aspects

Two sources are useful to consult here that offer practical advice in setting up an exchange or a visit (in many cases some of the same areas of concern occur): Claire Jones's (1996) article on organizing an exchange and Snow and Byram's (1997) book in the Pathfinder series on organizing a school study visit.

Factors to consider include:

- finding an appropriate exchange partner (Jones provides a useful sample letter);
- choosing the destination and accommodation for a visit;
- arranging appropriate transport;
- arranging appropriate insurance;
- checking the legal arrangements;
- costing the visit or exchange;
- holding an early pupils' meeting to outline plans for the exchange or visit, and contacting parents by letter;
- confirming bookings and collecting money;
- providing checklists covering health and dietary matters and giving telephone and address contacts;
- holding a parents' meeting prior to departure to allow for queries to be answered.

Comprehensive and careful organization on this level will do much to ensure the overall success of the trip.

Preparing for an exchange

Although general preparation is similar to that for a school visit, there are particular aspects of an exchange trip that need to be considered separately because of the experience involved for the student.

Unlike a study visit (and also a holiday experience), an exchange will involve a student being *alone* with a group of native speakers, maybe for an extended period of time. The experience of being in another country is likely to bring about some kind of culture shock anyway. Salvadori (1997: 21) in her article on Italian students on exchange in France points to this overall factor:

> The effect, the so-called 'culture shock', is inevitable, even for the more experienced and competent traveller. The physical world of perceptions (of forms and contours, of sounds, smells, tastes, movements, gestures and what they signify) is 'other' Added to this an exchange student has to cope with the new language and culture without the comfort zone of their peers or other mother-tongue speakers.

The language experience of the exchange student in a family is likely to be very different from that in the classroom. At school the student encounters language that is often presented in a highly structure and formalized way; the teacher is likely to speak clearly and without interference directly to the student; the language used is often predictable (in the textbook text and index). In a family the experience may be quite different: people may all speak at once (particularly in cultures that favour overlapping conversations); they may speak quickly and indistinctly and they may use colloquialisms that are quite unfamiliar.

It is helpful then to plan activities beforehand that might help students overcome fear or anxiety that may result from linguistic disjunction.

Salvadori suggests:

- help with listening (providing exercises to familiarize students with different accents, voices superimposed on one another; and adolescent's language);
- help with speaking (using paraphrases) – it could also be useful to learn strategic phrases asking for help;
- encouraging reflexive analysis so that students become less anxious and more focused on improvement.

It can also be useful to consider the response of the host family. Chambers (1997: 62) noted in his interviews with students who had been on German exchanges that 'Germans take the initiative in practising their English be they in Germany or England and some pupils lack the self-belief to counteract this.' It may be helpful for host families to be contacted to encourage them to speak in the target language (perhaps also slowly). Jones's (1996: 7) sample letter to host parents includes just such a message:

> *Finalement les jeunes Anglais ne sont pas capables de tenir de longues conversations, et entourés d'une famille étrangère, ils risquent de se sentir timides au début. Cependant ils se débrouillent assez bien en phrases courtes et je vous serais très reconnaissant de bien vouloir les encourager à communiquer.*

Students will encounter different cultural codes of behaviour with their exchange family and it will be helpful to prepare them for this. Codes relating to food, eating and general politeness will need to be discussed. It can also be useful to provide students with phrases to cover emergencies should they feel alarmed that they may not be able to communicate. Keeping a journal during their stay can also be useful.

Ideally students should be able to recognize cultural filters at work: seeing that their way of viewing their host family will be determined by their own cultural experiences. However, this may be too much to expect. General discussions in class about different ways of life, about tolerance and relativization may help in this respect. However, as Salvadori (1997: 21) points out, this may be very difficult for adolescents 'who are self-conscious … (and whose) daily sense of reassurance is based on habitual verbal and non-verbal communication with their surroundings, constructed on unambiguous meanings.'

Preparing for a visit

The linguistic and cultural aspects of a visit are likely to be slightly different for a student because:

PHYSICAL AND HUMAN RESOURCES

- a visit is likely to contain more structured activities;
- there are likely to be lower anxiety levels because of the contact with fellow students;
- contact with native speakers is likely to be more structured and focused.

Snow and Byram (1997) concentrate particularly on the potential afforded by a school visit to expand students' *cultural* knowledge and understanding. In their four-point analysis of cultural understanding (*savoir-être, savoirs, savoir-apprendre* and *savoir-faire*) they concentrate particularly on *savoir-être* (the ability to understand the target culture from a native speaker's point of view) and *savoir-apprendre* (understanding ways of learning). They suggest that these two aspects are particularly good to develop, as *savoirs* (knowledge) can be acquired in a classroom setting. They describe three different scenarios that encourage students to investigate their cultural surroundings: creating a travel brochure, investigating stereotypes and investigating setting up a twinning scheme. They also suggest sensitizing activities that can make students more aware of their own culture as well as the target culture. In all these activities students are asked to observe, collect information and reflect.

If teachers take students on day trips there can still be opportunities for cultural activities on a more modest level: observing how people behave, looking at shop windows, thinking about noise levels. Good preparatory exercises here would be to practise observing these things in their own local environment and to think about them critically before setting off.

If students are undertaking extended cultural activities, they are likely to need specific vocabulary: for example questions or asking for clarification. It will be good to prepare this kind of vocabulary in advance. Snow and Byram relate the kind of work done on a visit to content and language integrated teaching and learning (see Chapter 11) 'where the language is used as a medium rather than a subject' (1997: 31).

On day trips, opportunities for language practice will be more limited but nevertheless students can prepare questions to ask, and requests for help should the answers they receive prove difficult to understand.

Follow-up activities

It will be important to capitalize on what students have learnt not only to consolidate their learning but also to make the experience feel worthwhile.

If students have kept journals, these can be discussed. Students can make posters, give presentations or produce written accounts. In some cases this may contribute towards examination coursework.

Task 4.5

Talk to your mentor about experiences in your school relating to exchanges and visits and see whether this matches up with the ideas put forward in this section. (If not, why do you think this is?)

> **Task** 4.6
>
> Plan a preparatory activity for a family-to-family exchange for year nine students and discuss it with your mentor in terms of its appropriateness.

Links to teaching standards

Under *subject knowledge and understanding* trainees are asked to demonstrate that they are familiar with subject-specific health and safety requirements; under *planning and teaching and class management* they are asked to demonstrate that they: plan opportunities ... and keep all pupils engaged through ... exploiting opportunities to contribute to pupils' spiritual, moral, personal, social and cultural developments ... [and] to provide opportunities to develop pupils' wider understanding by relating their learning to real and work-related examples.

Investigating the role of exchanges and visits in a school context should help to contribute towards achieving this standard.

Working with a foreign language assistant

The school(s) in which you teach may or may not have foreign language assistants (FLAs). According to figures from the Central Bureau (1997 and 1999) the numbers of FLAs dropped significantly over the two-year period 1997–99: 2398 in 1997 and 1893 in 1999, a drop of 505 (21 per cent). The spread of languages has also diminshed with a higher percentage of French FLAs in 1999: 1417 out of 2398 in 1997 (59 per cent), 1291 out of 1893 in 1999 (68.4 per cent).

If, however, you are lucky enough to be able to work with an FLA then this can be of great benefit and it is useful to consider how to maximize the opportunities that then become available. The main advantages of working with an FLA are that there is:

- a genuine communicative partner and native speaker model;
- an additional source of the target culture often allowing for stereotypes to be challenged;
- an extra 'teacher'.

If we consider the requirements of the National Curriculum, then, two linked aspects of learning are particularly helped by working with an FLA: '*Social development* ... through delivering pupils' ability to communicate with others, particularly speakers of foreign languages, in an appropriate, sympathetic and tolerant manner' (p 8) and '*Developing cultural awareness* ... communicating with native speakers' (p 17).

There are two main areas where the FLA may be helpful: in lesson time, and out of lesson time.

In lesson time

It will be useful to check with your school what the normal procedures are for working with the FLAs. They may be shared across schools; they may be asked to help out during lessons or take small groups separately; there may be special arrangements for integrating the work done by the FLA; there may also be special arrangements for monitoring the work done by the FLA and recording what has taken place. There may also be different arrangements for work with different age groups.

Working with small groups

Traditionally working with small groups has been the main activity undertaken by the FLA. Rowles *et al* (1998: 16) in their guide to good practice in working with an FLA, suggest 20-minute sessions with four to six pupils as a workable norm. However, you will need to check what arrangements are usually in place in your school.

Possible activities that the FLA can undertake are:

- oral practice in general, particularly for examination groups;
- practising GCSE role plays;
- discussing A-level topics;
- acting as an interviewee to develop students' cultural awareness skills;
- acting as a mock oral examiner.

It will be useful beforehand to:

- liaise with the FLA;
- consider how the work to be done will integrate either in general with the scheme of work or in particular to the lessons you are teaching;
- provide materials or resources that the FLA may need.

One very important point to consider is how to run your own lesson if groups of students are working some of the time with the FLA. At best the lesson could be modular, with a carousel of activities, of which one is the session with the FLA. Another alternative could be a lesson based on reading (such as with the *Lesekiste* or *Bibliobus* resources) where absence from the classroom can be accommodated relatively easily. As a minimum, it will be important to consider how students can catch up on information and experience that has been missed while they have been out of the classroom.

Working as a partner during the lesson

There can be considerable advantages to team teaching with the FLA:

- the teacher-student ratio is improved;
- the target language can be modelled in an authentic way (role-plays for example);

- students, particularly for A-level topics, can have the benefit of different cultural inputs and viewpoints from two sources of instruction;
- the 'team' can in itself act as a good model for students in terms of how to operate collaboratively.

It will be helpful beforehand to have a planning meeting with the FLA to decide how the lesson will be handled and to consider what target language will be used during the lesson and any adjustments that will need to be made to ensure that the level is appropriate for the students.

Out of lesson time

There is likely to be considerable common ground between trainee teachers and FLAs:

- both are learning about how to teach (often FLAs have no teacher training);
- both need to familiarize themselves with national assessment procedures;
- both need to become familiar with the codes of the school.

It may then be mutually very helpful to share thoughts in these areas.

There are also several other ways in which the FLA can be an invaluable resource:

- as a target language partner;
- helping to prepare materials;
- providing up-to-date realia;
- providing up-to-date information;
- linking with schools in the target countries.

A target language partner

It can be very helpful to have a reciprocal arrangement with the FLA where you help each other with your languages. It can be an ideal arrangement to fix times when you speak one or other of each other's languages. This will provide extra practice for both partners and correction is often easier in a reciprocal arrangement.

Preparing materials

It can be extremely useful if an FLA is willing to record listening tapes. In this way particular areas of difficulty can be targeted which may not be covered by the tapes provided with course books. Since dates, times and numbers can all be difficult listening items, a high-speed recording of these, where short extracts are used for revision, can be an invaluable resource. Rowles *et al* (1998: 34) also make the following suggestions for listening tapes:

- tongue twisters and nursery rhymes;
- listening discrimination exercises;
- 'attitude' tapes where things are said demonstrating different emotions (anger, sadness etc);
- picture dictations.

It may also be possible to work with FLAs on producing simplified versions of different texts, which still then remain authentic. This may be useful for example in the context of collecting texts for GCSE coursework or for A-level topics.

Providing realia

If FLAs return home during their stay at your school, they may be willing to collect target culture items (menus, brochures, timetables and so forth), which can provide authentic reality in the classroom. They may also be willing to show and discuss photographs relating to their own personal life, which again can make language communication more personal.

Providing up-to-date information

An FLA will be able to provide not only the most up-to-date information on language developments but also information on current affairs. This is clearly of particular benefit to A-level students. Other cultural information that FLAs can provide can allow students to discuss cultural issues in depth, challenging the stereotypes they may have. For example, FLAs might provide material relating to aspects of their own life, which they may feel are 'typical' or 'not typical' of the target culture.

An FLA may also be able to provide new information on particular customs and festivals that can be both a point of interest and a subject for discussion and cross-cultural comparison.

Acting as a school link

Finally the FLA may be able to act as a link person with schools and or institutions in his or her own home country. This can be of reciprocal benefit because the FLA will have knowledge of both schools or the suitability of students for work placements in different locations.

The FLA can thus be an invaluable member of the foreign language teaching team and can also feel valued by being given responsibility for specific tasks.

Task 4.7

Liaise with your FLA to take responsibility for a particular aspect of a lesson. Ask your FLA to evaluate the experience and evaluate it yourself and then compare your joint observations.

Task 4.8

Discuss with your mentor experiences of working with FLAs and list any points that have not been raised in this section.

Links to teaching standards

Under *planning* and *teaching and class management* trainees are asked to 'plan' and provide opportunities to develop pupils' spiritual, moral, personal, social and cultural development and to develop pupils' wider understanding by relating their learning to real and work-related examples.

Working with an FLA should help to contribute towards achieving these standards.

5 Using information and communication technologies

This third chapter on *content* introduces trainees to the ICT requirements in the MFL curriculum and explores the resources and activities relating to different ICT tools.

Objectives

By the end of this chapter the trainee will have an understanding and appreciation of:

- the requirements governing the use of ICT in subject teaching;
- the role of ICT in the MFL curriculum;
- using audio resources;
- using computers for language learning;
- using the Internet and e-mail.

Using ICT in subject teaching

In addition to the standards required for qualified teacher status (QTS), outlined in Chapter 1, trainees of all subjects are required to demonstrate their competence in applying ICT to their specialist subjects. In addition to their general document (TTA *et al*, 1999), the TTA has produced documents that relate the general principles to individual subjects (TTA, DfEE, WOED, DENI, 1999). The initial document is in two parts: section A relates to effective teaching and assessment methods and section B refers to teachers' knowledge and understanding of, and competence with, ICT.

The document states the importance of the use of ICT to enhance learning objectives and not simply to act as a motivating tool. It requires teachers to be aware of the best ways of incorporating ICT in lesson planning and to be aware of ways in which students' progress in the subject can be enhanced by using ICT.

In terms of the teachers' own knowledge of ICT, section B sets out what teachers are required to be able to do with ICT, including word-processing, e-mail, presentation software and data handling. It states that teachers should be able to use ICT for administrative purposes in addition to teaching. The document is quite prescriptive and trainees are required to be thoroughly familiar with using ICT with a view to implementing its various functions in subject lessons. The Northern Ireland document *Northern Ireland Strategy for Education Technology* (DENI, 1999) subdivides this into:

- personal competence;
- subject competence;
- teaching competence.

The more useful document for trainees and teacher is the second of the TTA guides *Using Information and Communications Technology to Meet Teaching Objectives in Modern Foreign Languages: Initial Teacher Training*. This is divided into four sections:

- Section 1 explains how ICT contributes to students' learning.
- Section 2 sets the use of ICT in subject teaching in the context of the ITT National Curriculum.
- Section 3 presents a case study in the context of MFL.
- Section 4 lists sources and examples of using ICT in modern languages.

This document is extremely useful in helping the teacher of modern languages come to grips with the implementation of ICT within the framework of subject teaching and should be referred to at the planning stage of lesson development.

ICT in the MFL curriculum

Information technology (IT) has existed for some time as a separate subject area. However information and communication technology (ICT) is now a key skill and as such is a statutory requirement for every subject area from key stage three upwards. Modern foreign languages teachers and pupils will need to provide evidence of including this dimension. At the end of the 1990s it was evident that, where ICT had been used, this has been motivating, particularly for boys (Johnston,1999b; Nuffield Foundation, 2000: 46). However, use of ICT has not been fully developed in all schools and provision is uneven (Nuffield Foundation, 2000: 46; Dobson, 1998: 26).

ICT in the National Curriculum

In the MFL National Curriculum documentation ICT requirements are outlined in three different ways:

- the general requirements, which apply across the curriculum;
- specific requirements relating to MFL;
- suggested implementations.

General requirements

These are as follows(DfEE/QCA, 1999:30):

> 1. Pupils should be given opportunities to apply and develop their ICT capabilities through the use of ICT tools to support their learning in all subjects.
> 2. Pupils should be given opportunities to support their work by being taught to:
>   a. find things out from a variety of sources, selecting and synthesizing the information to meet their own needs and developing an ability to question its accuracy, bias and possibility.
>   b. develop their ideas using ICT to amend and refine their work and enhance its quality and accuracy.
>   c. exchange and share information, both directly – through electronic media
>   d. review, modify and evaluate their work, reflecting initially on its quality, as it progresses.

The emphasis in ICT requirements for MFL is mostly on *assessing* and *communicating* information. In other words, the exploration suggested in 2a above is not highlighted. Exploring and questioning data is an aspect highlighted more in A-level ICT requirements. In the introductory section on MFL in the National Curriculum, where learning across the National Curriculum is addressed (in particular the promotion of key skills), ICT is highlighted as follows:

> MFL provides opportunities for pupils to develop the key skills of ... IT, through using audio, video, satellite television and the internet to access and communicate information, and through selecting and using a range of ICT resources to create presentations for different audiences and purposes.
>
> (DfEE/QCA, 1999: 8).

In the programme of study for key stages three and four (DfEE/QCA, 1999: 16–17), ICT is mentioned three times in the content section 'knowledge, skills and understanding'. Under 'developing language skills', ICT sources are required for reading techniques (2h) and ICT is also required as a means of redrafting written work (2j). Under 'developing cultural awareness', ICT sources are required as a source of authentic materials in the target language (4a).

In the activities section of the programme of study, 'breadth of study', ICT is required as a means of producing written texts (5d, cf 2j) and as a resource for accessing and communicating information (5e, cf 2b, 2j and 4a).

Suggested implementation

In addition ICT is suggested as a possible dimension in the content section 'developing cultural awareness' where e-mail could be a means of 'communicating with native speakers' (4b), particularly those in more distant countries. E-mail is also suggested as one means of 'using the target language for real purposes' (5h) in the activities section of the programme of study.

ICT in AS/A-level syllabuses

Documentation from the three examining bodies quotes the relevant section of the key skills specifications from the Qualifications and Curriculum Authority and then relates these to the particular aspects of their own examinations where evidence may be generated (these examinations are described in greater detail in the section on A-level in Chapter 6).

Thus OCR describe in some detail how their syllabus relates to three levels of IT Level 2. (1999: 44–46) where candidates are asked to 'Search and select information for *two* different purposes' (IT 2.1) Unit 1 (Speaking), Unit 4 (Speaking and Reading) and Units 6 or 7 (Culture and Society by examination or coursework) are suggested. In other words, information is used for oral or written purposes. The Internet is also recommended as a resource.

For the second component (IT 2.2) where candidates are asked to 'explore and develop information and derive new information for *two* different purposes', Unit 1 (Speaking) and Unit 7 (Culture and Society, coursework) are recommended. Both units require students to research topics – in particular the coursework option requires visible evidence of research.

For component three (IT 2.3) where candidates are asked to 'present combined information for *two* different purposes (including text, images and numbers), Unit 1 (Speaking) Unit 4 (Speaking and Reading) and Unit 7 (Culture and Society coursework) are mentioned. The oral presentation may be backed up by documentation including images and numbers, and coursework may require word-processed presentation of materials.

AQA quote the same three IT components but at Level 3 (IT 3.1; IT3.2; IT3.3) and point to two modules that can be used to generate evidence: Unit 2 (Writing) and Unit 5 (Writing by examination or coursework. This information is given in a table (AQA, 1999: 39)) but with no follow up or detailed information.

Edexcel provides both a table mapping key skills on to units (2000: 102) and detailed information as to how their modules can provide evidence for the three components of ICT level 3 (2000: 107–09). The units they suggest are as follows:

- for skill IT 3.1: unit 3 (prepared oral topic); unit 4 (oral discussion or interpreting); unit 5 (topics and texts, or coursework);
- for skill IT 3.2: unit 1 (listening and responding); unit 2 (reading and responding); units 3, 4, and 5 (listening and responding, reading and responding and writing in registers);
- For skill IT 3.3: units 5 and 6: suggestion for activities include using the Internet and CD ROMs; word-processing, including generating images; and e-mailing drafts of documents to tutors for feedback.

There is clear guidance, then, in official documentation pinpointing ICT as an essential dimension of the curriculum. The detail will depend on the teacher and the resources available in the school. There are of course other pedagogical and education benefits in using ICT.

Task 5.1

Check through the ICT requirements for either the National Curriculum or A-level and consider how you can incorporate one of these into a lesson that you are teaching.

Using audio resources

Audio resources can be seen as belonging to ICT (the National Curriculum mentions it – specifically: DfEE/QCA, 1999: 8). There is further legitimization in that audio has moved away from just recording equipment and is now also a dimension of computer software.

Types of audio resources

The most familiar audio equipment is the cassette recorder and this is usually part of the equipment owned by the MFL department; CD players and mini-disk players may also be available. Students themselves may own these items (or a Walkman) so it can be useful to take advantage of these. Computers may have facilities to play CD ROMs or DVD ROMs, which can provide audio input. Television and the videorecorder also provide both visual and audio information.

Publishers often produce audio-cassettes to accompany textbooks. Cassettes can also be made up from recordings (using the foreign language assistant can be useful here) and students can be issued with blank cassettes to record themselves. New CD ROMs and DVD ROMs are coming on to the market. Caldwell describes a CD ROM program which helps students with pronunciation: TeLL me More (1999b) and a DVD ROM that allows learners to dub their own voices on to a TV series in the target language (2000).

Ways of using audio resources

Four important ways of using audio resources are:

- for listening purposes;
- for speaking purposes;
- for cultural awareness;
- as a stimulus for other activities.

Audio for listening

Audio cassettes and (videos) can be used to listen for information. This is often the basis of examination listening exercises. It can be helpful to train students to listen both for gist and detail (a language skill identified in the National Curriculum – DfEE/QCA, 1999: 16).

Tapes can also be used for developing students' ability to discriminate between sounds in the target language. It may be that tapes will need to be made for this purpose as most course book tapes do not include aural discrimination exercises.

Students can also listen to tapes while reading the written version of a text to help with linking written and spoken language items. This activity can be made more interesting by blanking out key words or using sections as sources for dictation and allowing comparison with the written text.

Audio for speaking

Students will often be taped in their oral examinations and it is useful to familiarize them with this procedure as early as possible. Students can prepare presentations to be taped and played back; they can make their own recordings and these can be used as a source for error correction for both language and pronunciation; audiotapes can also be made to send away to a partner school as a way of communicating with native speakers (cf 4c in the National Curriculum, DfEE/QCA, 1999:17).

Audio for cultural awareness

As well as using audio tapes to foster closer contact with a target culture, taped material of native speakers in itself should bring about greater cultural awareness. Students can be exposed to a variety of different voices and the foreign language can become real.

Audio as a stimulus

Audio material does not have to be spoken dialogue: sounds (particularly music) can also act as a stimulus for other activity. It was suggested in the section on creativity in Chapter 2 that music could act as a stimulus for creative writing. Playing different kinds of music (particularly if selected by the students) could also serve as a stimulus for discussion.

The value of audio resources and activities

Using audio resources can be helpful for some learners if this coincides with their preferred learning style. Audio resources are usually examples of authentic language use (although students may need support if there is too much external noise or the speech is too rapid). Listening to audio resources can help students to concentrate in lessons and has the effect of quietening them down in lessons (Halliwell's 'settling' activities, 1991). Audio resources are also good for encouraging learner autonomy, an aspect of all ICT resources. One problem can be that overlong listening tasks can be difficult if no support is available.

Task 5.2

Create an audio resource with the help of a native speaker to support an aspect of one of your lessons.

Task 5.3

Critically evaluate an exercise on a coursebook cassette that relates to your lessons, questioning its viability, relevance and efficacy. Consider how it could be improved if necessary.

Using video resources

Video resources, like audio resources, are likely to be available to trainees in schools. Many of the advantages mentioned in the previous chapter relating to using visuals also apply to video. Students are familiar with video: they know the format of the television experience and appreciate the authentic and lively contribution that video and television can bring. Three significant advantages of video are that:

- it can provide an authentic experience;
- it is up to date;
- many non-verbal cues are provided.

Dobson (1998: 26) comments on the usefulness of authenticity for cultural awareness purposes:

> Where teachers are able to incorporate a range of media including video and satellite television in their lessons, this normally motivates pupils and enhances their cultural awareness by providing real images of another way of life.

Stempelski and Tomalin (1990: 3) also comment on the usefulness of authenticity: 'using a video sequence in class is the next best thing to experiencing the sequence in real life'. It may be that in building up students' cultural awareness, a video experience represents a safe first encounter with cultural differences.

The fact that video or satellite television can provide up-to-the-minute information and up-to-date vocabulary can be useful for both teachers and students. This can be particularly relevant for sixth form topic work.

The abundance of visual clues is also helpful for understanding. Information that is relayed through an audiotape may be difficult for a student to grasp. The same information presented on video will be much easier, not only because the context is visible, but also because non-verbal signals can be added in. It may thus be possible to pitch the level of language higher for students when using video.

Four different areas of video use are described in this section, two relating to *using* video resources and two to *creating* video resources. These are:

- foreign language video material;
- satellite television;
- videoconferencing;
- using a video camera.

MFL video material

Two main sources of video material are from publishers such as course book extras or stand-alone resources, and off-air recordings of UK television programmes.

Many course books offer a video as part of the range of extra accompanying resources. Publishers also publish stand-alone videos. Besides the normal run of UK publishers it is helpful to look at those distributed by European Schoolbooks and by the Goethe Institut. The information sheet on videos published by CILT provides useful details of videos in French, German and Spanish including telephone numbers. The videos they list are those held in the CILT Resources Library. The French Embassy also provide a catalogue of videos which can be borrowed and where only postage needs to be paid for. These videos are often useful for sixth form work.

Most schools will have facilities for off-air recording and there should be no copyright problems providing recordings are made for educational purposes. The BBC Learning Zone and Channel 4 school programmes both provide a range of different programmes at different levels and teachers' booklets can be purchased to use with the programmes. Video packs can also be purchased if off-air recording is not possible. These television broadcasts are in French, German and Spanish.

Satellite television

Bering able to use satellite television will depend on the facilities available at the school. Clearly, being able to tap directly into television networks in other countries allows for an immediacy not present in video from UK sources. However, using satellite television does have problems. Mohr (1997), in his overview of the use of satellite television, provides a useful systematic approach, which overcomes two of the main difficulties: overload of programmes and knowing how to select effectively. Mohr adopts a four-point action plan of:

- classification;
- selection;
- identification;
- utilization.

He suggests undertaking an initial time-consuming classification exercise in order to identify what programmes are available: 'a one-off exercise, which will pay handsome dividends over a long period of time' (p 13). He provides his own list of German TV channels available on ASTRA (pp 14–16). He then suggests selecting particular programmes, not forgetting the value of commercial and sports channels. Programmes need to be identified that offer the best value in terms of what can be used from them. These programmes then need to be edited in terms of their language suitability and cultural acceptability, bearing in mind that programmes can be used with different groups.

Hill lists particular kinds of satellite TV programmes that may be suitable (1991):

- news broadcasts;
- advertisements;
- documentaries;
- drama
- humorous programmes.

He suggests particularly that programmes with short extracts are useful (holiday or magazine programmes, weather forecasts); that learning outcomes need to be identified;

that recordings to be kept should be catalogued but that it is useful also to discard recordings where appropriate.

Using video resources

With both foreign-language videos and satellite television recordings there are a large number of activities that can be undertaken to contribute to language work and to cultural awareness. Stempelski and Tomalin (1990) give recipes for 75 activities in their book on using video in an English-as-a-foreign-language context and many of these ideas can be transferred to a UK context for teaching a foreign language:

- with the vision on and the sound off;
- with the sound on and the vision obscured;
- freezing a frame on the tape;
- playing through a short extract.

If too long a sequence is played then students may lose concentration.

Students can concentrate on interacting with a video clip at the time of showing (answering comprehension questions, noting down information or vocabulary, filling in gaps in a transcript, for example); or they may use what they have seen on a video clip as stimulus for further language work (predicting what may come next or discussing what has happened, for example). This can operate at different levels: pre-16 prompting class discussion for example or sixth form work tying the video into a text or topic.

Language heard on a video clip can act as a good model for pronunciation, and as mentioned earlier can provide insights into the culture of another country (although items will be selected and presented in a particular way).

The fact that a video clip can be shown several times means that the video experience can have distinct advantages over a real experience in terms of learning. Students will have several opportunities to hear the same thing.

Videoconferencing

Videoconferencing is likely to be possible only if these facilities are available at school (occasionally telecommunication firms are willing to set up videoconferencing between schools). A link with another school abroad, which also has videoconferencing facilities, will have to be arranged. In practice it is very often only specialist (language) colleges that have the technology available. However, this is likely to be an area that will develop in the future so the benefits are worth bearing in mind.

Videoconferencing will allow students from one school to communicate directly with students in another school (a visual form of e-mail as it were). This could be as a group or as a sequence of individuals who will then be visible on the screen in the other classroom. Students will need to prepare carefully for the interaction and it is likely that the most effective links will be those that focus on a particular topic (as described in the sections on videoletters and e-mail below). There can be temporary disconnections in the link and teachers will need to be prepared for handling the frustration that can ensue.

Another use of videoconferencing can be as a source of teaching. The Nuffield Inquiry suggests that online teaching can be useful for learning another foreign language if this is not catered for in a school (Nuffield Foundation, 2000: 49 and 53). In the East Riding of Yorkshire a videoconferencing link has been set up to link sixth formers with foreign language assistants to allow for discussion of A-level topics (Stork, 2000).

Using a video camera

Students can create their own video resources by using a video camera (if this is available in the school). A useful outcome here can be the creations of video letters, which can be sent to a partner school. If this can be part of a video letter exchange then a kind of diluted videoconferencing will have been set up. Seidler (1989) describes his own video-letter exchange project between his school in Germany and a link school in the US. He gives useful details of how to organize students, how to arrange the filming and editing and discusses the problems that may arise. His most useful advice is to ensure that videos are exchanged *quickly,* so that momentum is not lost. (This was also the experience in the intercultural project described in the cultural awareness section of Chapter 2).

Using a video camera will need careful planning (checking light, sound, the battery, the tape and the tripod). Students will need to experiment with different kinds of shot (zooming, panning etc) so that balance and continuity is achieved. Some students may already be experienced in using a video camera and be able to help others.

It will be helpful to plan for a particular topic presentation. If this is part of a video-letter exchange then there can be follow up from questions from the partner school, perhaps a presentation of aspects of local interest. Students can prepare a topic, which will be part of an oral examination and then have the chance to review their own performance. They may wish to prepare role-play sequences.

Using the camera is likely to be a motivating experience for some students. Preparing to be filmed can be a helpful rehearsal for students who will have to take oral examinations. The sense of occasion in performing for the camera can bring out the best in students. One of Seidler's students' comments: 'most pupils in our class are excited when they are filmed (1989: 34)'.

Video, then, in all its forms can be a motivating dimension to foreign language teaching. It is likely that whatever form it takes it will involve the teacher in considerable preparation. However this will be rewarded in several ways:

- the building of a reusable resource;
- engagement and motivation of the learners;
- allowing time for interaction with individuals during the lesson.

Task 5.4

Evaluate the use of a video activity that you have observed in any lesson.

Computer assisted language learning (CALL)

The current situation

Provision and use of technology in schools still varies considerably despite the clear requirements for ICT in pre-16 and post-16 curricula outlined earlier. Dobson (1998: 26) notes from his 1996/97 OFSTED inspection that 'provision is still underdeveloped and uneven across schools' and that 'many struggle to provide an adequate experience of word processing for all pupils'. Caldwell (1999a) comments that 'there is little doubt that many schools have expert and enthusiastic ICT linguists. However, a sizeable number of modern languages technophobes and sceptics still need to be convinced of the advantages of their computers and reassured about their motivating value in the classroom.' Trainees and teachers may thus have to operate in quite different circumstances in different schools: these differences are likely to relate to attitudes in general to using computers, to provision (how many computers there are) and to availability and access. As a trainee you will need to be creative with what is available. It may also be that the department looks to a new member of staff to take over the responsibility for integrating CALL into lessons if other members of staff are reluctant to do so.

 There is considerable support available beyond the school: CILT now publishes a regular newsletter on ICT issues for language teachers on schools (*What's on-line for languages*); the government is offering training in ICT for language teachers up to Spring 2003 (£400 per teacher funded by the National Lottery – New Opportunities Fund training). Lists of providers have been issued to schools and these include CILT; the special organization for ICT, the British Educational Communications and Technology Agency (BECTa, formerly the National Council for Educational Technology, NCET) publishes information sheets on the Internet and satellite TV as well as very useful vocabulary sheets in different languages: '*Say it in …*' These sheets are available for Bengali, Cantonese, German, Gujarati. Hindi, Italian, Japanese, French, Spanish, Turkish and Urdu; BECTa has also produced a video: *Accent on IT: Practical training and support,* with seven illustrative case studies for using IT at key stage three. Moreover, CILT have produced a special series of publications: *Infotech* (similar to their Pathfinder series) which focuses on using communications technology in language learning. Sue Hewer's (1997) book on text manipulation is particularly useful in considering how best to use computers in MFL teaching. Software is also held in the CILT Resources Library.

 It will be helpful then to consider using as many sources of support as possible beyond the school. Within a school it will be helpful to talk to the IT co-ordinator and also to investigate arrangements for accessing computers, because these may be complicated. It is likely that it will only be in specialist colleges (particularly language colleges) where funding has been specially provided for enhanced technology, that extensive and comprehensive facilities will be available. In most schools there will be computers in a special computer suite and/or one or several computers in a classroom.

Using computers for MFL teaching

There are three main ways that computers may be used:

- for word-processing;
- for text manipulation (computer exercises);
- as a source of information.

Where computer facilities are extensive it may also be possible to have integrated multi-media activities.

Word-processing

Computers can be used to provide finished pieces of work that are attractive to look at and which incorporate graphics and tables/diagrams etc. Appropriate accents can be used and different fonts (such as italics or bold) used to add to the aesthetic appearance of the text. Word-processing is useful for both students doing coursework and for teachers preparing their materials.

Text manipulation

A number of authoring packages exist which allow word games or exercises to be set up with the teacher writing in the text. *Fun with Texts* (Camsoft) is the package most commonly found in schools (Gray, 1996). Wida are also a large MFL software producer. Major packages for sequencing activities are *Fun with Texts: Text Salad* (Camsoft) and *Matchmaster* (Wida); for gap filling activities: *Fun with Texts: Cloze* (Camsoft), *Gapkit* (Camsoft), *Gapmaster* (Wida) and *Choicemaster* (Wida). For text reconstruction *Storyboard* (Wida), *Fun with Texts: Copywrite Hard and Easy, Predict* (Camsoft). Word games or exercises can also be created by word-processing but the feedback facilities will not then be available. In these games (whether on software or word-processed) students will be manipulating texts by guessing the right answers to various language puzzles (Hewer provides extended examples and discussions, 1997).

A source of information

Students can consult references on CD ROMs (if the facilities in the school allow for this). Dictionaries are now available as CD ROMs and Walker describes the successful use of *Encarta*, a multi-media encyclopaedia, in a language college in Berkshire (1999). This Microsoft software comes in ten languages of which four are currently being used at the school. Pupils use the technology to support their coursework. One pupil comments: 'It is a very good resource. You find information that isn't in books.' It is also a resource that allows for access to information more quickly than by using the Internet. One problem mentioned by Walker is 'the temptation simply to copy chunks … and attempt to pass the work off as … [your] own'. This is clearly a danger both with using reference sources such as *Encarta* and the Internet and will need to be monitored.

USING ICT

For both reference resources and text-manipulation packages it is useful to consult the CILT information sheet on software. It may also be the case that the course book used in the school has accompanying software.

Integrating IT into the lesson

It is helpful if activities with computers link specifically with the scheme of work being followed and the activities in any one lesson. This will need to be taken into consideration when planning lessons and could take various forms. For example teachers could:

- take a text from the course book and set this up with different exercises;
- find or create parallel text with similar exercises;
- set up exercises to practise particular grammar points or structures;
- ask pupils to use the word-processing facilities to create texts, exercises or to do their homework.

If authorizing packages are used this may be more motivating because students will receive automatic feedback.

An important aspect of working with computers is that the teacher guidance and input is often done *before* the lesson: in looking through material to check out difficulties; in planning appropriate activities; in planning appropriate support and deciding on sequencing and grouping. In the actual lesson the teacher will then have more time to work with individuals since their work will be more autonomous.

ICT as a different dimension

Using ICT in lessons is generally popular, particularly with boys. Thus using IT can be beneficial not only because it is a curricular requirement but also because it is motivating. It is worth considering how ICT is different because much of the content offered in software packages is not that different to what could be provided on a work sheet. Specific points of consideration are:

- ICT as part of a range of sources;
- the content of IT software packages;
- the process of using IT.

ICT as part of a range of sources

The National Curriculum focuses particularly on ICT acting as an extra source. Here the focus is on *all* the different kinds of technology: audio, video, satellite television, the Internet. Thus under 2h in the *programme of study* 'written texts for information, including those from ICT-based sources' are mentioned as appropriate for 'techniques for skimming and for scanning' (DfEE/QCA, 1999: 16); 4a concentrates on 'authentic materials in the target language including some from IT-based sources' as being appropriate for developing cultural awareness. Specific suggestions are made for these 'authentic materials' (these are non-statutory): 'video, satellite television, texts from the Internet' (1999a: 17). 5d mentions ICT texts again in the context of ways of learning (*Breadth of Study*): 'pupils should be taught the knowledge, skills and understanding through ... producing and responding to different types of spoken and written language including texts produced using ICT'. Here then ICT-based texts are seen as valuable in the sense that they represent part of the range of texts with which students should be familiar. Video texts, audio texts, computer texts and Internet texts add to the range of handwritten and printed texts that students will already have encountered. It is also helpful to remember that this further range of texts will need different kinds of understanding: visual literacy and computer literacy.

The content of IT software packages

If we take Hewer's list of types of text manipulation: sequencing (reordering jumbled pieces of text), gap filling, text reconstruction and unscrambling or decoding words, then it is clear that three of these four activities could be done using different means. Jumbled pieces of text can be cut up and reordered or they can be numbered on a work sheet; gaps can be left in a text on a work sheet; scrambled words or words with letters replaced as a code can also be reproduced on a work sheet. Text reconstruction though is only feasible on a computer. This is an exercise where the student predicts vocabulary in a text (having seen the text briefly) with all instances of the word being reproduced simultaneously.

If the *content* is not very different, two significant questions can be asked: 'What is it about the *process* that makes IT activities motivating?' and 'Why not transfer other kinds of exercise on to a computer, if IT activities are motivating?'

The process of IT activities

Five aspects mark IT activities out as different:

- immediacy of feedback;
- success orientation;
- possibilities for differentiation;
- learning through repetition;
- opportunities for reflection.

With regard to *immediacy of feedback*, students operate in a cultural context where immediacy is given a high profile: mobile phones offer immediate contact in any location; TV controls allow viewers to swap channels instantly; information can be gained quickly by dialling or surfing. There may, then, be an expectation of receiving very quick feedback that cannot be gratified in the normal classroom procedure where students hand in work and have it marked. Trying out answers on a computer will provide instant feedback and can maintain the momentum of learning and interest.

Another important aspect of computer-based activities is that the orientation is towards success. Wrong answers can be deleted and replaced with little physical reminders of failure (apart from notching up minus points). Success will come with persistence. Help is often available and activities are not public (even if small groups are working together). There are, then, plenty of positive experiences for the student, compared with say, receiving back a piece of work with a low mark requiring many corrections.

Exercises on a computer can be differentiated fairly easily. For example, in a cloze exercise where every 'nth' word is deleted, texts could have a different ratio of deleted words according to the level of the learner. It will, for example, be less apparent to others what particular exercises are given to students or whether they have chosen to do extra exercises.

Being able to repeat procedures and work at your own pace will also help with differentiation. There is, however, a more general point related to repetition. Drills where vocabulary and structures are repeated can be experienced as boring. However, repetition of a computer exercise has a different function. The learner is repeating a language item in order to eventually find the right answer (whilst receiving positive rewards). Repetition then is happening here incidentally and is thus not so noticeable or so dreary.

Because computer language exercises are success-oriented students may be willing to try out several versions of a language item. Hewer (1997: 7–8) suggests that three students to a computer is often seen as ideal, one to type, one to monitor and one to look up items in a dictionary. It is likely, if students work in small groups, that they will talk together about what answers might be appropriate. Each discussion, even if in English, which is likely, can help students think through what they know about the language and to test out their ideas against each other's. This should help learning to become embedded. Hewer (1997: 25) herself suggests that, particularly in text reconstruction, there is long-term retention of the vocabulary and grammar practised. Hewer outlines different kinds of learning strategies that are useful (cognitive, metacognitive and social) and sees IT text manipulation exercises as being particularly beneficial in promoting these. (Chapter 9 deals with the role of learner strategies in MFL learning in greater depth).

The process of word-processing as opposed to writing items by hand has clear advantages. Not only is the end product always legible but it can be aesthetically pleasing.

The National Curriculum (2j) emphasizes the language skills of knowing 'how to redraft … writing to improve its accuracy and presentation' (1999a: 16) and mentions ICT in this context. Clearly the facilities available when word-processing allow for relatively painless redrafting with moving text, deleting and replacing.

It could be argued that using a computer and doing language exercises is not a communicative activity and therefore that this does not sit well with the current emphasis on communicative language learning. However, as we saw in Chapter 1, views are changing in terms of students' learning and a move towards autonomy. Certainly the new curricula for the National Curriculum and A-level reflect a greater interest in grammatical accuracy. Language exercises, which help to improve accuracy, can thus be seen to support the trend towards greater emphasis on form.

There is, then, a strong case for using IT even if this were not a curricular requirement. In working through many of the items in the National Curriculum programme of study it is clear that many of these requirements could be fulfilled by using ICT even when this is not stipulated. The added motivation that derives from using this dimension should help student learning.

> ### Task 5.5
> If you have two parallel classes design a written work sheet and an authored computer text containing the same language exercise, and monitor how pupils react to the two media. If you do not have two parallel age groups, try this out with teaching a similar grammar point or structure.

Using the Internet

A survey in late 2000 showed that 96 per cent of all secondary schools had been linked to the Internet following the government's drive to establish the National Grid for Learning (Johnston, 2000). However, the same survey showed that only 47 per cent of teachers felt confident to handle it (casting doubt on the higher percentage suggested by the government). As with CALL, it may be that schools will turn to newer members of staff to assume responsibility for some of the newer technologies.

It is unlikely, as a trainee, that you will be involved in decisions regarding setting up either a computer system or choices to be made regarding Internet provision (the service provider for example), nevertheless it will be important to consider how to use the Internet effectively in an MFL teaching context, and to know (even if you are already familiar with the Internet) what is available that is appropriate for MFL learning.

Four different functions can be identified:

- learning;
- accessing information;
- communication;
- publishing.

Learning on the Internet

There are sites available on the Internet where students can learn directly from the Web. The BBC, for example, offers free language instruction at a basic level with video clips from the *Learning Zone* at www.bbc.co.uk/education/languages (TES, 2000). The BBC also offers a GCSE revision package (*GCSE BITESIZE Revision*) in French, German and Spanish, which combines television broadcasts, books and the Internet (www.bbc.co.uk.gcsebitesize). A Web-based training course project (ICT4LT) for European languages teachers in English, Italian and Finnish is an example of online possibilities for teachers. (http://www.ict4lt.org/). This course itself is for teaching ICT (Fawkes, 1999).

However it may be that, in the area of learning, the Internet does not have a significant contribution to make. Mckenna and Mckenna warn of two dangers: that 'in practice, such [learning] material rarely offers much that could not be more conveniently obtained in the form of "actual" paper materials along with standard audio and visual resources' (2000: 9) and that 'what is billed as teaching material frequently turns out to be reference to teaching material or a list of further links to the same "teaching material"' (2000: 10).

Accessing information on the Internet

One of the most significant roles of the Internet is providing information. This can be a resource for both the teacher and the student.

It is important to consider how to search the Internet for information, whether this is for yourself as a teacher or whether it is an activity you wish to set up for your students. Two important practical points are that the Web is particularly congested in the afternoon and evening so you may have difficulty accessing it then; Web-site addresses also need to be regularly checked since these are often updated and changed.

Ways of searching the Internet are:

- using a search engine;
- using a Web guide with links to other Web pages;
- accessing Web sites directly.

Using a search engine

There are many different search engines. Atkinson (1998: 16–17) lists over 40 Web-page addresses or universal resource locations (URLS) for different languages. Two of the best known are Altavista and Yahoo!, which operate in several languages (http://www.yahoo.fr/; http://www.yahoo.de; http://www.altavista.com/). The search engine will require you to narrow down the areas for your search by typing in categories and subcategories (Atkinson provides diagrams for this process, 1998: 18–19).

Using a Web guide

Some institutions and organizations have already carried out searches and provide guides on specific topics that the Internet user can tap into. Thus, for example, the Lingu@NET site acts as a virtual language centre for teachers with shared resources and information on teaching (http: www.becta.org.uk/). The University of Sussex offers a particularly helpful site (http://www.susx.ac.uk/langc/) to language resources on the Internet.

By checking on different items in the text, links can be made to other relevant Web sites (these items will usually stand out from the text by being in a different colour or by being underlined).

Accessing Web sites directly

It is possible to access foreign newspapers (http://www.lemonde.fr/ and http:www.spiegel.de/ for example) or cultural sources (railways, art galleries, weather centres) or tourist resources. All of these sites will yield different kinds of materials useful for the learner.

Using and accessing information from Web sites

Accessing information from Web sites raises various issues, significant among these are:

- the appropriateness of the site;
- the status of the information;
- the cost of access;
- developing appropriate tasks.

Because the Internet is an unmonitored forum there will be Web sites that are unsuitable for students. Atkinson (1998: 13) suggests several ways of dealing with offensive or inappropriate sites including:

- using an Internet service provider that screens material;
- monitoring students closely;
- creating an intranet from Internet materials.

An intranet is a Web of materials downloaded from the Internet. König (1998) and Lamb and Fisher (1999) both describe projects where intranets were created within schools. Lamb and Fisher comment that: 'Intranets restrict pupils to working with a limited number of relevant sites … and therefore enable the teacher to be more directive and the learning to be more focused' (1999: 35).

Because the Internet is an open forum, some materials published will not have been reviewed and reliability may be questionable. This will be something for the teacher to consider but can also be a study skill, valuable for students as well: they will need to consider how to evaluate the validity and reliability of sources by checking with other reference sources.

Internet access can be costly but there will be ways that this can be minimized. Downloading texts and saving them will allow for offline activities. Preparing a specific focus beforehand can mean that browsing or searching can be more directed.

The project on the World Cup for year nine reluctant learners described by Lamb and Fisher (1999) used downloaded Internet pages (on star players, teams, stadia, merchandise and administration) pasted on to billboards so that language learning activities took place offline. These Internet pages were complemented by the World Cup intranet set up in the school, mentioned earlier.

Information available on the Internet is generally not structured for teaching purposes. The teacher then will need to devise appropriate accompanying tasks. The Internet material for the World Cup project described above provided a resource for the teacher who could then use the texts for activities in class.

Another possibility is giving students direct access to the Internet materials either on an intranet or on the Internet proper. Clearly, unstructured browsing is not desirable, not only because of the cost involved but, as Atkinson (1998: 14) suggests, because of limited learning outcomes:

> Surfing the Internet is an image that has some accuracy and relevance. There is a temptation to jump from link to link taking in the superficial aspects of each page and not reading or absorbing the material. If used on-line in this way, the Internet may lead to limited learning.

There can be real value in students searching for authentic materials to use for coursework (particularly at A-level), although here the same caveats apply as mentioned earlier with CD ROM reference material, namely that work needs to be monitored to ensure that items are not copied wholesale. In other words students will need to write their own summaries of what they find. Clearly activities such as these fit into the National Curriculum requirements for developing language skills: 2j '[knowing] techniques for skimming and scanning written texts for information including those from ICT-based sources' and for developing cultural awareness 4a, 'working with authentic materials, including some from ICT-based sources' (DfEE/QCA, 1999: 16 and 17).

Communicating on the Internet by e-mail

Another major function of the Internet is to provide a means of communication. This can be by e-mail or through a discussion forum. The skills that you will need to use e-mail are:

- logging on;
- preparing text beforehand and saving it on disk;
- uploading this text and sending it;
- receiving text and saving it (Townshend, 1997: 11).

E-mail can serve quite a different function from accessing information on the Internet. The National Curriculum requires students to communicate 'with native speakers' (4b) when developing their cultural awareness. (DfEE/QCA, 1999: 17). E-mail will allow for this to happen in a lively and interesting way, also allowing access to countries beyond Europe.

The advantages of this direct contact are the same as those mentioned earlier in the video letter project and in the intercultural project described in Chapter 2:

- there is an immediacy of contact;
- contact is with real people, students will have a sense of audience;
- students can experience a sense of ownership of the medium, the content and the language.

In practice there will, however, also be areas that will need attention. As with Internet browsing, unstructured correspondence is likely to have several disadvantages. Townshend notes that 'pen friend exchanges die out quite quickly for most children' (1997: 9). It is likely to be more beneficial to have a structured approach with:

- links to the teacher in your partner school;
- decisions made as to whether *all* pupils send e-mails;
- choosing topics for discussion that can integrate into schemes of work;
- monitoring e-mails for content and language;
- preparing material in advance which is to be sent in order to cut down online costs and in order to be able to monitor texts.

The presence of a link school is assumed here. If your school has no e-mail partner then a partner school may be found by contacting the Central Bureau for Educational Visits and Exchanges. Their newsletter offers plentiful information, as does their Web site for finding partners: Windows on the World (http://www.wotw.org.uk).

Townshend (1997: 7–11) offers a 13-point action plan which provides an excellent framework for setting up an effective e-mail link:

- contact teachers in the link school personally (telephone or videoconferencing);
- agree topics (linked to curricula);
- decide on the language of exchange;
- decide text length, number of texts and level of language;
- discuss objectives;
- agree project duration and deadlines for sending and receiving;
- consider a viable number of projects;
- devolve content and handling to students as much as possible;
- involve other departments (geography, mathematics, English, religious education (RE));
- involve senior management;
- involve parents;
- cope with glitches;
- have planning documents.

Townshend includes an excellent planning sheet, which covers topics, free times (dates of holidays), examination dates, details of the class, (age, interests). Getting the practical aspects of an e-mail exchange sorted will ensure a much greater chance of successful outcomes for the students.

Monitoring students' work need not be too prescriptive – students can be taught how to spell-check (a useful study skill anyway) and can prepare texts well in advance of sending them by e-mail.

Johnston (1999a) describes an interesting example of a project supported by e-mail where pupils in a language college worked with a French school and a German school. In two design and technology projects (one making an Oxo cube dispenser and one making a pinball machine) pupils communicated with each other regularly by e-mail (also meeting together, and with the English and German school videoconferencing once a week). The head of technology at the school comments 'they've learned a lot about the importance of real communication' (Johnston, 1999a). Townshend also provides several examples of e-mail projects in her useful overview of e-mail use.

Other possibilities for e-mail can be for learning a minority language. Cassidy (2000b) reports that Internet-based courses for Latin and Japanese were piloted from autumn 2000 in around 60 schools. Students work on their own and send work to be marked by specialists by e-mail.

Online forums can also provide an invaluable resource for teachers, where they can exchange ideas and resources. Lingu@NET (www.mailbase.ac.uk/lists/linguanet-forum) and the Early Language learning forum (www.mailbase.ac.uk/lists/ell-forum), co-ordinated by the CILT, both offer this opportunity.

USING ICT

Publishing on the Internet

If your service provider offers you Web space then publishing your own home page can be of real benefit in celebrating the work done by your students and opening up the possibilities for other contacts.

Your ICT co-ordinator should be able to help with preparing a home page. Atkinson provides several case studies and a step by step guide (1998: 37–46). The activity of preparing a homepage should be motivating for students and in itself would be a cross-curricular skill. It will be helpful if the site is interactive if it is to attract contact from others. Atkinson (1998: 39) though mentions a useful caveat, namely that care needs to be taken to ensure an appropriate level of privacy, because the Internet is a highly public medium.

The Internet, then, can provide several fruitful opportunities for learners which offer the chance of using language in quite new and different ways.

Task 5.6

Use the Internet to find a text appropriate to one of your lessons and structure some suitable accompanying tasks.

Task 5.7

Consider how an aspect of your scheme of work might be enhanced by an e-mail project with a link school. Devise appropriate activities that could be undertaken by e-mail.

Links to teaching standards

These have been provided globally for all four aspects of ICT in this chapter.

Under *knowledge and understanding*, trainees are asked to demonstrate that they 'know and can teach the key skills required for current qualifications relevant to their specialist subject (s) for pupils aged 14–19 and understand the contribution that their specialist subject(s) makes to the development of key skills', and that they 'have for their specialist subject(s) a secure knowledge and understanding of the context specified in the ITT national curriculum for information and communications technology in subject teaching'.

Under *planning*, they are asked to demonstrate that they 'have a secure knowledge and understanding of and know how and when to apply in relation to their specialist subject the teaching and assessment methods specified in the ITT National Curriculum for information and communications technology in subject teaching'.

Under *teaching and class management*, they are asked to demonstrate that they 'use teaching methods which sustain the momentum of pupils' work and keep all pupils engaged through ... selecting and making good use of ... ICT ... resources which enable teaching objectives to be met' and through 'exploiting opportunities to improve pupils' basic skills in ... ICT ... needed for effective learning, including information retrieval'.

Understanding the four aspects of ICT outlined in this chapter and understanding some of the related tasks described should help trainees to achieve these standards.

Other useful Web sites are:

www.learn.co.uk
www.linguaweb.co.uk
www.modlangs.co.uk
www.puzzlemaker.co.uk
www.reallyusefulfrench.co.uk (links into reallyusefulgerman)
www.studyspanish.com
www.travlang.com/languages
www.turpsoft.co.uk
http://web.ukonline.co.uk/canonave/
http://utc.ngfl.gov.uk/resource/cits/mfl/inpractice/index.html
http://utc.ngfl.gov.uk/resource/cits/mfl/materials/cartoon

6 Assessment

The aim of this final chapter on *content* is to help the trainee become familiar with different types of assessment in state schools in England and Wales.

Objectives

By the end of this chapter the trainee should be able to:
- understand assessment procedures at key stage three;
- understand assessment procedures at key stage four;
- understand assessment procedures at A and A/S level;
- be aware of developments in Scottish qualifications;
- appreciate the role of homework in assessment and as an integrated extension of classroom study.

Introduction

Assessment is a crucial part of the teaching process. Assessing students' work is part and parcel of lesson planning and is important for various reasons:
- It enables the teacher to gauge whether what has been taught has in fact been learned by the students.
- It provides information for the student on his/her progress in a subject.
- It provides information for parents.
- It is used as an outcome measure for further study or for leaving school.

There are different forms of assessment and the good teacher will incorporate various types of assessment into units of work and lessons. In the context of language lessons, Buckby *et al* (1992) list the following sub-divisions of assessment:

- *Formative assessment* is ongoing assessment, conducted at regular intervals by the classroom teacher. It enables the teacher to take stock of what the students have learned.

- *Diagnostic assessment* is also formative but it is used usually to identify particular areas requiring work. On the basis of the results of diagnostic assessment, a remedial programme for specific elements of the course can be tailored to individual or group needs.
- *Evaluative assessment* is based on feelings and experience rather than objective criteria – for example, giving a mark for 'effort'.
- *Motivational assessment* is designed to provide learners with short-term, achievable goals that motivate them to continue achieving. Assessing students at the end of a unit of work is formative, diagnostic and should be motivational.
- *Summative assessment* is the final stage assessment and the term is usually applied to end of key stage tests or to GCSE. Such assessment may be carried out by the school, or may be externally controlled by an examination board. Elements such as coursework in GCSE and the option to submit coursework have provided more flexible alternatives to the traditional summative terminal examinations.

Nicholls (1999a) highlights the distinction between internal and external assessment. Internal assessment relates to tasks that are drawn up and marked by the class teacher. These types of tasks relate very closely to the work being covered in class and provide information for the department and for the school. External assessment, on the other hand, is set and marked by external bodies, such as central examination bodies.

The Assessment Reform Group (ARG), set up by the Nuffield Foundation, has recently published its report (ARG, 1999) which develops the work carried out by Black and Wiliam (1998). In this latest research, the group reiterates the clear distinction that exists between assessment of learning and assessment for learning (ARG, 1999: 2ff). The former is used for grading and reporting, whereas the latter is more wide ranging and should promote learning. The Assessment and Reform Group distinguishes assessment for learning from straightforward teacher assessment, which, they state, is not necessarily formative. The group identifies seven characteristics of the type of assessment that promotes learning:

- It is embedded in a view of teaching and learning of which it is an essential part.
- It involves sharing learning goals with students.
- It aims to help students to know and to recognize the standards for which they are aiming.
- It involves students in self-assessment.
- It provides feedback, which leads to students recognizing their next steps and how to take them.
- It is underpinned by confidence that every student can improve.
- It involves both teacher and students reviewing and reflecting on assessment data (ARG, 1999: 7).

This latest analysis of assessment in schools points out that what is termed formative and diagnostic assessment in schools is sometimes only another term for what is, in effect, summative assessment in purpose. Assessing for learning incorporates observing students, using open questions, setting tasks that require students to use certain skills, asking students to communicate their thinking in a variety of ways, through drawings, actions, role play, writing, concept mapping and discussion words and how they are being used (ARG, 1999). The most important element of this, however, is involving students in decisions about their work and involving them in the process of the assessment. The focus of learning and assessment is changing and there is a recognition that learners need to be involved in taking responsibility for their own learning, which, by implication requires involvement in assessing their own work. In designing assessment as part of the teaching/learning process, it is necessary for the teacher to find ways of giving the students more opportunities for learning from assessment. The introduction of the key skill of 'managing one's own learning' must incorporate the assessment dimension.

Self-assessment

Students can be given the task of identifying parts of their work which they mark themselves. This can be achieved by giving them self-contained materials, such as reading, listening or writing tasks or those involving a combination of skills with mark sheets.

Peer assessment

By establishing in advance criteria with the class for the assessing of a particular piece of work, such as a role play or dialogue, it is possible to involve students in assessing each other's work. This is not only motivating for those assessing, it also is a learning experience for both parties. Those being assessed learn from the comments of their 'assessors' who also learn how to improve their own work by identifying areas of improvement in the work of others. Teachers at first may be reluctant to give the students this responsibility for fear that they would 'cheat'. Experience has shown, however, that by giving the students the responsibility of establishing the marking criteria and the guidelines for applying the criteria, they have greater ownership of the process. It would also result in the assessment being formative and motivational for all students in the class. With more sophisticated learners, it could also become diagnostic.

The type of assessment chosen by teachers as most appropriate must be related to various factors:

- the purpose of the assessment;
- the time of year;
- school and departmental policies;
- statutory requirements.

Assessment at key stage three

The teaching of modern languages at key stage three (KS3) is governed by the Programme of Study. The assessments required at the end of the key stage are not set by external agencies, as is the case for other subjects. The assessments at this stage therefore are internal. In this section we look at how assessment relates to students at KS3. During the course of the language classes at KS3, it will be necessary for a record of students' achievement in these levels in all four ATs to be compiled. At key stage four, as the student progresses towards a final examination, be it GCSE or any other syllabus, continuous assessment of the four ATs needs to be kept up.

Assessment, with rubrics and test questions and answers required in the target language, involves an integrated approach to both teaching and testing. Thus, in assessing a listening exercise, there may be some element of the other skills that will be involved, for example, reading or speaking. It is necessary, therefore, to ensure that what is being assessed is not masked by the inability to cope with other factors. In assessing listening, for example, an exercise involving ticking boxes or completing a grid of visuals would provide less contamination of the skill being assessed.

Record keeping is essential to producing a profile of each individual student. A pro forma could prove useful.

Attainment target one – listening

Assessing listening can be done as a *whole class activity* where everyone listens to the tape at the same time and either they all attempt the same task or differentiated tasks by outcome are given to individuals or groups. It can also be assessed by distributing a compilation of tasks on a cassette that students can attempt during independent learning sessions when they can work on the peripheral audio learning equipment (PALE) system or in a language laboratory or in groups at a listening station. (The PALE is a set of self-standing cassette boxes around a classroom, which enables students to work independently of the teacher, either speaking or listening, individually, in pairs or in groups.) If possible, they could be allowed to take the cassette with them to work on during a homework hour or at home and to submit at some prearranged time. Obviously this demands some degree of trust between teacher and student, but if there is an emphasis on students taking responsibility for their own learning and if they are trained in this system from year seven, it will become standard practice. By giving parents/guardians/other adults the responsibility of verifying that their child has completed the tasks unaided, similar to asking them to sign homework, it raises awareness of the work and gives the family ownership of the assessment process.

Attainment target two – speaking

In assessing speaking, it is necessary to involve the students in a variety of tasks that allow them to demonstrate various skills, such as delivering a monologue or radio broadcast, speaking with a partner, contributing to a group discussion, conducting a role play in a communicative setting, responding to questions. Again, if a school has a PALE system, it would be possible to allow them some freedom in compiling their own portfolio of tasks and submitting them (or a selection thereof) when they feel ready. Alternatively they could be permitted to take the tasks home to do on their own personal cassette players, or if they do not possess one, using the school's resources in the lunch hour or after school. This encourages the students to take a pride in their own work and gives them experience of independent learning and encourages them to take more responsibility for their own learning skills, which feature in the programme of study. Each student in the class would receive a cassette on which they would record their work and hand it in for correction at the end of a unit or the end of a week, according to the system you devise.

The assessment of speaking lends itself to peer assessment, particularly if the focus is on communication. The class, in conjunction with the teacher, establishes the criteria that would be evidence of a particular mark or grade. In the early stages of using peer assessment it is better to keep the criteria simple. For example, you might use a three-point scale:

3 = task achieved, full communication;
2 = part of the task achieved;
1 = some doubt as to whether task achieved.

The class would then listen to some sample role plays in order to check the consistency of application of the criteria. Following these 'trials' they could be given the responsibility of working in groups and reporting back to each other. When the process becomes routine, and with older classes, the criteria for assessing could be developed to incorporate other aspects, such as use of language or range of language.

Attainment target three – reading

Traditional tests of reading usually involve texts with activities based on them. In addition to these tests, students could be given the option of a reading for pleasure exercise, where they choose a reading book from a suggested list and complete a project on it. An integrated skills approach could involve providing students with books that have accompanying tape material, for which worksheets could be adapted. Materials such as those produced by InterNationes, for German, are very useful for this kind of assessment, in that they have self-check sheets that encourage independence in the learners. This approach would be motivational in that the students have a degree of choice in what they read. It also provides some differentiation according to interest.

Attainment target four – writing

All of the types of activities suggested for writing tasks can be assessed: lists, letters, completing blanks, articles, reports, form filling, note-taking. In assessing writing, there are two components that have to be taken into consideration: communication and accuracy. Whilst, in speaking, it is quite possible to communicate relatively successfully but not in accurate target language, in writing, accuracy assumes a more important role. When assessing a piece of writing, therefore, it might be useful to allocate some of the marks for communication and others for accuracy in the language. Extra marks can be allocated for the range of vocabulary and the variety of structure used.

At the moment in modern foreign languages there is no external assessment on the eight levels as set out in the Programme of Study, although in English, mathematics and science this has been common practice for a number of years. It is useful, however, to use the level descriptors as an indicator of how the students in your class are progressing. Evidence from formative assessment should be used to review your lessons and to remedy any deficiencies. If half of the class is not achieving very high marks at the end of a unit, it may be that something has gone wrong, although more frequent formative or diagnostic assessment tasks should raise problems much earlier on so that some diagnostic measures can be taken. Assessment throughout the key stages is an essential part of lesson evaluation.

Assessment at key stage four (GCSE)

At key stage four, assessment has normally been the summative GCSE examination. Assessment at this level has undergone several changes since it was introduced in 1989. There has been a change from basic and higher levels to foundation and higher, with overlapping tiers. Although organized according to the skill areas (speaking, listening, reading and writing), the test types require a more integrated skills approach. The rubrics are now entirely in the target language and there is a greater variety of test type questions. This section first of all looks at the general issues related to GCSE and then analyses some of the features of the major examination boards' syllabuses, with an outline of some of the most frequent test types. There is then a final section that looks at the awarding of grades in the final examination.

General issues

General Certificate of Secondary Education examinations are governed by regulations laid down by the government body, the Qualifications and Curriculum Authority (QCA), which ensures that there is a common framework according to which all the examination boards have to work. The QCA is the body responsible for ensuring consistency across examination boards and it monitors the process of setting and conducting examinations in each of the examination boards. A code of practice sets out the core to which all examination syllabuses and question papers must adhere. It also contains the assessment weightings that should be common to all examination papers. Guidelines are presented that stipulate the amount of English permitted in answers (currently 10 per cent in total) and the procedures to be adopted in setting of questions and awarding of grades. There is also guidance given on the grammatical structures to be targeted at each level and there are regulations governing how spelling, punctuation and grammar in English are to be assessed.

Number of examining bodies

In England there are now only three examining bodies:

- Assessment and Qualification Alliance (AQA subsuming the Associated Examining Board, Southern Examining Group, City and Guilds and the Northern Examination and Assessment Board);
- Oxford Cambridge and RSA Examinations (OCR) (combining the Oxford Delegacy, University of Cambridge Local Examinations Syndicate, the Oxford and Cambridge Board and Royal Society of Arts);
- Edexcel (combining the University of London Examinations and Assessment Council and BTEC).

This has simplified matters considerably and brought about greater coherence. In Scotland and Northern Ireland and Wales the national examination body has the dual function of defining the curriculum and of setting the examinations. These bodies are: the Scottish Qualifications Authority (SQA), the Council for the Curriculum, Examinations and Assessment (CCEA) in Northern Ireland, and in Wales the Welsh Joint Education Council (WJEC), although schools in those areas are free to enter their students for examinations in other boards.

Within the statutory guidelines each examination board has some freedom to design subject specifications that meet the needs of their client groups. As it is a free market in that schools can choose to enter their students for any examination board, there is a great deal of competition to make the examinations user friendly and attractive. Reasons for choosing a particular board above another might relate to the weighting of skills, or even the perception that it is easier to gain a higher grade. Procedures are designed to ensure that there is comparability of standards across boards and across time.

Specifications (formerly known as syllabuses)

From 2003 all GCSE syllabuses will have to conform to new specifications that will take into account the recommendations set out in the review of the National Curriculum and the establishment of the National Qualifications Framework. The changes at GCSE have been summarized by QCA as follows:

- There is a shift away from topics linked to specific key stages towards students' knowledge of language and their ability to apply it in a variety of contexts.
- Topic areas have been reduced and will be more relevant to candidates' level of maturity.
- At least 20 per cent of the total marks will be allocated to knowledge and application of grammar and structures (integrated into the tests of speaking and writing).
- No dictionaries will be allowed in the examination.
- ICT will be integrated into the examination (Maynard, 2000).

Teaching for the new examinations will begin in September 2001 for those courses that last two years. In addition to the terminal examinations, there also exist modular courses and coursework elements which mean that there is greater flexibility of types of assessment within the system. Schools can choose which option best suits their students. Guidelines are laid down as to the maximum percentage of any subject that can be taken by coursework alone.

Short courses, available with some examination boards, are designed to be half a full GCSE and will be suitable for students who are perhaps specializing in other areas of the curriculum but who wish to keep their options open.

The specification sets out the percentage of assessment allocated to the various papers (usually 25 per cent for each of the four skills), details of each of the papers, the topics to be taught, the language content to be covered, the grammatical items with which candidates should be familiar, both receptively and productively, a defined vocabulary for foundation tier, target language rubrics and details of how the final grades are awarded.

The examination in each of the four skill areas is offered at foundation and higher tiers, with overlapping questions that are common to both foundation and higher tiers. A candidate must be entered for one level in each of the skill areas. A candidate entered for the foundation tier attempts all the questions targeted at foundation level and in addition the overlapping questions. Those attempting the higher tier also take the overlapping questions and proceed through the higher tier questions. The questions are not necessarily presented in the papers in a hierarchy of difficulty so that it is possible for candidates to find questions at their level throughout the papers.

The topics for each of the boards for all languages used to be based directly on the five areas experience or contexts for learning in the National Curriculum programmes of study, thereby facilitating links between key stages three and four and providing a coherent progression for students. The current list included in the GCSE exams for all boards is:

- A Everyday activities.
- B Personal and social life.
- C The world around us.
- D The world of work.
- E The international world.

Following the curriculum review, boards now have greater flexibility in that it is not necessary for students taking a full course to study all five areas nor is it necessary to do two areas for those taking the short course.

Boards are opting for different topics in which to examine students. AQA, for example, presents four themes:

1. My world.
2. Holiday time and travel.
3. Work and lifestyle.
4. The young person in society.

Edexcel will be testing the following topics:

- At home and abroad.
- Education, training and employment.
- Health and fitness.
- House, home and daily routine.
- Media, entertainment and youth culture.
- Social activities.

At the time of writing no details are available on the topics that will be offered by OCR, CCEA or WJEC.

The specification defines the sub-topics that should be covered at both tiers and will give a detailed breakdown of the areas that are required for each level. For example, an excerpt from the current syllabus for French (CCEA) subdivides Shopping thus:

Foundation
Types of shops/facilities
Location of shopping facilities
Types of items
Availability of items
Number/quantity/quality/size/colour
Cost/payment
Shopping announcements

Higher
Commenting on the cost
Asking for change
Exchanging an item
Requesting delivery of an item
Refund/special offers
Trying something on

Candidates at the higher level would be expected to be able to cope with the content at the higher level in addition to the specifications for foundation. In order to give students the opportunity to score high marks it is necessary to ensure that they are familiar with all of the defined content areas and that they are able to function independently in a variety of attainment targets. The list above would require, for example, that they be given experience of role plays in shops, asking to try on clothes, to bring back damaged or unsatisfactory goods. They would also have to have had experience of writing letters of complaint, asking for refunds and stating the reasons for their dissatisfaction.

The various items of grammar that have to be learned are set out, again for each of the tiers and subdivided according to whether they should be receptive or productive. In French verbs, for example, the candidates entering for higher tier are required to be receptively familiar with every tense, but productive only in the main tenses. They are not required to produce the conditional, the conditional perfect, the subjunctive or the past historic. Candidates at foundation level are required to be productive with the present, the imperfect, the perfect and *aller* + infinitive for the future. The teacher must ensure that the students are able to recognize and use all the required structures, especially if they expect a high grade to be awarded. Realistically speaking, however, it is likely that the students will need to be familiar with a set number of verbs, particularly in the less common tenses.

In terms of the TL rubrics, it is essential that students be completely familiar with the instructions that they will find in the examination papers. These should be given to students to learn and should feature consistently over a period of time in the department's examinations and assessment tasks.

The subject specification also sets out how the assessment contributes to the wider curriculum such as:

- social, cultural, spiritual, moral and ethical issues;
- education for citizenship;
- information and communication technology;

- environmental education;
- health and safety;
- european dimension.

In addition boards will be required to ensure that key skills are assessed in all of the GCSE and above examinations and that, in following the examination syllabuses, students have opportunities to develop the skills of:

- communication;
- information and communication technology;
- application of number;
- improving own learning and performance;
- working with others;
- problem solving.

Generally modern languages will contribute to most of these areas. Individual boards will give precise details of the extent to which the various papers cover the key skills.

Types of questions at GCSE level

From a survey of the various examination boards, the following questions have been used. These can be adapted to focus on a variety of skills:

- ticking boxes;
- true/false;
- matching pictures with letters/numbers/words/phrases/headlines;
- completing forms;
- completing sentences or phrases (no manipulation of language necessary);
- filling in blanks (manipulation of language necessary);
- putting statements in correct order;
- multiple choice;
- advantages/disadvantages – positive/negative statements;
- role plays (speaking only) – usually with visual support;
- open-ended role plays with prompts;
- writing lists, postcards, letters, articles, short reports.

It is essential that students have practice in the different types of questions. Use of past papers and specimen papers for forthcoming new examination specifications is important. These can be purchased from the various boards and are available online.

Marking of examinations

When the examinations are completed they are sent to the boards where they are distributed amongst a team of examiners who are trained each year specifically on the marking of particular papers. In the case of the oral examination, some boards give schools the option of marking their own set of tapes and forwarding a sample for moderation or of sending all of the tapes to the central board for *ab initio* marking. There is no advantage or disadvantage for candidates who are marked by their own centre, in that lenient or severe marking is generally picked up at the moderation stage.

For teachers with a few years of experience behind them, being part of a marking team as assistant examiner is a good opportunity to gain some insight into the process of marking and it can have an impact on the way they prepare their candidates for the examination in future.

Some more experienced teachers value the challenge of being part of the team of principal and chief examiners who set and co-ordinate the marking of the scripts and who are involved in the final stage of awarding the grades.

Awarding of final grade

Points are awarded for each of the assessment components. The final grade for the overall examination is awarded on the basis of the aggregate number of points. Each of the four papers has a total of eight points that can be awarded (a total of 32 points are thus available). On the basis of how the total number of points awarded are calculated, a grade is awarded as follows:

0–1: U
2–5: G
6–9: F
10–13: E
14–17: D
18–21: C
22–25: B
26–29: A
30–32: A*

The relationship between the level a student takes (either foundation or higher) and the final grades is as follows:

Foundation (grades E, F, G)
Overlap (grades C, D)
Higher (grades A*, A, B)

Candidates who are entered at foundation level and who achieve 100 per cent of the marks cannot gain higher than a grade C. There is a degree of risk in deciding at which level a student should be entered and discussions are usually held with the students and/or their parents before any final decision is taken. If candidates are entered for a higher tier but fail to reach the minimum grade, they may not be awarded anything for that skill. It would therefore be better for someone to gain a better score at the foundation level than to gain no grade at all by failing the higher tier.

Appeals procedure

For candidates who fail to achieve the grade expected by the school, there is the opportunity to have a re-mark and recheck conducted by the board. This is requested by the school and a fee is usually charged for this facility. This is only useful if some major discrepancy arises and there would be relatively few instances where a grade change would be awarded.

Candidates whose personal circumstances at the time of the examination would seriously have affected their ability to perform at their best can be given special consideration if the school presents a case for this.

Mark schemes and examiners' reports

The examination boards publish each year the mark schemes for the papers and a detailed report from the chief examiners of the subject on each of the components. These documents are invaluable to help you prepare your candidates for the examination, in that they give detailed insight into the type of answers the examiners were asked to accept and those that were unacceptable. They give some details of the types of common errors that candidates made and the weaknesses that were perceived across centres; these can form the basis for preparing students for the following year's papers. The final report also lists the grade boundaries and the percentage of candidates awarded each of the grades. Such information is useful to heads of departments who are deciding which board to choose for their students.

Conclusion

Assessment is one area that constantly changes according to government regulations. It is necessary, as a teacher, to keep up to date with the requirements and proposed changes.

Links to teaching standards

Under *subject knowledge and understanding* trainees should demonstrate that they 'are familiar, for their specialist subject, with the relevant KS4 ... examination syllabuses and courses'. Under *planning* trainees are asked to demonstrate that they 'ensure coverage of the relevant examination syllabuses and National Curriculum Programmes of Study'. All of the standards included under *monitoring, assessment, recording, reporting and accountability* are covered in this chapter.

Task 6.1

Familiarize yourself with the subject specifications for modern languages from at least two of the examination boards in order to make an informed choice about the examination that you consider would be most appropriate for your students.

Assessment at A-level

Foreign languages are currently not a popular option at A-level and numbers have been dropping steadily over the last few years (Morgan and Freedman, 1999). The Nuffield Inquiry suggests that only 10 per cent of sixth formers choose languages, (Nuffield Foundation, 2000). In terms of choices languages comes low in the ranking (Morgan and Freedman, 1999). An acceleration in decline in A-level foreign languages is noted in the *CILT DIRECT 1999 Languages Yearbook*. Figures for French for example read as follows: 1995: 48,9112; 1996: 50,343; 1997: 48,752; 1998: 46,316;1999: 42,335. It is likely then that sixth-form groups will be small, especially for languages other than French, and also mostly female, according to OFSTED inspection findings for 1996/97 (Dobson, 1998). It was also the case in 1996/97 that 90 per cent of MFL A-level candidates were studying French, German and Spanish. Although a further range of languages is offered by examining bodies (see below), take-up is low. The Nuffield Inquiry particularly rues the omission of languages such as Japanese and Portuguese (Nuffield Foundation, 2000: 51).

In terms of teaching there is likely, then, to be the bonus of a small group, and of course a group that is motivated because they will have opted for this subject choice. However, teaching at this level will be different and there will be several significant factors to take into consideration. These include:

- the new A-level specifications;
- the different linguistic demands after GCSE;
- the different context demands after GCSE;
- teaching literature and topics.

New A-level specifications

There have been several major changes coinciding with the end of the 1990s and the new millennium:

- the number of examining bodies has been reduced;
- the pattern of A-level study in general has altered;
- key skills have become a feature of the A-level programme;
- examining bodies have produced new specifications, which give grammar a much higher and more visible profile.

Number of examining bodies

The same situation applies as mentioned earlier for GCSE, namely that there are three main examining bodies besides those in Wales and Northern Ireland. This has brought about not only greater coherence but also the added advantage that the bodies responsible for vocational qualifications are also part of these academic examining bodies.

Pattern of A-level study in general

'Curriculum 2000' implemented in September 2000 is the new A-level curriculum, which is modular in structure and means students will take several subjects (QCA, 2000a). This allows for qualifications to be taken at different intervals over years 12 and 13 in school. For MFL this means that the first three units or modules of the course can be taken at the end of year 12 as an advanced subsidiary (AS) qualification. Government announcements in May 2000 also suggested that talented 14 to 16 year olds could take AS level as an alternative to compulsory GCSEs (Cassidy, 2000a).

Key skills

Key skills are now part of both GCSE courses and A-levels. Thus the specifications from the new A-level examining bodies all contain sections that explain how MFL can contribute to students' development of key skills.

Of the six key skills mentioned earlier (communication, application of number, information technology, improving own learning and performance, working with others), application of number and problem solving are the two not mentioned by any of the examining bodies as areas that may be enhanced by MFL. Each set of specifications offers specific advice on how evidence for the other four key skills may be obtained and developed. 'Communication' cannot be assessed through MFL A-level performance so, therefore, it is a question of developing skills that can then be transferred to English, Welsh or Irish as a mother tongue.

The new specifications

Each of the three main examining bodies has produced a modular specification. These specifications are similar but not identical. In each case:

- language skills are integrated;
- the first three units constitute an 'AS' qualification;
- there are further language skill assessments contained within the second set of modules (A2);
- there is a module that represents the 'old' literature or topics paper, which can be assessed either by a final examination or submitted as coursework.

Edexcel offers a modular course in six languages (French, German, Italian, Russian, Spanish, Urdu) with six units as follows:

1. Listening and writing.
2. Reading and writing.
3. Prepared oral topic.
4. Oral discussion or interpretation.
5. Prescribed topics/texts or coursework.
6. Listening and writing; reading and writing; writing in registers (creative writing, discursive essay or task-based assignment).

Five different general topic areas are given (of which three apply to the AS modules); six topic areas and seven set texts are given for Unit 5. This examining body offers considerable choice with the different options for Unit 4 and a choice of one section from the three given in Unit 6.

AQA offers a modular course in seven languages (French, German, Spanish, Bengali, Modern Hebrew, Punjabi and Polish) with six units as follows:

1. Listening, reading, writing.
2. Writing.
3. Speaking.
4. Listening, Reading, Writing.
5. Writing (topics, texts) or coursework.
6. Speaking.

Five general topics are given, three of which are applicable to the AS modules. The topics and texts for Unit 5 are given under the title *The cultural and social landscape in focus* with three set texts, three areas of study with suggested literary texts and six non-literary topics.

OCR offers a modular course in French, German and Spanish with six units as follows:

1. Speaking.
2. Listening, reading and writing.
3. Reading and writing.
4. Speaking and reading.
5. Reading, listening and writing.
6. Culture and society (written paper or coursework).

For Unit 6 there are eight literary texts, six literary topics with no prescribed texts or seven non-literary topics. Eight General Subject areas are given for AS and five further topic areas for A2.

For all three examining boards there is a much more transparent system of marking provided than was previously the case and grammar lists are given indicating expectations at both AS and A (A2) level. The grammar areas given are those prescribed by the QCA. The rubric given in each case is virtually identical: 'AS and Advanced GCE students will be expected to have studied closely the grammatical system and structures of the … language during their course. In the examination they will be required to use actively and accurately grammar and structures appropriate to the tasks set down from the following list.' (Edexcel, 2000: 47).

The subject criteria prescribed by the QCA specify eight aims and eight areas of knowledge, understanding and skills for AS students, with a further five for A-level students. These all relate to developing language, cultural and cognitive competence.

The four assessment objectives given are:

- A01: understanding and responding in speech and writing to spoken language.
- A02: understanding and responding in speech and writing to written language.
- A03: showing knowledge of and applying accurately the grammar prescribed in the specification.
- A04: demonstrating knowledge and understanding aspects of the chosen society.

These are weighted differently for the different levels: AS: 30 per cent, 30 per cent, 25 per cent, 15 per cent; A-level: 25 per cent, 27.5 per cent, 25 per cent, 22.5 per cent. (Edexcel, 2000: 8).

Communicative skills are thus given a higher profile at AS level and cultural understanding a higher profile at A-level.

In previous A-level schemes the emphasis on grammar was not so explicit and no lists were prescribed. In all examinations dictionaries are also now not allowed.

The different linguistic demands of A-level

Clearly the heavy emphasis on grammar will be significant for A- and AS-level students (although the revisions to GCSE will now also include 20 per cent of marks for accurate application of grammar and structures (Maynard, 2000). There will also be several other areas that will be different from GCSE: students will be expected to handle language in a different way and they will also need to think, analyse and argue differently. It is useful here to refer to two different sources: research done by Suzanne Graham on the switch from GCSE to A-level (1997) and OFSTED inspection findings for 1996/97 (Dobson, 1998).

Graham (1997: 2) identifies six areas of linguistic difficulty (extensive reading, writing accurately and at length; using grammar correctly, vocabulary acquisition; listening comprehension; oral discussion work) plus two general areas of weakness (effective study skills and time management). Dobson confirms some of these linguistic problems (1998: 17): 'Where progress is more limited it is usually manifested in an insecure grasp of grammar, written work and hesitancy in speech.'

Looking at both these sources and the new A-level specifications there seem to be six significant new areas:

- developing study skills;
- improving grammar;
- integrating language skills;
- acquiring discourse competence;
- coping with long texts;
- using language for discussion rather than function.

Developing study skills

The chapter on learner strategies (Chapter 9) talks in greater length on this topic. It is vital for students to be able to manage their own time effectively, to review their own work and build their own language reference resources (Lonsdale, 2000 offers an extremely helpful framework for this). Students will have to work on their own and will need to know how to use dictionaries and reference materials (even though the former are not allowed into examinations).

Improving grammar

It may be that students will need an intensive period of grammar work in the first term of year 12, particularly if grammatical structures have been undertaught in key stage four. Students will not only need to understand structures but will have to keep their own bank of grammar resources, to which they can refer.

Integrating language skills

Skills at key stage four are assessed as discrete items. It will be helpful then both at KS4 and at the later stage to organize activities, that integrate skills. The new specifications emphasize responding to written language and spoken language. It can be useful to explore with students', differences between the two kinds of language. Meiring and Norman (1999) also provide a useful example of an integrated topic.

Acquiring discourse competence

It will be useful for students to develop skills in decoding texts and constructing their own texts. Learning the importance of headings (titles), subheadings, punctuation, connectives and so forth will help students to map the content of a text and will also help with structuring their own written work.

Coping with longer texts

Up to GCSE, most texts that are encountered are short. The long texts, with which students must cope at A-level, can come as quite a shock, and students will need support. It can be useful to ask students to skim-read a long text quickly to get the general gist; or to scan a text to identify particular information. In this way a student can become more used to encountering unknown vocabulary without this being a hindrance to some understanding. Progression can then be made using clues in the text to help guess the meaning. (Barnes, 2000 offers some useful suggestions).

Using language for discussion rather than function

Cummins (1984) describes two kinds of language competence: basic interpersonal communicative skills (BICS) and cognitive academic language proficiency (CALP). The former represents the kind of spontaneous language used in interpersonal communication and the latter the more abstract language considered necessary for academic study. Cummins' contention is that skill in the former does not predict skill in the latter. Graham relates these two types of language to GCSE and A-level (1997: 18 and 33) and it is easy to see that a student who has been fluent with predictable functional language items pre-16 can exhibit the hesitancy in speech mentioned by Dobson, when asked to produce personal complex thoughts in quite different sorts of language in a post-16 course.

There are two main linguistic problems here: students will need a much wider vocabulary and knowledge of structures and will need to manipulate these structures to produce their own sentences. Help can be provided by learning writing or speaking frames (language structures and vocabulary of opinion); by building up a systematic store of language items and by using sensibly models of writing, for example authentic texts (Lonsdale, 2000 and McLachlan, 2000 provide useful suggestions).

The different content demands at A-level

As well as having the language capacity to engage in discussion and analysis, students will also need to have developed the skills of analysis and debate in order to produce mature and interesting content. Dobson (1998: 17) notes that:

> Students find the intellectual challenge of applying language to the more abstract ... ideas associated with 'A' level study demanding after the restricted scope of GCSE requirements. For some, the challenge is daunting and their writing shows a lack of the maturity, complexity and range expected for advanced study.

Students then will need to develop their own ideas and be able to defend them. McLachlan (2000: 19–20) in her review of necessary oral skills for A-level points to the value of debate and presentation in helping students develop, and also offers an illustrative case study on *La violence à la télé* (pp 21–23).

In order to help students develop their own opinions it will also be helpful for teachers to consider whether the whole class will study the same texts or topics or whether these should be individualized.

Teaching literature and topics

A major difference for MFL teachers at A-level is that they will have to teach content as well as language. Each examining body has one unit, that requires written answers on literary texts or non-literary topics. This may require a great deal of background work for the teacher if the area is unfamiliar.

Teaching literature

A literary text can be daunting as a long text. It can be useful to isolate key sections of the text for close analysis and combine this with much faster reading of the sections in between. Sheila Barbour provides an excellent example of how this can be done in practice using the text *Boule de suif* (2000). She illustrates, in particular, the value of very close analysis in alerting students to the complexity of a literary experience: understanding metaphorical links and appreciating irony.

Karen Turner (1999) suggests a similar approach of detailed selective analysis plus an overview of the whole text. She provides useful suggestions for supporting the independent reading of a whole text with glossaries of key vocabulary, signpost questions and transference of key ideas into grids, diagrams, timelines and so forth.

Studying literature can also be combined with language work (Collie and Slater, 1987, and Wicksteed, 1993, offer some useful ideas here).

Teaching a topic

Useful sources of material are suggested on the CILT information sheets for A-level topic materials. Particularly recommended are the set of resources for languages (*Thématique, Thematisch* by Stanley Thornes) and the newspaper/audio resources prepared by Authentik in French, German and Spanish.

ASSESSMENT

Links to teaching standards

Under *subject knowledge and understanding,* trainees are asked to demonstrate: that they are familiar with their specialist subject(s) with the relevant ... post-16 examination syllabuses and courses; and also that they know and can teach the key skills required for current qualifications relevant to their specialist subject(s) for pupils aged 14–19, and understand the contribution that their specialist subject(s) make to the development of the key skills.

Under *monitoring, assessment, recording, reporting and accountability,* they are asked to demonstrate that they 'understand the expected demands of pupils in relation to ... post-16 courses' and that they 'understand and know how to implement the assessment requirements of current qualifications for pupils aged 14–19'.

Familiarizing themselves with A-level work as suggested in this section should help trainees achieve this standard.

Vocational A-levels

The old GNVQ qualifications are now no longer part of the curriculum being taught. They were replaced by vocational A-levels as from September 2000.

> **Task 6.2**
>
> Devise an activity or find a text to make an A-level text or topic relevant to the students.

> **Task 6.3**
>
> Select a study skill and devise and practise an activity related to this in a sixth form lesson.

Qualifications in Scotland

At the time of writing the national structure of qualifications in Scotland is undergoing substantial change. Until now the structure of the Scottish Certificate of Education has been as follows:

- Standard grade (at foundation, general and credit levels) for students at the end of S4 (ie aged 16) – equivalent to GCSE.
- Higher grade – equivalent to the present AS-level.
- Certificate of Sixth Year Studies. The structure and name are set to change significantly within the next two or three years. It will be called the Scottish Qualification Certificate, the structure of which will be as follows:
  - access;
  - intermediate I (for S4 students);

TEACHING MODERN FOREIGN LANGUAGES

- intermediate II;
- higher (for S5 students);
- advanced higher.

Full details as they develop can be found on the Web site of the Scottish Qualifications Authority (www.sqa.org.uk).

Homework

Homework is work undertaken by a student unsupervised by the teacher and usually in an environment beyond the classroom. It is useful to think of these circumstances and consider the advantages that out-of-school work provides and how these may be exploited, and also what appropriate activities are for an unsupervised student.

The out-of-school context

Two major advantages of an out-of-school context are the elasticity of time and space arrangements, and the lack of public scrutiny.

Students can take as much (or as little) time as they want for homework activities and they can practise and study without their efforts being commented on by others. There is, then, an excellent opportunity for differentiation and this is worth bearing in mind when planning homework. It will also be possible for pupils to use resources from different places because they are not confined to the classroom.

It is worth considering that not all students have the same out-of-school opportunities. In the mid-1990s there was a government drive to set up homework facilities in libraries. It may be sensible to see what is available locally for your students.

Lack of supervision

It will be sensible to plan homework so that there is complete clarity in terms of the task being set because the student will have no recourse to the teacher for further clarification. Several useful suggestions are:

- allowing plenty of time for setting homework in the lesson;
- checking in the lesson that the homework is thoroughly understood (if necessary using English);
- providing very structured guidelines for the homework (writing on the board as well as talking it through orally);
- starting the homework in the lesson so that students' work can be checked.

One problem may be that the students copy each other's work (where there is written homework). Leman (1999) also mentions the problem of middle-class parents' contributions to pupils' coursework. With post-16 students there may be an additional problem if material is downloaded from the Internet without this being acknowledged. Another way of viewing this problem is to see that these kinds of activities can also be opportunities for collaboration and exploitation of resources. It will be useful to talk to your mentor about departmental views on this issue.

ASSESSMENT

Key questions

Before planning homework it is useful to consider some key questions:
- What is the homework policy in the school and department?
- What is the purpose and function of this homework?
- How will it be integrated into my lessons?
- What kind of feedback will I give?

School/departmental policies

It is important to establish early on what homework policies exist in your school. You need to know:

- how long students are expected to take for homework in your subject and in different year groups;
- when 'homework nights' are;
- how homework marks are recorded;
- what sanctions exist if students fail to do their homework; and
- favoured styles of homework in your department (students in parallel year groups can become most indignant if they are asked to do very different things from their peers).

The purpose and function of homework

Homework represents special opportunities for both the teacher and the student. For the *teacher* there is the chance to:

- check that students have learnt something;
- provide evidence for assessment;
- collect examples of 'good work' to act as models and points of discussion (suggested by Buckland and Short, 1993);
- have a link with parents.

For the *students* there is the opportunity to:

- have more ownership of the work being done;
- develop skills for autonomous learning;
- build up confidence.

Besides these global functions, homework can also fulfil more specific objectives, in particular:

- revising and extending what has been covered in lessons;
- finding out and preparing for lessons to come;
- practising skills not used during lessons.

Integrating homework into lessons

It is useful to think of homework, not as a bolt-on extra but rather as an integrated component of a planned series of lessons. It will be useful to consider integration on two levels: as part of the lesson content, and in terms of time allocation within the lesson.

With regard to lesson content, it will be important when planning a lesson to think how homework can support what is being covered in the lesson in the ways suggested above. It can also be useful to consider whether any individual piece of homework is just related to a single lesson or whether it is part of a series perhaps relying on different language skills.

We have already mentioned the importance of allowing sufficient time in a lesson to give instruction about the homework being set. It is also important to consider timing issues related to collecting in homework and dealing with problem areas that become evident through homework. Students may respond well to a set pattern of homework procedures (vocabulary learning is always tested at the beginning of the next lesson; there is always a five-minute slot to discuss homework). Again it will be useful to discuss with your mentor whether such procedures are common practice in your department.

Buckland and Short (1993) in their extremely useful book on homework offer some helpful ideas on integrating homework into the lesson (pp 28–34).

Homework can be *summative* (in providing assessment data for the teacher); *diagnostic* (in demonstrating what students do or do not know) and also *formative* (in helping students understand errors through feedback).

Feedback can be given globally to a class by the teacher commenting on how a particular piece of homework has been done. This is often helpful for students so that they do not feel as though they are working in a vacuum. A kind of global feedback can also be given if generic errors are identified within a piece of homework and followed up in some way.

Individual feedback can also be given, particularly for pieces of written work. Issues to consider here are:

- Should there be positive feedback as well as error correction?
- If there are errors should they *all* be identified or only some of them?
- How will errors be identified (by noting or should a correct version be given)?
- Will you use English or target language for feedback?

It will be useful to discuss these points with your mentor both in terms of favoured departmental practice and also in terms of possible advantages and disadvantages.

It may also be helpful to think about opportunities for students to write feedback on their own work. Trenchard-Morgan (1999) gives some useful ideas on helping students extend their range of teaching strategies (see also suggestions in Chapter 9 on learner strategies) or on each other's work.

Homework content

A final area to consider is what to set as homework: which activities work well? Buckland and Short provide many examples of imaginative ideas for each of the four different language skills (1993).

They also include useful tips in terms of managing different kinds of homework: providing tapes for listening; getting students to write exercises; setting up a bank of reading materials etc. It may also be helpful to think of foreign language homework as being in three different categories:

ASSESSMENT

- learning;
- producing;
- discovering.

Learning

Students can be asked to learn items of vocabulary for testing; they can learn dialogues to be spoken in a following lesson (and perhaps be taped); they can learn short texts to write or sing.

Producing

Students can, for example, produce written or prepared oral work in response to various stimuli (such as pictures, drawings, diagrams, outlines or extensive reading); or they can produce diagrams, pictures etc linked to written items. They can produce audio or video tapes to use in class or send to a link school.

Discovering

Students can be asked to find out information about language (by consulting dictionaries or skimming through texts). They can also discover cultural information either about their own culture or the target culture by surfing the Internet or investigating in libraries and so forth.

There are, then, a wide range of different activities that can be set for homework and these can serve different purposes. Worksheet copy-masters may be useful and publishers are now beginning to produce homework handbooks. Channel 4 have set up a Web site to help students with French and other subjects at www.homeworkhigh where students can ask teachers questions.

Task 6.4

Set a 'learning' and a 'discovering' homework with the same set of students and see how different pupils respond. This should provide useful information on the types of learner in your class.

Task 6.5

Consider some common error or errors that occur in homework from one of your classes and consider how to provide global feedback on this in your next lesson.

Links to teaching standards

Under *planning* trainees are asked to 'demonstrate' that they 'plan their teaching to achieve progression in pupils' learning through ... setting tasks ... including homework which challenge pupils and ensure high levels of pupil interest'. Under *teaching and class management* they are asked to: use teaching methods which sustain the momentum of pupils' work and keeps all pupils engaged through ... careful attention to pupils' errors and misconceptions and helping to remedy them ... [and through] providing opportunities for pupils to consolidate their knowledge and maximizing opportunities ... through setting well-focused homework to reinforce and develop what has been learnt.

Concentrating on homework as suggested in this section should help to achieve these standards.

7 Equal opportunities and special needs

This chapter is the first of four tackling *key issues* related to modern foreign language teaching. It deals with the questions of equal opportunities and students with special educational needs in the modern language classroom.

Equal opportunities

As was seen in the introductory chapter, modern languages used to be a subject studied only by the most able. Since the introduction of the National Curriculum and the policy of languages for all, the issues of equal opportunities and the inclusion of children with special educational needs (SEN) into all areas of the curriculum have become important considerations for teachers of modern languages.

Objectives

By the end of this chapter you should:

- have an awareness of the influence of gender in modern language education;
- have an awareness of what special needs are;
- be familiar with the arguments in favour of and against teaching modern foreign languages to SEN children;
- be aware of a range of strategies for presenting material.

Introduction

Since languages for all became policy, students who would normally have dropped languages after year nine are now forced to continue with language study until the age of 16. Many arguments could be made in favour of this situation and language teachers fought vigorously to have languages retained as a core. The negative side, however, is that there are now many students in languages classes at key stage four who have neither ability in learning languages nor the inclination to try. There are also many who do have ability but find the language curriculum less than challenging. The word 'equality' and the term 'equality of opportunity' have long been bandied about. It is clear, however, that, because people are not all equal, giving them equality of opportunity does not necessarily imply treating them all equally.

Arguments for languages for all

Several arguments have been put forward in favour of compulsory language learning and several developments in language teaching which have taken place over the past two decades were designed to make modern languages both more attractive and more accessible to a wider range of students.

The government would argue that the UK lags far behind the language capability of other European states, a fact confirmed in the Nuffield Inquiry (p 15). Part of the problem lies in the fact that, unlike our European partners, modern languages have not been a major feature of the school curriculum here. It should be noted, however, that to compare modern foreign languages such as French, German or Spanish with English as a foreign language in other European countries is an unfair comparison; English is a global language and it is easily accessible in the media throughout the world. Anecdotal evidence would suggest that German is no more popular in French schools than it is in the UK, despite the proximity of the target country.

Comparative statistics on performance in a wide variety of school subjects suggests that UK students are far down the league table in basic literacy and numeracy. However as Brown (2000) suggests these figures can be misleading. The study of a modern foreign language not only enhances communication skills and a number of transferable learning skills but encourages a revision or a learning of the basics of the mother tongue.

As was seen in the initial chapter, languages in schools have developed considerably since the days when it was an elitist subject for only the best students. The more attractive aspects of MFL are summarized briefly below:

- a move towards a communicative curriculum;
- a topic-based approach as opposed to a grammar focus;
- more attractive textbooks;
- use of multi-media;
- syllabuses more relevant to the needs of students;
- more flexible examinations.

Despite these changes and despite teachers' efforts to make languages more attractive, the problems of lack of motivation and poor performance concerning boys in languages and the teaching of languages to some students with special educational needs are still areas which are giving rise to concern.

Boys and languages

Languages have generally been perceived as feminine subjects (Callaghan, 1998) with feminine topics (home, family and so forth) being studied, and, while boys no longer have the choice to drop languages before key stage four, figures for A-level languages suggest that they do disappear from language classrooms at the first possible opportunity (Clark, 1998). Other research has shown that subject choice differs in single-sex schools from that in mixed schools, and this may relate to boys' perceived susceptibility to peer pressure (Thomas, 1998). Elwood and Gipps (1999) describe studies which show that, in single-sex settings, boys were more keen on languages than their counterparts in mixed-sex schools. Morgan and Freedman's feedback from 219 teachers on provision and uptake in MFL contained a large number of comments relating to low achievements in boys (1999). Other research carried out in the UK, which examined both teachers' and students' perspectives on languages for boys, showed some of the factors as to why boys are not motivated in languages to be the following:

- language study is irrelevant;
- languages are too difficult;
- the learning of languages puts a burden on memory;
- studying languages requires concentration;
- the lack of knowledge and their inability to express themselves leads to frustration;
- they dislike listening;
- the syllabus for languages is uninteresting. (Based on Clark, 1998: 6ff.)

A later study by Downes (2000) in which boys were interviewed about their perceptions of language learning uncovered similar opinions and reactions. The findings of this study are particularly relevant because it was conducted after the introduction of TL testing. They are summarized below.

The boys perceived languages as different from other subjects in the curriculum in that:

- there is pressure to be accurate;
- grammar is difficult;
- languages are both the subject and the medium of instruction;
- demands are put on memory;
- they do not necessarily like the target culture;
- homework is difficult.

They stated that they did not understand what they were expected to do:

- they do not like the excessive transactional nature of the activities;
- they are not interested in the topics;
- the use of the target language for instructions causes problems;
- the enthusiasm in years seven and eight has all but disappeared by years nine and ten;
- once they start to lose the thread, it is difficult to get back on track;
- they do not like taking responsibility for their own learning. (Adapted from Downes, 2000: 2.)

What the boys in both of the studies seem to be saying is that the content of the curriculum has done little to change boys' attitudes over time. It would seem, therefore, that all the changes mentioned above to try to make language learning more attractive have done little to convince boys of the value of languages. It is not all negative, however. The boys interviewed in Clark's study mentioned the following positive features:

- the relationship with the teacher was crucial in affecting their attitude and motivation;
- variety of activity is important;
- games are popular as are role play and drama.

They suggested that the following might be helpful:

- more contact with native speakers in terms of visits to the target country;
- more use of ICT, video-conferencing etc desirable;
- more group-work activities;
- more help with learning strategies (Clark, 1998: 11f).

The following positive aspects were mentioned in the Downes study:

- they like a variety of activities;
- some tasks are relevant and enjoyable;
- they like pairwork;
- external examinations provide some challenge;
- their achievements are recognized and rewarded (Downes, 2000).

By comparing the perceptions of the students in both these studies, it is possible to identify some key elements. The learning environment should encourage variety of activity, skill, task, resources and pace. The rapport with the teacher is crucial and teachers should be exploring ways of developing students' awareness of learner strategies. Boys need reinforcement and rewards and the tasks should be relevant and challenging and the topics not too feminine.

Many teachers reading this and other documents on equal opportunities and encouraging boys in languages will no doubt say that they are doing all of these things but with little effect on boys' behaviour, motivation and attitude to languages. Admittedly, certain aspects cannot be changed, such as the biological and socio-economic factors influencing boys' learning, their attitudes to it and the factors relating to the content of the curriculum and external examinations. It is necessary for teachers, however, to adopt strategies that work for them with the students in their classes and that cater for both boys and girls in the class. Although Downes makes only tentative suggestions as to how to manage the classroom in order to encourage more effective learning by boys, the teachers in his study noted that the following factors went some way to meeting the needs of boys in the modern language classroom:

- a variety of activity and tasks is necessary and a variety of approach to different ATs;
- there should not be too much frantic activity and activity change as this is unsettling;
- use activities that involve physically moving round the classroom;
- create activities which harness the competitive element;
- create a sense of fun;
- explain grammar clearly to enable boys to build a system;

EQUAL OPPORTUNITIES AND SPECIAL NEEDS

- get a balance between TL and English explanation in grammar;
- give clear explanation of the purpose of activity;
- use target setting as a means of motivation;
- good rapport between teachers and students is essential;
- be aware of the link between motivation and success, especially for boys (Downes, 2000: 4ff).

Given the evidence that suggests that boys do better in languages in single-sex schools, it might be worth experimenting with single-sex groupings within classes or even single-sex language and science classes in schools. The danger with this is, however, that classes consisting of all boys in languages may lack some of the elements that are regarded as good practice, such as variety and challenge.

The issue of equal opportunities with regard to gender at key stages three and four is not one of inclusion but one of meeting the needs of one group, namely boys, whilst encouraging girls to go on to greater success. At the upper school, there is still a need to persuade boys to continue with language study beyond the compulsory level. Language classes at post-GCSE level in mixed schools usually have more female students than male students. One of the concerns remains how to encourage more males into language professions with the competition from the sciences and other subjects that are seen as having a more masculine image.

Task 7.1

Look at your school's equal opportunities policy and discuss with your mentor the implications for the modern foreign languages classroom.

Special needs

The Warnock report (1978: 41) stated:

> that a teacher of a mixed ability class of 30 children even in an ordinary school should be aware that possibly as many as six of them require some form of special educational provision at some time during their school life and about four or five of them may require special educational provision at any given time.

In this regard:

> A child is said to have Special Educational Needs (SENs) if he [sic] has a 'learning difficulty that requires special educational provision to be made for him; and a child is said to have a 'learning difficulty' if:
> a) he has a significantly greater difficulty in learning than the majority of children his age; or
> b) he has a disability which either prevents or hinders him from making use of the educational facilities of a kind generally provided at an Ordinary school. (NI Order, 1986: par. 33 (2).)

Only a small proportion of the children with SEN is educated in special schools, and the current moves are towards integration and inclusion, so it is necessary for teachers of all subjects to have an awareness of some of the major issues relating to SEN. Indeed the Code of Practice (DfEE, 1994) states that all teachers in a school have a responsibility towards children with SEN. The main aspects of this complex area of identifying, assessing, planning and monitoring students with SEN have been dealt with in detail in Alsop and Luth (1999). Some reference will be made to this article in the following sections.

Disapplication

The reviewed National Curriculum has provision for 'disapplication' – schools will be able to exempt certain students from parts of the curriculum if it is felt that they would benefit from other aspects (DfEE, 2000). At key stage four, in particular, the regulations state that up to two NC subjects may be disapplied for any one student. The three conditions that are attached to this are that the student is:

- participating in extended work-related learning;
- pursuing individual strengths to emphasize a particular curriculum area;
- making significantly less progress than other students of his/her age to consolidate the learning and progress across the curriculum.

Modern foreign languages can be disapplied for students in any of the three categories above. This will certainly have implications for students who have special needs and it may result in an absence of students with learning difficulties from the language classes above KS3. This is almost a return to the elitist days of language teaching. In the lower classes, however, there will still be students with special needs or learning difficulties.

The following paragraphs present a definition of the kinds of special needs that a teacher is likely to encounter in the classroom and suggest some strategies that might be appropriate.

Types of SEN

There are various types of special needs that might be encountered in students in a classroom and some students will have more than one special need. Students might have one or more of the following:

- severe learning difficulties (such as multi-sensory impairment; autism; Asperger syndrome);
- mild learning difficulties;
- moderate learning difficulties (MLD) (for example, difficulties with literacy and numeracy);
- specific learning difficulties (SPLD) (for example, dyslexia; dyscalculia);
- emotional and behavioural difficulties (EBD);
- physical impairment;
- sensory impairment;
- exceptional ability. (Adapted from Alsop and Luth, 1999: 139ff.)

As a teacher of modern languages, you will be responsible for ensuring that you meet these students' needs first and foremost in the delivery of the curriculum. You will receive help and guidance from the special needs co-ordinator (SENCO) in the school but ultimately you are responsible for ensuring that your lessons are inclusive in that they are accessible to all the students in your class.

Modern languages and SEN

The aims of language teaching for SEN students can be, *inter alia*, cultural, social, intellectual or affective, according to Lee (1991). The teaching of languages also offers a linguistic dimension that can aid students' literacy and numeracy by giving them a second chance at acquiring the basics. The other aim of language teaching important to SEN students is that it should be enjoyable and a rewarding experience in order to enhance their learning self-esteem. For students who have experienced so much failure in their schooling, the learning of a language can create an environment for them where they feel they have a fresh start.

The problem with teaching modern languages to students who possess a limited attention span, however, is that learning a language is a cumulative process. It is necessary, for example, for students to have a knowledge of numbers before they can deal with the topic of shopping which involves prices. Because students with special needs have difficulty retaining information, the teacher has to find ways of presenting a limited amount of language in a variety of different ways. There has to be repetition disguised as different activities that engage the interest and attention of the SEN students. For this to be successful, the material has to be pitched at a more mature level, as students with special educational needs do not respond well to being presented with activities and tasks that they consider to be below their level of maturity.

Materials

Much of the commercial material designed specifically for children with SEN or low ability groups is in French and, to a lesser extent, German. In schools where Spanish or other languages are offered to the whole ability range, it will probably be necessary to adapt and borrow from the materials in other languages. Various LEAs throughout the country have produced packs of materials designed to help teachers adapt languages to suit the lower levels of ability. Many of these have been produced by ad hoc groups of teachers who were faced with the challenge of teaching SEN students but with little, if any, resource support. CILT produces a regular bulletin on languages and SEN, which presents reports on materials, projects and other support material.

Problems and strategies

The main difficulty in talking about SEN students is that no two students' needs are the same and, even if they were, what might be required to meet one person's needs may not be appropriate for the other. Nevertheless, there are some factors that may be common to many learners in the modern language classroom such as:

- poor motivation;
- short concentration span;
- low self-esteem;
- fear of something new;
- fear of failure based on past experiences.

They may have specific difficulties such as:

- reading problems;
- inability to work without supervision;
- no retention of information;
- inability to monitor their own progress;
- inability to solve problems;
- difficulty in copying;
- difficulty in organizing material.

As a result of these difficulties, either individually or in combination, behaviour may become disruptive with frustration manifesting itself in a number of ways, for example by:

- shouting out and being aggressive;
- distracting others, throwing pieces of paper round the class;
- refusal to work;
- withdrawn behaviour.

These behaviours may manifest themselves in a mixed-ability classroom and can pose particular problems for the teacher. The following sections provide some advice on techniques and strategies that may be appropriate for some students with special needs.

Holmes (1994b: 5ff.) lists some of the problems experienced by children with special needs and suggests some solutions:

Problem	*Solution*
Poor auditory discrimination.	Frequent repetition of sounds and regular exercises in repetition/vocal games.
Weak visual memory.	Colour coding/using shapes. Adapt print on to colour pages.
Visual disturbance.	Avoid dense typeface.
Difficulty reading.	Show one line at a time.
Conceptual difficulties.	Be aware that certain behaviours might be masking conceptual problems.
Writing difficulties.	Use of movable mini-flashcards/charts/grids.
Poor attendance.	Providing materials for independent learning.

There are various ways to get students involved in the work of the classroom. For example when language is being presented using flashcards, the students can:

- point at the card;
- pick up the card;
- hand over a flashcard;
- nod/shake their head;
- put cards in the correct order;
- hold up a card when they hear the correct word.

Repetition and imitation are vital for acquiring new language and even more is required by children with special needs. A variety of techniques is necessary for repetition, in order to avoid boredom. Teachers should try to make sure they include the following differences in presentation and activities:

- loud/soft;
- fast/slow;
- division of syllables around class;
- front/back of class;
- different expressions;
- tone of voice;
- boys/girls.

The teacher should make sure that the following are incorporated into lessons:

- visuals (clear use of symbols);
- multi-sensory approach;
- multi-media, if possible;
- clarity of speech;
- a lot of repetition;
- variety (of activity, of skill and of pace);
- gesture;
- mime;
- support;
- student involvement (hands-on approach).

The learning objectives must be clearly defined, they must be achievable for the students; they must be staged in small steps. Students must have a sense of purpose and they must feel that they have achieved something at the end of the lesson.

In conclusion, it should be stated that good teaching that encourages learning is the same for high achievers as for students with special needs. The focus should be on the learning of the students and every effort should be made to make the language lesson accessible, challenging, varied and enjoyable. Techniques and strategies that are found in the literature on teaching to special needs classes are equally applicable to mainstream classes.

Inclusion

In the programme of study for modern foreign languages a whole section is devoted to inclusion of all students. Inclusion is governed by three principles:

- setting suitable learning challenges;
- responding to students' diverse learning needs;
- overcoming potential barriers to learning and assessment for individuals and groups of students.

Setting suitable learning challenges

It is recognized that there are differences in students' learning ability and the programme of study takes account of these by stating that teachers will be required to adapt the content of the programme of study to meet the needs of individuals. It is stated that differentiation is crucial to meet the needs of students. For example, it states that material from an earlier or later key stage may be necessary either in order to enable the student to progress or to enable them to catch up with material that they may have missed. Reasons for this may be because of a medical condition or because they are travellers or refugees. Thus the needs of slower learners and more rapid learners are taken into consideration.

Responding to students' diverse learning needs

The programme of study notes that differences in groups may require significant adaptation of the teaching approach. It mentions boys/girls, children with special needs, disabilities, students from different social and cultural backgrounds, including different ethnic groups. It encourages teachers to be aware of the different needs such groups of individuals bring with them to the learning situation and to create learning environments that take account of their individual needs.

Overcoming potential barriers to learning and assessment for individuals and groups of students

This section emphasizes the point that some students will have learning requirements that demand some intervention which otherwise will become barriers to learning. It lists the students' needs under the categories of special needs, students with disabilities and those whose mother tongue is not English. Specific guidance is given as to what measures may be put in place to support the learning of such groups. Examples include allowing greater use of ICT, using symbols and signing or symbol systems to encourage language skills. It also suggests allowing more time for the completion of tasks and in assessment to discount aspects of the level descriptors when arriving at a judgement.

EQUAL OPPORTUNITIES AND SPECIAL NEEDS

Summary

This section has shown that learners differ in their motivation, ability, attitude and experience. It is the job of the teacher to ensure that all students in the modern language classroom have equal access to the learning of the subject. This will entail differentiation of some kind and adapting the material, conditions and assessment to suit the needs of the learners. Creating a climate of equal access and inclusion is achieved not by treating everyone equally but by tailoring the content and teaching approach to the needs of the group. By doing so the teacher will be providing an enriching learning experience to all the students in the class.

Task 7.2

Take a lesson from a textbook and adapt it to suit the students with specific special needs. Take the same lesson and adapt it to meet the needs of students who are exceptionally gifted at languages.

Links to teaching standards

Under *subject knowledge and understanding*, trainees are asked to demonstrate that they 'understand how pupils' learning in the subject is affected by their physical, intellectual, emotional and social development'. Under *planning*, trainees are asked to demonstrate that they 'plan their teaching to achieve progression in pupils' learning through: ... identifying pupils who have special educational needs, including specific learning difficulties, who are very able ... and knowing where to get help in order to give positive and targeted support'. Under *teaching and class management* trainees are asked to demonstrate that they 'use teaching methods which sustain the momentum of pupils' work and keep all pupils engaged through ... setting high expectations for all pupils notwithstanding individual differences, including gender, and cultural and linguistic backgrounds' and 'are familiar with the Code of Practice on the identification and assessment of special educational needs'. Focusing on equal opportunities and special needs, as outlined in this chapter, should help trainees to achieve these standards.

8 Using the target language

The aim of this second chapter on *key issues* is to examine the role of the target language (TL) in modern language classrooms. It presents some of the arguments for and against total use of the TL in lessons.

Objectives

By the end of this chapter you should understand the various issues related to using the TL and be in a position to make a reasoned choice about when and how to use the TL.

Introduction

One major area of controversy, particularly since the introduction of the National Curriculum guidelines, has been the debate on the use of the TL in a communicative teaching approach. There are arguments both for and against its use. This chapter outlines some of the main issues and presents a model for so-called 'judicial' use of the language in the modern foreign language classroom.

Modern languages are unique as a subject in the curriculum in that the language is at one and the same time both content and medium of instruction. This means that thinking about how the language should be used has implications on these two levels.

Another factor that must be taken into consideration is the context in which the teaching is taking place: the size of class, the age, previous experience and relationship of the students with the teacher, the number in the class, the time of day, the length and objectives of individual lessons and whether the teacher is a native speaker or not.

Issues

The main question is how much the TL should be used. Should it be 95–100 per cent as suggested in the guidelines?

Two factors must be taken into consideration before we advocate a policy of using TL 100 per cent of the time. Firstly, the classroom is an artificial setting, divorced from the target country (with the exception of geographical situations where the modern language is also spoken in the community). Secondly, there are other constraints imposed by the National Curriculum, examination syllabuses and the school situation, which impose restrictions on the time available and that prevent the creation of a naturalistic environment and where there may be varying attitudes to TL use.

In schools in the UK, however, a considerable emphasis continues to be placed on the use of the TL as the main medium of communication. Published documents on the foreign language curriculum state:

> The first essential is frequent contact with the TL through the teacher's continuous use of it and through tape recordings.
> (DES/WO, 1990: par: 9.5)
>
> The TL can be used both to practise specific language patterns and vocabulary and to communicate with the students on everyday topics in modern language classes.
> (NICC, 1992: par. 8.3)
>
> In pursuing [the aims of modern language learning] most teaching programmes incorporate the following features: the development of communicative competence among the students, the increasing use of the foreign language as the medium of the classroom.
> (SOED, 1991: 2)
>
> Students are expected to use and respond to the TL, and to use English only when necessary (for example, when discussing a grammar point or when comparing English and the TL).
> (DfEE/QCA, 1999: 16)

Sources of the TL

We can identify four main sources of the authentic TL available to students: the teacher, information and communication technology (ICT) (audio, video and e-mail), visitors to class and peers (Franklin, 1990a).

As mentioned in Chapter 4, visitors to a class can be useful if they are native speakers of the TL such as a foreign language assistant (FLA) or an exchange teacher who can contribute not only an authentic TL model but also provide a cultural perspective. Having TL visitors can also create a need for the teacher to communicate meaningfully with them in the foreign language, demonstrating to the students that there is a genuine reason for them as learners to use their TL as a means of communication (DfEE/QCA, 1999: par. 4b).

ICT resources such as audio and video sources are valuable in that they can bring authenticity into the classroom and provide cultural as well as linguistic input into the lesson. They can, however, also present problems to learners since they cannot interact with the native speakers and, in many cases, the quality of the sound recording prevents rather than helps understanding. In IT sources such as e-mail, the language will be clear but this does not mean that it will be understood, although as this is an interactive medium there may be a chance of checking meaning.

The National Curriculum documentation states that peers are an important part of the language learning process and that students should have opportunities to work together in pairs and in groups, using the TL (DfEE/QCA, 1999: par 5a).

The main provider of the TL, though, is the teacher, who has the task of providing a linguistically rich environment within the confines of the classroom.

Teacher use of the TL

Calls for greater use of the TL have resulted in the publication of books and resources designed to help teachers with the task (Halliwell and Jones, 1991; NCC 1993; Holmes, 1994a) and all the up-to-date textbooks contain lists of helpful suggestions of how to incorporate the language into lessons. McDonald's (1994) book also provides lists of useful TL classroom language. With the introduction of testing in the target language, syllabuses produced by examination boards also give lists of instructions that will be used in the exams. You are not being required, therefore, to reinvent the wheel, but all teachers of modern languages must ensure that they provide the learners with good models of the language. Whilst realizing that the TL need not be used 100 per cent of the time, it is imperative that students be given lots of opportunities to hear the language. These are some possible suggestions:

- Create a foreign language ambience in the classroom so that students realize they are entering a TL zone.
- Build up a repertoire of classroom instructions which you use systematically.
- Use mime, gesture, cognates, interpreters to ensure above all that the TL you use is comprehensible to the students.
- Use previously taught/learned structures for genuine communication.

Student use of the TL

In order to meet the requirements of the National Curriculum, students must be given opportunities for:

> Communicating in the target language in pairs and groups, and with their teacher
> Using the target language creatively and imaginatively
> Using the target language for real purposes (DfEE/QCA, 1999: 17)

You can create a bank of structures which students should be encouraged to use when dealing with the immediate classroom environment, such as 'I've forgotten …'; 'May I …?'; 'Could you …, please?' This bank of phrases can be added to in a systematized fashion during the course of their language learning classes.

Arguments against total TL use

Atkinson (1993) gives some reasons why 100 per cent TL use is undesirable.

Rapport

Total use of the TL with students can create a barrier between teachers and students and can have an adverse effect on the teaching and learning situation, which relies heavily on interpersonal communication. The result can be, therefore, that what sets out to be a communicative ideology can inhibit the communication it originally set out to promote.

Native speaker versus non-native speaker

Rapport can be a particular factor in situations where both the learners and teachers share the same mother tongue, and using the TL appears a rather artificial situation to both. If teachers try to pretend they do not understand English this can lead to a rather artificial situation, far from the communicative ideal. Small-scale research that examined the teaching of science through the medium of French, taught by a native speaker, found that the native speaker status of the teacher was a major factor in the students' positive reaction to the lesson and the target language (Salters *et al*, 1995).

Methodological argument

In terms of methodology Atkinson argues for an approach which considers all the variables concerned with maximizing students' learning. This will inevitably involve creating an environment in which both languages can be used.

Content

The emphasis over the past few years has been on the quantity of the TL to be used rather than on the quality or level of language. It is easy enough to state that all classroom instructions should be in the TL, but if the only language that was taught in classrooms was related to class language, learners would have a very limited set of vocabulary and instructions. Teachers need to develop strategies to recycle language structures with which students are familiar in more unfamiliar topics. For example, it is possible to introduce new items of vocabulary for a new topic using a past tense, rather than the present. In this way progression will be assured.

Use of English

As a reaction against the apparent overinsistence on total use of the TL in the UK classroom both by government publications and inspectors' reports some critics argue for a balanced view of the place of English in the foreign language classroom (Buckby, 1985; Harbord,

1992; Atkinson, 1993; Collins, 1993). Indeed there has been a softening of the insistence on total use of the TL most recently.

It is important to mention, however, that teachers must not give learners the impression that all the important work is done in English. The TL must still be regarded as the main means of communication by both teacher and student but English can and should be used for specific purposes. Collins argues for systematic use of the mother tongue for specific purposes such as:

- explaining the aims of a lesson;
- gaining feedback from students after something has been taught to see if the hypotheses they form are correct;
- to clarify points that arise in meaning;
- to draw comparisons between items (both linguistic and cultural) in the TL and in English;
- to give instructions, if TL use would be too time consuming (Collins, 1993).

Grittner (1977) argues that a distinction should be drawn between the proper and improper use of English in the foreign language classroom. English that leads to more practice in the foreign language by the students is regarded by Grittner as positive, whereas any English used which makes the student a passive listener may well have negative effects. It might be argued that using English to save time is, in fact, proper use of the mother tongue, since it frees time for more use of the foreign language. Buckby (1985) comments that a minute of English can prepare the way for a purposeful and fruitful session of TL use.

Harbord (1992) lists three occasions when one might use the mother tongue of the learners: to facilitate teacher-student communication, to facilitate rapport and to facilitate learning. Harbord concludes on this issue that the mother tongue should not be used merely as a time-saving device in order to allow more time for more useful activities. Rather, quoting Duff (1989) he states:

> [the mother tongue] should be used to provoke discussion and to develop clarity and flexibility of thinking and to help increase our own and our students' awareness of the inevitable interaction between the mother tongue and the TL that occurs during any type of language acquisition.
>
> (Duff, 1989, cited by Harbord 1992: 355)

Unless, therefore, the mother tongue can enhance the quality of the learning experience in the classroom, it should be avoided.

Motivation

One of the variables connected with the judicious use of English is that of student motivation of the students. Collins (1993) comments that the motivation, especially of lower ability children, may dictate that use of the TL has to be interspersed with English in order to keep their attention and to ensure they are following the lesson. Again, however, it is essential to ensure that such students are still given a sustained diet of the TL, simplified, explained and made comprehensible to them by whatever means.

One factor that must be taken into account when dealing with students studying a foreign language, and especially a second foreign language, at the present time in years 10 or 11, is that they must be relatively motivated to study languages in the first place. Chambers (1992) adds the practical difficulty in sustaining TL use when the teacher is particularly tired. If the teacher feels he/she has to revert to the mother tongue when tired, it is unreasonable to expect students to sustain their concentration at all times on the TL.

Age of students

Buckby (1985) recommends that in the early stages of foreign language learning the lesson should contain at least one 10-minute period of uninterrupted TL use. This should be extended until years 10 or 11 when, according to Buckby, it should be possible to conduct most of the lessons in the TL. For this reason he regards it as unreasonable to make a blanket policy of TL use, when learning contexts differ from school to school and class to class. Franklin (1990b) also comments that, particularly at the early stages of language learning when learners have few linguistic resources at their disposal, the mother tongue can be a helpful resource. Common sense would suggest that it is possible to use more TL with older learners, that is to say those who have been learning a language for some time, than with beginners, although recent evidence appears to indicate that this is not frequent in practice (Dickson, 1996; Dobson, 1998).

Codeswitching and decoding

A further point in the TL/English debate is the distinction between two ways in which English can be used. Codeswitching refers to the practice of switching between the TL and the mother tongue for specific purposes. Decoding on the other hand refers to the practice of making an utterance in the TL followed by the translation in the mother tongue. Buckby, however, recommends a type of 'English sandwich' as an example of good practice of TL use where the foreign language phrase is uttered, followed by the translation and immediately followed again by the TL version (Buckby, 1985: 51). Wong Fillmore (1985) comments that the type of decoding that encourages learners to wait for the translation deprives them of the process of 'figuring out' what the TL means. It is important to be consistent in the use of TL and MT for various functions and teachers will need to use their experience to guide them in finding a balance between both languages.

Avoidance of English

There are numerous ways the teacher can avoid using English, so that the students interact with the language. The following represent some of the strategies you can use:

- use a student to interpret in English;
- use non-verbal communication;
- be consistent with language and symbols;

- rephrase where necessary;
- use clear visuals;
- use cognates;
- use the TL to talk about events outside the classroom;
- give students strategic phrases to seek help;
- encourage students to ask for help in the TL from their peers;
- accept incomplete utterances and allow them to supplement with English;
- encourage inaccurate language which does not impede communication;
- refuse to accept English where it is not necessary.

Testing in the TL

Since 1997 the GCSE exams have asked the majority of questions through the TL, requiring the candidates to respond either with non-verbal responses or responses in the TL. At first there was some apprehension within the language teaching profession that this would prove to be too difficult for students and now this development is being reconsidered. Some researchers in language education felt that it was inappropriate to test students through the medium of the language as this might cause problems with the reliability of the tests themselves (Page, 1993) although one commissioned small-scale research project concluded that it was quite feasible to test in the TL (Neather *et al*, 1995). In order to meet the new requirements, textbooks now contain many more rubrics and questions in the TL and many provide examples of set phrases that students could encounter in examination papers. Examiners have developed more varied types of questions, which limit the amount of TL required by the students. Examples of such questions are: ticking boxes, multiple choice, table completion, matching pictures, true/false. As with all examination questions, students have to be trained how to cope with the demands of particular test types. Since the introduction of the tests in the TL, it is fair to say that teachers have continued to develop strategies for teaching their students how to succeed in GCSE through the TL.

Summary of arguments for and against TL use

The main arguments for a high level of TL use are that:

- learners are provided with a good model of the language;
- students have maximum opportunities to learn by doing;
- using the TL fits with a communicative approach;
- the TL should be used for important communications with students so that it is not seen as an unimportant medium.

The arguments against a high level of TL use are much more numerous but may not be more powerful:

- the rapport between teacher and learner may be inhibited;
- if teachers and learners share the same mother tongue, it may seem artificial to use the TL;
- using English may be more efficient (if there is something complicated to communicate);

- language awareness activities (comparing mother tongue and the TL) can usefully take place in English;
- using English may improve students' motivation, if their attention is sustained more keenly;
- using English may be a good idea if the teacher is tired.

Task 8.1

Make a list of the various aspects of a lesson and identify those that are best done in the TL and those that would be better done in English.

Task 8.2

Devise a list of phrases which students could be taught systematically in the TL. Include progression in your list.

9 Learner strategies

This chapter deals with a *key issue* that is currently of considerable interest to teachers of modern languages and researchers: the strategies that learners use.

Objectives

By the end of this chapter the trainee should:

- have an awareness of some research into learning strategies;
- have a knowledge of some strategies used by language learners;
- be aware of the importance of the learner in the learning/teaching process.

Learner strategies

There has always been an interest in why learners, all exposed to the same learning experiences in language classrooms, make differential progress. The Council of Europe offers no answer to the question: 'Why do learners not learn what teachers teach?'

> There is of course considerable variation among learners of different ages, types and backgrounds as to which [classroom conditions] they respond to most fruitfully, and among teachers, course-writers, etc. as to the balance of elements provided in courses according to the importance they attach to production vs. reception, accuracy vs. fluency, etc.
> (Council of Europe, 1998: 82)

The attempts to make the curriculum more relevant, materials more attractive and the language more accessible to learners have not resulted in better learning or more success in modern foreign languages.

For more than two decades researchers have been endeavouring to identify characteristics that were possessed by good language learners in an endeavour to train less successful learners to use such strategies (Cajkler and Thornton, 1999). Naiman *et al* (1978) were the first group to conduct empirical research to investigate why some learners were better at languages than others. They were interested in the relationship between the strategies and techniques developed by learners and their psychological characteristics. The study was conducted in two phases, the first involved interviews with successful language learners, followed by case studies. The second phase involved classroom observation of three classes and testing the learners for personality traits. The researchers classified the strategies according to certain types:

- an active task approach: learners sought out learning opportunities;
- realization of language as a system: they analysed the TL and formulated hypotheses;
- realization of language as a means of communication and interaction: they sought opportunities to use the TL and concentrated in the early stages on communication and fluency as opposed to accuracy;
- management of affective demands: for example, they were able to laugh at themselves;
- monitoring of performance in the form of asking native speakers for correction. (summarized by Graham, 1997: 39)

No correlation in the study was found between the learner strategies and the psychological characteristics of the learners. In a later study Rubin (1981) identified the good language learner as someone who:

- seeks clarification;
- makes guesses and inferences;
- practises silently and aloud;
- thinks through the language in her [sic] head;
- uses contextual cues;
- seeks to use the language as much as possible (cited in Cajkler and Thornton, 1999).

Skehan (1989) lists a number of individual psychological differences that may go some way to explaining why all learners do not learn what teachers teach. Other researchers have adopted a social constructivist approach and have suggested that it is not the differences between individuals in terms of motivation, learning styles and strategies, but the different sets of knowledge and experience that the learners bring to the learning that can account for differences in their learning (Williams and Burden, 1997).

Attempts to respond to individual learner styles have resulted in style-led teaching, whereby learners are taught in ways that best use their preferred learning style. In terms of language learning such an approach is advocated by Banner and Rayner (2000). Other theorists have looked at more general dispositions to learning and some recent work has identified four such predispositions. Some learners are precise processors, others sequential processors, others technical processors and some confluent processors (Johnston, 1996). Learners may prefer to learn in one mode as opposed to the others, or they may present a more balanced, eclectic approach.

In the literature a distinction is drawn between two types of strategy: learner strategies and communication strategies. Grenfell and Harris (1998) comment that these are distinguished as follows: *learner strategies* are those used by learners to help them learn a language; *communicative strategies* are used within discourse and are techniques used to establish conversation and to keep it going.

Teachers tend not to focus on how the learners learn but on how they themselves teach. Chamot (1987) and Cajkler and Thornton (1999) found that teachers confused learning strategies with teaching strategies. Grenfell and Harris (1998: 24) comment that the terms 'learner strategy' and 'learning strategy' are used synonymously in the literature. They list various definitions of learner strategies:

- special thoughts or behaviours that individuals use (citing O'Malley and Chamot, 1990: 1);
- strategies that contribute to the development of the language system that the learner constructs and which affect learning (citing Wenden and Oxford, 1987: 23);
- steps taken by students to enhance their own learning (citing Oxford, 1990: 1);
- specific actions, behaviours, steps or techniques that students employ to improve their progress in internalizing, storing, retrieving and using the L2 (citing Oxford, 1993: 175).

An extensive review of learning strategies is contained in the work of O'Malley and Chamot (1990) who set their theory within the area of cognitive learning theory. In this theory a distinction is made between declarative knowledge and procedural knowledge. The former represents the things we know about, whereas the latter is knowing how to do things (O'Malley and Chamot, 1990: 20, citing Anderson, 1985). According to O'Malley and Chamot, we can declare declarative knowledge; procedural knowledge, on the other hand, may be more slowly acquired and, over time, the learners may lose access to the rules that originally gave access to the procedure (p. 24). O'Malley and Chamot (1990) and earlier work by O'Malley *et al* (1985) also distinguish between 'metacognitive' and 'cognitive' strategies. 'Metacognitive' strategies involve activities such as planning, monitoring and evaluating learning, whereas 'cognitive' strategies involve strategies used for manipulating the language, such as memorization strategies or applying grammar. In addition they also identified social/affective strategies. They list the following under these headings:

Metacognitive

- advance organization;
- directed attention;
- selective attention;
- self-management;
- advance preparation;
- self-monitoring;
- delayed production;
- self-evaluation;
- self-reinforcement.

Cognitive strategies

- repetition;
- resourcing;
- directed physical response;

- translation;
- grouping;
- note-taking;
- deduction;
- recombination;
- imagery;
- auditory representation;
- keyword;
- contextualization;
- elaboration;
- transfer;
- inferencing.

Social-affective strategies

- co-operation;
- questioning for clarification;
- self-talk (O'Malley and Chamot, 1990: 44f).

Grenfell and Harris (1998) note several difficulties with this categorization in that some strategies might be either cognitive or metacognitive and they also argue that the strategies involved in actual language learning are subsidiary to those that refer to metalearning.

The current literature on learning strategies, however, is based heavily on the work of O'Malley and colleagues. In an empirical study Fleming and Walls (1998), for example, investigated which of these strategies six year nine students used in learning either French or German. Using the above taxonomy, they asked the learners which of the strategies they employed. They found that they used the whole range of metacognitive strategies, particularly those related to self (monitoring, evaluating, managing) and those involved in advance preparation. In terms of cognitive strategies, they found that these were grouped into three broad areas: active learning, language manipulation and abstract representation and reflection. That is to say that these learners were keen to learn independently that they worked with the language provided by the teacher and developed it and they employed individually adapted methods of learning, such as use of imagery, mnemonic devices and auditory representation. The conclusion of this study is that good language learners take an active role in their learning and that they use a broad range of strategies that enable them to plan, monitor, manage and reflect on the process of learning a language (Fleming and Walls, 1998: 20).

The National Curriculum Programme of Study makes mention of strategies but only as an 'add-on', in terms of language learning skills. No guidance is provided as to how these skills are to be integrated into the learning programme and no advice given as to how to train learners in their use. In an attempt to provide some practical guidance for teachers on how to apply strategies to the National Curriculum, Harris (1997) lists a variety of strategies that are used by learners, according to the four attainment targets. Some of the strategies would be regarded as 'learner' strategies whilst others would fall under the category of 'communication' strategies:

AT1

- recognizing the type of text;
- recognizing the topic;
- interpreting the gist;
- predicting;
- using tone of voice for clues;
- identifying cognates;
- identifying unfamiliar sounds;
- replaying tape;
- breaking down utterances into individual words;
- writing down sounds and relating to previously learned words.

AT2

- keeping it simple;
- being flexible in expressing yourself;
- approximating meanings;
- circumlocution;
- using all-purpose words;
- making up words;
- using mime, gestures;
- using strategic utterances to ask for help;
- using fillers.

AT3

- examining titles for clues;
- skimming;
- scanning;
- substituting English words;
- analysing unknown words;
- identifying chunk boundaries;
- identifying grammatical category words;
- breaking down phrases;
- identifying parts of words;
- using punctuation as clues.

AT4

- making the most of what you know;
- adding ideas as you start to write;
- recalling previously learned phrases;
- using set phrases;
- using markers;
- using clause links;
- trying out previously learned grammar in new contexts;
- drafting;
- redrafting. (Adapted from Harris, 1997: 7ff.)

LEARNER STRATEGIES

In a large study of 607 learners of French, German, Spanish and Italian, 461 learners of English in Spain and 546 learners of English in Italy, Cajkler and Thornton (1999: 47) found that the learners used the following in descending order of frequency:

- memorizing;
- listening to TL songs;
- reading textbook;
- reading exercise book;
- silent practice;
- testing self on words;
- repeating words;
- revising classwork;
- listening to TL radio at home;
- listening to cassettes;
- trying to use language wherever possible;
- practising with friend;
- watching satellite TV at home;
- reading TL books in class;
- reading TL books at home;
- watching TL videos at home;
- watching TL videos in school;
- watching satellite TV in school.

They conclude, as indeed other researchers have concluded, that if greater emphasis is to be paid to learner strategies, teachers need to have a greater awareness of these strategies and to be prepared to organize their teaching to concentrate more on learner than on teacher strategies.

In another study with more advanced learners the techniques of 'thinking aloud', retrospective interviews and learner diaries were used (Graham, 1997). The former were comments made by students as they performed a language task and the latter two were when they were asked to report on how they usually tackled a language learning activity. Graham identified the following strategies, which were used by learners when doing specific skills:

- listening;
- creating practice opportunities;
- naturalistic practice;
- self-management/philosophizing.

These strategies were used to enhance performance in listening tasks and involved, for example, taking part in exchanges or speaking to penfriends on the phone. The last skill involved thinking about the listening process. The following list of strategies were found to be linked to the various skill areas (the four attainment targets):

Listening

- selective and directed attention and problem identification;
- advance organization;
- comprehension monitoring;
- inferencing from context.

Reading

- double-check monitoring;
- comprehension monitoring;
- problem identification;
- substitution;
- interpretation;
- reading aloud.

Writing

- planning;
- drafting;
- monitoring production;
- substitution;
- translation;
- transfer;
- auditory or visual monitoring;
- production evaluation.

Speaking

- planning;
- selecting;
- using formulaic phrases;
- translation.

As in other studies the above research shows that effective learners have a bank of strategies that they use, sometimes interchangeably and according to the skill being practised.

The skill of the teacher is firstly identifying the strategies used by students and secondly finding ways of training the ineffective strategy-users to use more effective strategies. Graham (1997: 84) reviews the literature on training and notes that strategy training needs to be informed, integrated and to involve a high level of self-control and that the programmes should involve a high degree of metacognitive reflection. Several training programmes are reviewed in O'Malley and Chamot (1990) and some aspects may be useful to the teacher to encourage more effective learning in their learners. The main strands of the training programmes are summarised by Graham (1997: 84):

- investigation – an audit of learning strategies currently used by learners is taken and these are discussed by the class;
- presentation – the teacher describes and demonstrates the strategy;
- practice – students are given opportunities to practise using the strategy;
- evaluation – students are encouraged to review the strategy.

The question as to whether this should be done in the TL or in English is not resolved in the literature but, as with the teaching of grammar, it might be most effective if the discussion of the strategies were to be done in English whilst the practice using the strategy is done through the TL.

Teacher research

The first step in this process is to investigate what is going on in the heads of the learners in your classroom as they learn the language. You may want to conduct some empirical research of your own to find out what strategies your students use in the language class. You may find, as at least one of the studies quoted above (Fleming and Walls, 1998: 18), found that:

> We were impressed, if not a little surprised that the selected pupils were able to articulate so clearly their perceptions of language learning processes. They all presented as enthusiastic, conscientious and inquiring language learners who employed a range of the strategies that were of interest to us.

In identifying the strategies used by your students, you will be in a much better position to harness their learning potential and encourage independent learning on their part. The difficulty in researching learner strategies is that some of the traditional research techniques such as classroom observation cannot give the observer any insight into what learners are thinking or feeling when they are involved in a language lesson (Cohen, 1984, cited by Graham, 1997: 43). Ways of eliciting the strategies that have been employed in the studies cited here are semi-structured interviews and questionnaires. You could also ask your learners to complete learner diaries to note down their progress in learning the language (see, for example, Graham, 1997; McDevitt, 2000). Details of many appropriate research techniques can be found in the literature (Nunan, 1992). A study of your own classroom learners would be ideal for a project or for a dissertation at higher degree level (see Chapter 12).

Another way of highlighting learner strategies might be for the teacher in the first instance to learn a new language and to keep a diary of the strategies employed: those that were successful and those that were unsuccessful. Many initial teacher education courses incorporate a course of *ab initio* language courses. This could form the basis of a learning strategy awareness programme, which could be adapted by a language department.

Summary

The topic of learner strategies goes beyond the modern foreign language classroom and is one that is of interest to teachers of all disciplines. To answer the question 'how can we get learners to learn what teachers want them to learn?' (as opposed to what teachers teach) would be a major breakthrough in learning. The first stage is realizing that not all learners learn in the same way, that some learners are more successful than others and that there are

TEACHING MODERN FOREIGN LANGUAGES

certain strategies employed by effective learners that might be helpful to unsuccessful learners. The crucial factor is motivation according to Graham (1997): the teacher has to be motivated to change the way he/she teaches and to take an interest in the learners' perspective; secondly, the teacher has to create some enthusiasm in the learners to want to know how to learn; and thirdly, the learners must be self-motivated to focus on the strategies and to persevere with their learning. In doing all of this the teacher will be meeting many of the requirements of the National Curriculum Programme of Study that encourages variety of learning approach and the teaching of metalearning skills. Above all, the focus shifts from the teaching to the learning and, when this happens, the newly qualified or trainee teacher has made a transition that is crucial in terms of professional development.

Task 9.1

Conduct a small-scale piece of research with a group of learners at KS4. Select a text and ask them to write down in their own words how they tried to understand the text. Identify from their responses the types of strategies used.

Task 9.2

Try learning another language yourself, either by attending a class or by following a self-teach course book. Keep a diary of the strategies you used during the first few lessons.

Links to teaching standards

Under *subject knowledge and understanding* trainees are asked to demonstrate that they 'know, for their specialist subject, pupils' most common misconceptions and mistakes'. Concentrating on learner strategies should help trainees to achieve this standard.

10 Teaching foreign languages at primary level

This chapter introduces the trainee to *key issues* in the debate on teaching foreign languages at primary level. It tracks the history of initiatives to introduce languages at this level and considers what is involved in terms of implementation. The knock-on effect for teachers at secondary level is also considered.

Objectives

By the end of this chapter the trainee should have an understanding of:

- the history of early language learning initiatives;
- issues related to implementation;
- problems related to implementation;
- implications for teachers at secondary level.

Introduction

At the time of writing, teaching foreign languages at primary level is the aspect of foreign language teaching most prominent in the media and in government initiatives (along with concerns about recruitment). It is useful for trainees to be familiar with the context of this interest, both in historical terms and considering the context of European practice as a whole. Even if trainees are not involved with teaching at key stage two, there are implications for year seven teaching for most teachers at secondary level.

The context of early language learning

Although there are some sceptical voices about the desirability of primary level FL learning (Poole and Roberts, 1995), the majority of current research favours a 'younger is better' approach (Johnstone, 1994a). The following benefits have been identified:

- more time for language learning is made available;
- more positive attitudes to foreign language learning and to the target cultures;
- improvement to communicative skills;
- a link to literacy;
- better knowledge of Europe and the world.

The guidelines for modern foreign languages at key stage two comment on 'valuable educational, social and cultural experience' and draw attention to the additional cross-curricular benefits of primary MFL:

> The learning of a foreign language provides a medium for cross-curricular links and for the reinforcement of knowledge, skills and understanding developed in other subjects.
> (DfEE/QCA, 1999:32)

It is important to consider two aspects of MFL teaching at primary level in terms of context: its history, and European practice.

The history of primary MFL

There was considerable interest in the 1960s in introducing languages into primary schools in England (the 'French from Eight' programme supported by the Nuffield Foundation). Primary teachers received special in-service education and training for this. In addition Claire Burstall and her team investigated the language proficiency of students with and without a primary background. Her final report proved a death knell for these primary MFL experiments. She concluded that:

> it is hard to resist the conclusion that the weight of the evidence has combined with the balance of opinion to tip the scales against a possible expansion of the teaching of French in primary schools.
> (Burstall *et al*, 1974: 246)

Since the mid-1970s there has been some development of primary teaching but for the most part this has been in the form of one-off projects or language clubs. The major exceptions have been initiatives in Scotland and developments in the late 1990s.

Initiatives in Scotland

Government support for primary FL became particularly evident in Scotland in 1989 with a circular recommending the piloting of foreign languages in primary schools (Scottish Education Department, 1989). Six pilot projects were launched in 1989 and a further six in 1990, with a total of 12 secondary schools and 76 primaries covering four languages. In 1992 the Secretary of State for Scotland announced that foreign languages would be introduced into all primary schools in Scotland during the course of the following five years. In support of this programme some 2500 primary school teachers received 27 days in-service education and training from autumn 1993 onwards following a government commitment to train one teacher in every primary school (Low, 1999).

The Scottish initiative is interesting from many perspectives. It is interesting from a diversification point of view because four languages were introduced (French, German, Spanish and Italian). It is interesting from a teaching point of view because, initially, specialist teachers were brought in with a view to training primary teachers already in post.

Primary languages in Northern Ireland

There are several examples of good practice in primary languages across the five education and library boards in Northern Ireland, although there is no official support for them nor are there statutory programmes of study for key stages one or two. Many primary schools are involved with Comenius projects and a great deal of interest has been generated in languages at senior management level in the primary sector. Details of some of these initiatives are reported in the CILT *Primary Languages Bulletin* (1997).

In addition to these initiatives there is the presence of a large number of Irish medium primary schools (*bunscoileanna*) where some examples of good practice in language education are found.

Developments in the 1990s

In the late 1990s government support for FL teaching at primary level accelerated considerably:

- In 1999 a Good Practice Project with 18 primary schools was established supported by the government, DfEE and the CILT. This project was to run for two years with an evaluation report published in 2001.
- A national advisory centre was established in CILT (the National Advisory Centre for Early Language Learning – NACELL) with library facilities, a bi-annual bulletin and Web site (http://www.nacell.org.uk).
- Non-statutory guidelines for key stage two provided both suggestions for understanding and using the foreign language and links with other subjects, together with suggested attainment target level descriptions for levels one to four.
- The Qualification and Curriculum Authority (QCA) announced a major research project looking into the feasibility of extending the teaching of MFL in key stage two (CILT, 2000: 14).
- The QCA also developed sample schemes of work for key stage two teaching, with materials for French published in September 2000, available at the Web site www.standards.dfee.gov.uk.
- In August 2000 the Teacher Training Agency announced its support by allocating up to 100 extra places on primary postgraduate courses with French as a specialist subject.

In addition to government support there is evidence of interest and support elsewhere:

- The Nuffield Inquiry foregrounded early language learning as a priority (Nuffield Foundation 2000: 8, 40–43 and 89). For their 'flying start' they particularly recommend setting up bilingual primary schools or 'international primary schools' (pp 8, 42 and 89).

- A growing number of resources are being published for use in primary schools. At the time of writing CILT has eight books in its Young Pathfinder series.
- In some parts of the country there is considerable activity. Naysmith reports on research carried out in all of the 158 key stage two schools in West Sussex in 1998 where over 60 per cent of schools had some foreign language activity take place (1999: 16).

The beginning of the new millennium appears, then, to signal a resurgence of interest in early language learning in England.

The European context

Foreign language learning at primary school is common in other European countries. Two publications reviewing research on languages at primary school provide a wealth of detail of these initiatives (Blondin *et al*, 1998; Edelenbos and Johnstone, 1996). Johnstone (1994a) also provides a comprehensive overview of European practice.

France, for example, piloted primary MFL with pupils aged 10 (*cours moyen* 2), providing video in-service education and training resources for primary teachers. In Germany primary languages are well established although practice may vary between the different *Länder*. Austria has a strong tradition of foreign languages at primary level, recently confirming this as part of all primary schooling. In Austria too there are primary bilingual schools, the so-called Lollipop project.

Daniel Tierney provides an interesting overview of primary MFL projects in France and Scotland in his research undertaken in 1996 (Tierney, 1997).

Implementation of early language learning initiatives

It is useful to consider issues relating to implementation on two levels: a macro level with issues relating to teachers and curriculum, and a micro level with issues relating to classroom practice and possible out-of-school activities.

The global issues

There appear to be two major questions that are of interest to those who are involved in primary MFL projects and those evaluating and researching projects (other issues that have been identified as more problematic are discussed in the section below). The first is 'who should do the teaching?' The second is 'how can foreign languages best be integrated in the primary curriculum?'

The teachers

There are two main groups of teachers who can and do teach foreign languages in primary schools. There are specialist foreign language teachers who visit the primary school(s) and who have a degree in languages, or are native speakers, and a postgraduate teacher training qualification, with experience of secondary school teaching. Then there are primary teachers *in situ* who have undertaken in-service training in FL teaching. Naysmith also identified 'volunteers' as a group (parents for example). In his survey 62.2 per cent of the teachers were qualified foreign language teachers (1999: 17).

There seem to be strong arguments for both kinds of teacher. The language specialist is clearly likely to be more confident in speaking the target language. Research by Driscoll, looking at the two different types of teacher, noted that specialist teachers demonstrated more continuous, relaxed use of the target language, whilst the generalist primary teacher's use of the target language was more formulaic (1999b: 30). Other advantages are that the secondary school specialists have constant reinforcement and practice from a variety of sources (Frost, 1999: 181–82). Frost suggests, in his article on primary MFL and the community, that there may be real benefit in schools sharing scarce resources such as teachers with expert knowledge and expensive curriculum materials. Low notes that specialist teachers are also likely to have a guaranteed timetable slot (1999: 57).

Although there are clear advantages in terms of subject knowledge with a specialist teacher there may be disadvantages in terms of human relationships. A teacher coming in for short periods of time will have little time to build up knowledge of individual pupils. Driscoll also noticed in her classroom observations that specialist teachers may be embarrassed or constrained in what they can do in a classroom, as they are operating on someone else's territory (1999b).

Added to this is the question of supply. There is already a shortage of foreign language teachers at secondary level. If these teachers were also to take on extra duties in primary schools then clearly the situation would be exacerbated. It is the current lack of specialist teachers that has led to initiatives in Scotland and France seeking teachers within primary schools, who would then receive extra in-service training.

There are currently few courses for primary MFL training. Sharpe (1999: 167), however, comments, interestingly, that the current shortage of applicants for MFL secondary teacher training places may not be worsened if more places were made available for MFL specialists on primary courses. In other words it may be different people who apply to come on the courses.

In Naysmith's (1999) survey of primary schools the 'specialist primary foreign language teacher' was seen as the ideal teacher by 65 per cent of the respondents. This 'ideal' is rather sidestepped in the comments in the Nuffield Inquiry, where it is suggested both that existing primary teachers be retrained and also that people entering ITT would have 'an accredited study of a language beyond 16' (Nuffield Foundation 2000: 43). However, with the Teacher Training Agency special initiative it does seem that there is now more government support for the specially trained primary MFL teacher.

Although the generalist teacher in the primary school is currently not likely to have specialist MFL training, there are nevertheless several advantages that he or she can offer. The generalist teacher will have a much better holistic knowledge of his or her class and will be able to differentiate work accordingly. It will also be much easier to incorporate MFL into the day-to-day curriculum because this can be done whenever a suitable opportunity arises. Moreover, it is the generalist teacher who oversees daily classroom business, which can be an ideal vehicle for MFL (dealt with in more detail in the section below).

Rumley (1999: 115) points to the fact that the generalist class teacher 'is a very significant person' in the lives of the children in his or her class, and the enthusiasm of such teachers can be truly influential. However, the generalist teacher teaching MFL may feel isolated. The teachers interviewed by Driscoll spoke of different experiences with teaching French: in all other subjects they were able to discuss their classroom practice with other teachers and share ideas. Frost points to the usefulness of networking between schools, to pool ideas and as a source of professional learning (1999: 193). In the Good Practice Project just such a network has been established (an e-mail forum), and NACELL has also a wider e-mail network: the Early Language Learning Forum (www.nacell.org.uk/networking/ell_forum) for more general use.

The curriculum

It will be of some concern to teachers of MFL in primary schools as to how to integrate the foreign language into the curriculum. Two important issues are: the number of languages, and the 'separateness' of the foreign language component.

There seem to be two main models of incorporating foreign language into the curriculum: *sensitization,* where several languages are covered but in less depth; and *language acquisition,* where only the language is studied and the progression is built in (Driscoll 1999a). 'Language awareness' programmes may just raise questions relating to language in general.

The number of languages is important in terms of continuity. If several languages are touched on in a sensitization programme it does not matter which languages are then available in secondary school. If only one language is used as a reference point and pupils progress in that language then, clearly, being able to continue with that language at secondary level is very important (Morgan, 1999).

The current key stage two curriculum does not allow for a great deal of flexibility and teachers must include a 'literacy' and 'numeracy' hour each day. It may then be difficult to incorporate MFL as an 'extra' subject.

Johnstone (1994a: 5–10) provides five alternative approaches in his useful review of primary teaching:

- awareness;
- encounter;
- subject teaching;
- embedding;
- immersion.

Awareness and encounter correspond roughly to 'sensitization'; 'embedding' and 'immersion' to using the foreign language as a medium for communication with 'embedding' as a partial form of immersion. 'Embedding' is the kind of teaching that was included in the Scottish pilot studies and is described in Muir (1999). Teachers will use the foreign language for any aspect of the curriculum that appears suitable. Muir gives examples from mathematics, expressive arts, religious and moral education and environmental studies. By using the foreign language across these subjects pupils are encouraged to:

- make cross-curricular links;
- relate the foreign language to what they are studying already;
- use language authentically.

The generalist primary teacher will be able to exploit these cross-curricular links more easily than the visiting specialist teacher because the pupils will usually have only the one teacher for most subjects.

Johnstone (1994a: 9) points to some problem areas with embedding. Firstly, there may be fragmentation because the language learnt is likely to be unconnected; secondly, using 'embedding' as a foreign language approach does not help with continuity into the secondary school, where foreign language is taught as a *subject*. It may also be difficult to assess foreign language competence in an embedded model.

Another way of 'embedding' language is to use the foreign language for classroom business: what Rumley calls 'incidental language use' (1999: 116–17). Teachers can use the target language for greetings, attendance register and general classroom routines. Driscoll describes these general classroom activities in her research on primary teachers in Kent (1999b). The advantages of this incidental language are that:

- pupils will have plenty of repetition and practice;
- the target language is being used for authentic purposes;
- the foreign language component is not taking up extra time.

Classroom practice

As well as global issues relating to teachers and integration into the curriculum there are also issues on a micro level which relate to classroom practice. The following can be particularly useful to consider:

- types of suitable activity;
- types of suitable materials;
- support for learning;
- links with other subjects.

Suitable activities

Any book on primary language teaching is likely to emphasize games and multi-sensory activity (Argondizzo, 1992; Halliwell, 1992; Rumley, 1999; Rumley and Sharpe, 1993). Rumley and Sharpe (1993: 35) provide some helpful reminders of the advantages of games:

> They foster interest and motivation, they provide opportunities for real communication in a meaningful setting, and they facilitate plenty of repetition without it seeming tedious ... Game formats ... are already known, understood and enthusiastically enjoyed by students ... [they can inspire] confidence in both teacher and pupil.

Rumley and Sharpe provide 25 useful examples of games in their article.

Songs can be equally effective. Phin (1992: 4) mentions added benefits of videoing these or adding art and craft work in his description of teaching German at primary level.

Storytelling can also be a useful appropriate activity for primary level teaching, although care will need to be exercised in terms of the level of language. Janie Mireylees (2000) notes some of the advantages of storytelling in her article (on using stories in Primary French and finding appropriate related tasks):

- the environment is usually positive with teacher and pupil sharing the experience;
- stories follow a familiar pattern so that pupils feel secure;
- you can use body language and props to help with meaning;
- listening can be interactive with pupils repeating part of the story.

Suitable materials

As well as the eight Young Pathfinders available at the time of writing (Tierney and Dobson, 1995; Satchwell, 1997; Satchwell and de Silva, 1995; Martin, 1995; Martin and Cheater, 1998; Skarbeck, 1998; Biriotti, 1999; Cheater and Farren, in press) there is also a growing number of other resources. Details of these can be found in Rixon (1999), and recent publications are regularly reviewed in CILT's publication *Early Language Learning Bulletin*. It is helpful to remember that resources produced for teaching English as a foreign language also sometimes have versions in other European languages. The video animated cartoon series 'Muzzy' for example has been produced in French, German, Italian and Spanish.

Support for learning

The suggestions made in Chapter 4 for using visuals will all be very helpful when teaching in a primary context. In addition Hurrell (1999) has many useful suggestions to make in her analysis of integrating the four skills into early language lessons. In general she suggests:

- exaggerating the voice (pitch and volume);
- using simpler grammar;
- focusing on individual words (with flashcards for example);
- using facial expressions;
- using mime and gesture.

In relation to specific skills, helpful suggestions include:

- allowing the written form to be seen while listening;
- building up speaking skills into fuller utterances;
- using 'phonic clouds' with groups of words with similar sounds grouped as a series of clouds;
- tracing words on the body;
- building up written sentences.

All of these strategies will provide invaluable scaffolding for the learner.

Links with other subjects

There should be no problem with links with other subjects if it is the generalist teacher who is in charge of primary MFL. He or she will be teaching most of the subjects anyway and will be in an excellent position to make cross-curricular links.

Problems of implementation

Although strong government support for primary FL teaching emerged in the late 1990s, there are several areas of accompanying difficulty. As well as the need for suitable resources, mentioned earlier, there seem to be three key areas that are problematic:

- teachers' lack of time;
- the need for suitable training;
- a lack of continuity and progression.

The evaluation of the Good Practice Project mentioned earlier, where 18 nationwide initiatives are being investigated, has been helpful in identifying these areas (Cassidy, 2000c).

Teachers' lack of time

The demands of the National Curriculum already mean that teachers have full timetable commitments. Including an extra subject will thus need imaginative planning. If teachers are able to follow the example of teachers in the Scottish initiatives, who have embedded the foreign language in their existing curriculum, then this should help to overcome some of the problem.

Suitable training

Teaching foreign languages at primary level makes particular demands on the teacher because of the expectation of teaching in the target language (see Chapter 8). Teachers may lack the confidence to be able to sustain the foreign language in the classroom and may also have worries about their subject knowledge, given that there is some expectation of accompanying cultural knowledge (Driscoll, 1999a) and that young learners will echo the teacher's pronunciation almost exactly (Danks, 1997). Frost (1999: 184), in his overview of the radical changes that are likely to be necessary if primary foreign language is to be adopted nationally, highlights this problem:

> Primary MFL requires a massive commitment in terms of cultural values, political beliefs and personal knowledge on the part of those teachers who may have only GCSE ... French.

His recommendations include collaboration between teachers and action research where teachers reflect on their own practice. The forums and networks mentioned earlier, which have been set up by NACELL, seem to provide for this kind of contact. The Nuffield Inquiry team also suggests that expert teachers could share experience and expertise online with others (Nuffield Foundation, 2000: 43).

A further area of training that could be of interest is where foreign language assistants could be seconded or trained to help in primary schools. Again the Nuffield Inquiry has a helpful suggestion, namely that 'Primary schools should be offered incentives to recruit foreign language assistants as classroom helpers' (Nuffield Foundation, 2000: 43).

As well as the welcome government support for training specialist primary MFL teachers there will clearly be other areas where extra training will be needed.

Continuity and progression

Problems of continuity and progression between primary and secondary schools exist for all curriculum areas: the cultures of the two schools are likely to be different in terms of teaching style and focus, and there is often insufficient liaison between the parties concerned (Morgan, 1999). For modern foreign languages the problems are exacerbated with the existence of the mixed-feeder-school system where some of the primary schools feeding into a local secondary school may have done foreign languages, whilst others have not. Independent schools may be in a position to solve this problem if they have their own junior schools (Morgan, 1998); language colleges too may liaise directly with clusters of feeder schools and help to support them (CILT, 1998: 8). This, too, was the principle underpinning the Scottish pilot project where a secondary school would support its feeder primary schools by seconding one of its teachers to teach in its feeder school cluster (Tierney, 1997).

However, in a great many cases there are real problems. In Naysmith's (1999: 17) survey there was a high level of concern over continuity: 42 per cent of the teachers reported that there was no regular exchange of information between primary and secondary schools and this also was an area of concern voiced in the Nuffield Inquiry, which pointed to the 'frustration and disillusionment for both teachers and learners' because of the elusive continuity of learning (Nuffield Foundation, 2000: 1).

Low (1999: 60) points out that even where it is the *same teacher* teaching in both primary and secondary schools there may be discontinuities in practice: 'the same teachers operating in primary – secondary were observed to teach in quite different ways and did not necessarily build on what their pupils had done in primary'.

There may then be problems with varying levels of proficiency in a foreign language from students from different feeder schools; there may be no continuity between the foreign language learnt at primary and the one learnt at secondary (Low, 1999); there may be problems in terms of teaching style (Morgan, 1999; Naysmith, 1999).

It is clear that long-term strategic planning and frequent liaison are key factors in overcoming these difficulties.

Receiving primary pupils into the secondary school

If you are teaching in a secondary school then you will experience the difficulties associated with continuity at the other end of the transfer process. We have seen that it may be problematic for the primary school teacher in terms of preparing pupils for the transition to secondary school, but it may also be difficult for a secondary school teacher if due consideration is not given to previous primary school experiences, whether or not these include foreign language learning. Low (1999: 61) comments that:

> Evidence from evaluations of the earlier experiments in the UK and the national pilot in Scotland have shown that failure to take account of pupils' prior language learning can have a demoting effect on pupils with implication for their subsequent attainments in the foreign language.

Areas to consider could include the following:

- teaching style;
- work on literacy and language awareness;
- levels of proficiency in the foreign language;
- project work done in a European context.

Teaching styles

Teaching styles in a primary context are likely to focus on child-centred, multisensory fun activities and in a secondary context on more subject-centred activities with a greater emphasis on reading and writing (Willcocks, 1983). Children in a secondary school will need to understand abstract ideas that lie beyond classroom experience (Bruner, 1974) and which are encapsulated in language used (in Bruner's terms) 'symbolically'. Earlier learning is likely to have been supported by actions and pictures (Bruner's 'enactive' and 'iconic' levels of learning, 1974). The symbolic language of abstract concepts will be new.

It will be helpful, then, for the foreign language teacher in the secondary school to consider the levels of language being used (both mother tongue and target language) and the suitability of activities, pitching these at different levels from the beginning of year seven to the end.

Literacy and language awareness

All students will have had literacy training in the primary school and it will be vital for teachers to be familiar with what is covered in the literacy programme (This aspect of FL teaching has already been covered in greater detail in Chapter 2.) If students have already studied a foreign language in their primary school then this may have been a sensitization programme. If the foreign language studied was different to the one being offered in the secondary school, then this experience may be exploited for language awareness purposes.

Whatever the background of the students may be, it will be important for the secondary teacher to investigate it. This could be by:

- liaising with the different primary schools;
- talking to students;
- asking students themselves to gather the information.

Depending on the language background and experience of the class it will then be up to the teacher to exploit this as fruitfully as possible. This may be by:

- discussing key language problems;
- explaining key language terms;
- comparing languages.

It is likely though that discussions and reflections will need to be in English if students are to gain maximum benefit. Levels of the target language are not likely to be sufficiently advanced to allow for in-depth discussion and investigation.

Target-language proficiency

A major problem of a year seven class with mixed primary foreign language experiences is likely to be boredom, if work is being done that is already familiar to some students. However, this is not a different problem to that of differentiation in general which will occur in a mixed ability class. It may be though that assumptions in the school will be that a year seven class will be treated as a whole.

Strategies to overcome varying levels of language proficiency could be:

- dividing the class into groups of differing ability;
- using students with existing knowledge to act as mentors or teachers for other novice students;
- providing differentiated materials;
- providing extra work of a different level.

There will be a delicate balance to be struck between maintaining the interest of students who already have a certain level of proficiency and not favouring them too much, thereby alienating the other students.

European project work

It may well be that students in a year seven class have taken part in European projects even if they have not learnt any foreign languages at primary school. Evans (1999), in his overview of European school links at primary level, gives some examples of projects and describes the different SOCRATES arrangements.

Primary pupils are excluded from LINGUA Action A projects, which support joint educational collaborations, but they may be involved with LINGUA Action D projects where teaching materials are produced. *Primary Goes Europe* for example has brought together teachers from many different countries and produced materials in different European languages (Stadtschulrat 1997, 1998 and 1999). Comenius projects, which link schools, also have no lower age limit but here the emphasis is on the linking rather than on language.

European links may have taken place in a primary school, even without funding from SOCRATES. For example nine primary schools in South Gloucestershire that form part of the Good Practice Project have linked with primary schools in France and exchanged audio tapes and posters (Central Bureau, 2000: 9). An independent school in Kent also plays host to a small number of French primary pupils from Calais who visit the school each Wednesday (O'Shea, 1999).

There are then European projects happening in primary schools and it will be helpful to establish whether any students have taken part in them and to encourage them to share cultural or linguistic insights which they have acquired.

Conclusion

The teaching of foreign languages at primary level is an area of growing importance and interest in the new millennium and one where there are likely to be many new changes. Secondary teachers will be involved in some way in these changes, whether they are seconded to teach in a primary school or whether they have to deal with the new situations from which students will now come. Primary MFL is a focus for positive views on foreign language learning and may indeed offer one avenue for a more general change and improvement in attitudes towards foreign languages and cultures.

Task 10.1

Take an early section of a year seven foreign language textbook and imagine how you might adapt it to suit a class of students with mixed primary language backgrounds.

Task 10.2

Plan an activity that would investigate the primary foreign language and European experiences of year seven pupils.

Links to teaching standards

Under *subject knowledge and understanding*, trainees are asked to demonstrate that they understand for their specialist subject, progression from key stage two programmes of study. Spending some time considering the teaching of MFL at primary level should contribute to achieving this standard.

11 Future subject developments in modern foreign languages

The final two chapters deal with development: both subject development and personal/professional development.

The aim of this chapter is to introduce the trainee to areas of development related to MFL. Major issues will be discussed and indications of small-scale initiatives will be given where these exist. Above all note will be taken of the European context: both as a comparison where initiatives may be more fully developed and also as a contrast in terms of differing attitudes to foreign language learning, given that teachers in the UK operate in a climate where the majority mother tongue is a world language of high status.

Objectives

By the end of this chapter the trainee will have an understanding of:

- the Nuffield Inquiry;
- the Council of Europe framework for foreign language teaching;
- the nature of content and language integrated learning.

The Nuffield Inquiry

Key information

The Nuffield Inquiry was a major independent investigation (funded by the Nuffield Foundation) undertaken during the period 1998–2000, taking stock of the current situation with regard to foreign languages in terms of needs, provision and planning and making

FUTURE SUBJECT DEVELOPMENTS IN MFL

recommendations based on research and consultation. These often radical recommendations could have a major influence on the teaching and learning of foreign languages.

The Inquiry committee consisted of two chairmen, a secretary (male) and ten members (six male and four female) representing the fields of education and the world of business (Asian as well as European languages were represented). Evidence was gathered from a wide range of sources: surveys by NIACE and FEDA; an online e-mail chat line, interviews with employers in the public and private sectors and written contributions from 177 individuals and 191 institutions (listed in the final report, 2000).

The fifteen main recommendations of the Nuffield report are:

1. Develop a national strategy for languages as a key skill.
2. Appoint a languages supremo.
3. Raise the profile of languages in the UK.
4. Establish business–education partnerships.
5. Provide schoolchildren with a sound basis for language learning for life.
6. Invest in an early start.
7. Raise the quality of the provision for languages in secondary schools.
8. Ensure wider participation beyond school.
9. Promote languages for the majority of 16–19 year olds.
10. Develop a strategic approach to languages in higher education.
11. Develop the huge potential of lifelong language learning.
12. Intensify the drive to recruit more language teachers.
13. Exploit new technologies to the full.
14. Ensure policy is reliably and consistently informed.
15. Establish a national standards framework for languages.

Task 11.1

Look at the detail of recommendation 5 or 13, which relate directly to school-based practice, and consider how you might implement change in your classroom.

Link to teaching standards

Under *subject knowledge and understanding* trainee teachers are asked to demonstrate that they 'are aware of and know how to access recent … classroom-relevant research evidence on teaching secondary pupils in their specialist subject(s) and know how to use this to inform and improve their teaching'. Knowledge of the remit of the Nuffield Inquiry and the content of its final report should contribute to achieving this standard.

The Council of Europe framework

The Council of Europe Draft 2 Framework, *Modern Languages: Learning, Teaching, Assessment, a Common European Framework of Reference* (1998) is an important European document, which is likely to affect future foreign language teaching in Europe. The Nuffield Inquiry (2000: 29) talks of the Council of Europe's 'distinguished record in promoting and supporting language learning'. The research and documents produced by the Council of Europe in earlier research in the 1970s resulted in the 'threshold level' benchmark, which relied on an identification of language needs expressed in the form of language function and notions (Van Ek and Alexander, 1975). This 1970s research was extremely influential in informing the communicative syllabuses in place today. It is likely, then, that the current Council of Europe research will also be influential in future foreign language developments.

The 1970s Council of Europe (1975: ix) research focused on the language needs of adult learners in a context of social mobility in Europe, looking particularly at the usefulness of learning 'one of the major languages of international intercourse' (English) and at what kinds of language items and structures could be relevant. In the new Council of Europe research (undertaken during the 1990s) social and professional mobility are again seen as the important relevant context, but the focus has moved away from *language content* (and one language) to a much broader picture of *language-related issues*. Four main issues can be identified:

- diversity of languages;
- diversity of levels of language;
- coherence between identified levels;
- transparency of description.

Diversity of languages

An extremely important aspect of the document is the emphasis on plurilingualism and pluriculturalism (Council of Europe, 1998: 95–102). A plurilingual, pluricultural competence is seen as particularly useful for three main reasons:

- (a social reason) it gives a 'richer repertoire' of language items for communicating with other Europeans;
- (a linguistic reason) learning one language already provides a basis for competence in learning languages;
- (a cultural reason) learning several languages provides a good experience of diversity and prevents a narrow, national (ethnocentric) point of view.

Particularly interesting is the suggestion that: 'it is not uncommon for the learning of *one* language and contact with *one* foreign culture to reinforce stereotypes and preconceived ideas rather than reduce them' (Council of Europe, 1998: 97).

There is also the further suggestion that plurilingualism is the norm in *any* complex society: 'if … the concept of plurilingualism and pluriculturalism is extended to take into account the situation of all social agents who in their native language and culture are exposed to different dialects and to … cultural variation … it is clear that … imbalances … are the norm' (Council of Europe, 1998: 96). There is the implicit suggestion here then that pluricultural competence can work within countries as well as across countries.

Diversity of levels of language

One of the consequences of learning several languages is likely to be varying levels of proficiency in the different languages. The framework suggests that the uneven and changing nature of plurilingual/pluricultural competence should be accepted in a positive way as the kind of flexibility well suited to the rapidly changing needs of members of the European (and international) community. This is seen in terms of learners' identity, helping them:

- to construct their language and cultural identity through integrating into it a diversified experience of otherness;
- to develop their ability to learn through this same diversified experience of relating to several languages and cultures.

(Council of Europe, 1998: 97)

Partial competence in any one language may mean overall limited competence or it may mean proficiency in a limited language activity (just reading, for example). In any event partial competence is seen in a positive light 'as forming part of a plurilingual competence which it enriches' (Council of Europe 1998: 97).

Another way in which diversity of language levels is celebrated is in the overall framework of different achievable levels of language proficiency. The suggestion is that an instrument be devised (the *European Language Portfolio*, see below) which will allow 'all forms of language learning and teaching' to be described (Coste *et al*, 1998: 138). This will mean not only describing lower levels of achievement in positive terms but also seeing the language learning process as one of lifelong learning taking place beyond as well as within the classroom (Council of Europe, 1998: 13–14).

Coherence of the framework

The Nuffield Languages Inquiry suggests that the UK should adopt a national standards framework based on the Council of European framework (Nuffield Foundation, 2000: 9). One of the criticisms levelled at the current UK system is the lack of coherence or 'joined-up thinking' (Nuffield Foundation, 2000: 5). Coherence is a feature particularly emphasized in the Council of Europe document. This is sought not only by integrating all levels of language learning as mentioned earlier, but also in three further ways:

- by identifying sub-categories of language-related competence;
- by identifying sub-categories of general competence;
- by identifying sub-categories of communicative language competence.

The comprehensiveness of this approach not only allows all the different kinds of language learning to be encompassed, but also provides a sufficiently flexible framework for this to be adopted Europe-wide. A future sophistication is to provide a 'branching approach' that allows the six common reference levels (discussed in more detail below) to be flexibly further subdivided to accommodate local differences in different countries (Coste *et al*, 1999: 144).

Overall categories

The overall categories of competence are seen in the context of learners engaged in life tasks (an 'action-oriented approach'). A variety of factors are at work in determining success in achieving different tasks (Council of Europe, 1998: 12–13):

- general competences;
- communicative language competence;
- the language activity – what is required by any particular task or situation (the domain).

Here then the overall complex context of any activity is understood, recognizing that all dimensions may also interrelate with each other. Thus in dealing with telephoning abroad to book a hotel room the following group of competencies may be called into play:

- general competence in dealing with the unfamiliar;
- communicative language competence, knowing a range of vocabulary, structures and appropriate usage;
- language activity skills in listening to and producing a foreign language.

The domain of hotel room-booking will require particular kinds of language and the task of making a phone call particular strategies (being particularly explicit because no visual signals are available, for example).

General competencies

Four kinds of knowledge are identified in this category:

- *savoir-être:* being confident or streetwise;
- *savoir:* having a bank of knowledge built up from experience or learning;
- *savoir-faire:* having a range of skills that have been mastered;
- *savoir-apprendre:* knowing how to use the first three skills appropriately when faced with a new situation.

These general competencies can be seen to link into the key skills and other aspects of the curriculum identified in the 1999 National Curriculum document (DfEE/QCA, 1999: 8–9) but perhaps provide a more robust framework in terms of understanding foreign language mastery.

Communicative language competence

Three different levels of competence are identified:

- linguistic;
- socio-linguistic (knowing appropriate forms);
- pragmatic (using appropriate forms in particular contexts).

Extended examples are given of how these might translate into actual language performance (Council of Europe, 1998: 14–15, 47–58). These competencies draw directly on established research (Coste *et al*, 1999: 139) and perhaps provide a more comprehensive picture than the rather disparate presentation of linguistic and cultural knowledge in the 1999 National Curriculum documentation.

Transparency of description

Transparent description is seen as a central aspect of the framework in order for this to be appreciable across a range of contexts. This range is not only conceived as spanning different European education systems but also systems within countries. Council of Europe team members provide a useful explanation in their synopsis:

> Learners, teachers, course designers, examiners, inspectors and administrators each see foreign language learning from different perspectives. A common framework ... will make it easier to establish common ground and situate their efforts relative to each other. (Coste *et al*, 1999: 139)

The six common reference levels are clearly set out using vocabulary that is easy to understand, ranging from the Basic User (A1–A2) to the higher levels of the Proficient User (C1–C2) (see Table 11.1).

There are two advantages of using the European framework in a UK context. Firstly, it offers useful holistic criteria which are currently missing from documents, such as the 1999 National Curriculum booklet. Secondly, one can see that these holistic judgements would also accommodate the subcategories of itemized attainment targets for the four language skills, incorporated into the National Curriculum.

The European Language Portfolio

The *European Language Portfolio* is the instrument suggested for measuring language competence. This is an imaginative instrument, which aims to be both flexible and comprehensive. The portfolio is seen as a way of recording both formal and informal achievements and experiences in the foreign language. In other words an evaluative element of self-awareness is built into the document.

In the description of changes that have taken place, in terms of developing the portfolio, Christ (1998) emphasizes that many questions have not yet been settled. The preferred options she mentions are for:

- a set of portfolios to meet different age-related needs;
- a flexible loose-leaf format;
- the use of various languages of description including the learner's mother tongue.

The portfolio will comprise three sections:

- a language 'passport' detailing all language achievements (including intercultural experiences);
- a language 'profile', giving details of different language and intercultural experiences and including self-evaluation;
- a 'dossier' of personal work, including also contextual documents (learning diary, school curricula and so forth).

Proficient User	C2	Can understand with ease virtually everything heard or read. Can summarize information from different spoken and written sources, reconstructing arguments and accounts in a coherent presentation. Can express him/herself spontaneously, very fluently and precisely, differentiating finer shades of meaning even in more complex situations.
	C1	Can understand a wide range of demanding, longer texts, and recognize implicit meaning. Can express him/herself fluently and spontaneously without much obvious searching for expressions. Can use language flexibly and effectively for social, academic and professional purposes. Can produce clear, well-structured, detailed text on complex subjects, showing controlled use of organizational patterns, connectors and cohesive devices.
Independent User	B2	Can understand the main ideas of complex text on both concrete and abstract topics, including technical discussions in his/her field of specialization. Can interact with a degree of fluency and spontaneity that makes regular interaction with native speakers quite possible without strain for either party. Can produce clear, detailed text on a wide range of subjects and explain a viewpoint on a topical issue giving the advantages and disadvantages of various options.
	B1	Can understand the main points of clear standard input on familiar matters regularly encountered in work, school, leisure etc. Can deal with most situations likely to arise whilst travelling in an area where the language is spoken. Can produce simple connected text on topics that are familiar or of personal interest. Can describe experiences and events, dreams, hopes and ambitions and briefly give reasons and explanations for opinions and plans.
Basic User	A2	Can understand sentences and frequently used expressions related to areas of most immediate relevance (for example very basic personal and family information, shopping, local geography, employment). Can communicate in simple and routine tasks requiring a simple and direct exchange of information on familiar and routine matters. Can describe in simple terms aspects of his/her background, immediate environment and matters in areas of immediate need.
	A1	Can understand and use familiar everyday expressions and very basic phrases aimed at the satisfaction of needs of a concrete type. Can introduce him/herself and others and can ask and answer questions about personal details such as where he/she lives, people he/she knows and things he/she has. Can interact in a simple way provided the other person talks slowly and clearly and is prepared to help.

Table 11.1 Common reference levels

Conclusion

The *Common European Framework* is still a draft document and consultation will not finish until the end of 2000 with further dissemination envisaged in 2001, the European Year of Languages (Christ, 1998: 216).

Given the powerful influence of previous Council of Europe research it is likely that this framework conceived by a European team will have repercussions in the foreign language classrooms and assessment systems in the different member states of Europe.

Task 11.2

Look at a set of levels for one of the attainment targets and track how this could be matched to the six levels of the *Common European Framework*.

Links to teaching standards

Under *subject knowledge and understanding* trainees are asked to demonstrate that they are 'aware of and know how to access recent ... classroom-relevant research evidence on teaching secondary pupils in their specialist subject(s) and know how to use this to inform and improve their teaching'.

Under *monitoring assessment, recording, responding and accountability* they are asked to demonstrate that they 'use different kinds of assessment appropriately for different purposes, including National Curriculum and other standardized tests and baseline assessments, where relevant'.

An understanding of possible developments in line with the *Common European Framework* may help to contribute towards achieving these standards.

Framework documents are available on the Internet: www.culture.coe.fr/lang.

Content language and language integrated learning

'Content and language integrated learning' (or CLIL) is the latest way of describing a teaching/learning situation where the foreign language is used as a medium for teaching another subject. Examples of this technique are and have been in existence in this country but it is growing, particularly in popularity in other European counties. *Sections bilingues*, 'bilingual sections' or 'bilingual teaching' are other titles used, although one needs to be careful here not to include situations where immigrant children are learning in a school environment using a language that is not their mother tongue. CLIL initiatives on the whole are seen as extensions to foreign language teaching and involve using a foreign language as a medium of instruction for subject lessons in addition to the foreign language being a subject in its own right.

Why use CLIL?

The popularity of this kind of initiative relies on the belief (backed up by research into Canadian immersion and other programmes) that:

- students will have improved language skills;
- subject learning will not be impaired;
- students will have improved cognitive flexibility;
- students will access the genre language of subjects more easily;
- the problem of 'content vacuum' and 'girlie topics' will be avoided.

Where are the CLIL initiatives?

Although there were several initiatives in the UK in the 1980s when there was more interest in and possibility of doing different kinds of teaching, it is not common now to find CLIL programmes in place. This contrasts sharply with other European countries where bilingual sections are becoming increasingly popular. In France and Germany the Adenauer–De Gaulle 1963 friendship treaty resulted in some 'bilingual strands' (*bilinguale Züge*) and *sections européennes* being set up in 1970. In Austria, in particular, bilingual sections and schools are flourishing (at the time of writing there are eight secondary bilingual schools, and six primary bilingual schools, plus many other bilingual initiatives). There are also other initiatives in Central Europe and Scandinavia (Thürmann, 1995; Masih, 1999).

There are bilingual schools in Britain in the form of Welsh-medium schools (Giles-Jones, 1994) and more isolated instances: business studies in Spanish at Millais School; geography in Spanish at William Ellis School; science in French at Ashfield School; geography in French at Craigroyston High School; history and geography in French at Hockerill Anglo-European School; 40 per cent of the year seven timetable is in French at Hasland Hall and 40 per cent of years 4/5/6, 7/8 at Bolitho School. A video issued by the Central Bureau (*Teaching with Foreign Languages*) provides further information on some of these initiatives. Suggestions have been made by government bodies as to the desirability of CLIL teaching: the DFE in 1995 (in its recommendations for language colleges) but these recommendations have not resulted in any major initiative. Even the independent Nuffield Inquiry hides its suggestions for bilingual section teaching at primary level under the vague term of 'international primary school', although it does recommend rewarding secondary schools for bilingual sections (Nuffield Foundation, 2000: 49 and 90, Recommendation 7.8)

The UK context is also not helped by the current assessment situation. The National Curriculum is prescriptive. Examination boards will not allow subjects to be taken in a foreign language. Even the specially negotiated 'Spanish and business studies' GCSE examination in Spanish is now due to be axed. In other countries the question of assessment is partly resolved by schools having their own internal assessment procedures and by, for example in Germany, some schools combining the German *Abitur* with the French *baccalauréat*. The International Baccalaureat does offer some possibilities at post-16, since there is now some discussion of being able to take subjects in different languages.

Possible small-scale implementation

It is unlikely that you will be able to bring about any large-scale implementation of a CLIL programme; Ullman (1999: 97–101), for example, describes the conditions he needed for setting up his project:

> There are many major issues which need careful consideration, and I am outlining here those that I consider to be of paramount importance and without which a successful bilingual section could not have been set up.
> A supportive senior management team ...
> Convincing parents and pupils ...
> Curriculum implications ...
> Resourcing ... staffing ... Textbooks ...

However it should be possible to try out a small-scale CLIL initiative. Johnstone (1994: 8) in his overview of primary school FL teaching suggests an 'embedding' approach where:

> Rather than teach the foreign language as a separate course ... attempts are made to relate it to other aspects of pupils' primary school curriculum ... A class that is doing a project ... might exploit an aspect of the project through activity in the foreign language ... The embedded approach ... represents a small but significant step towards immersion.

Indeed in the favourable context of Austria, initial CLIL attempts started out in the *Fremdsprachenhauptschulen* with 'project weeks', where a native speaker would work with a subject teacher to teach a subject-related week-long project in the foreign language.

In thinking, then, of trying out a small-scale CLIL initiative there are several issues to be considered:

- approval and collaboration with others;
- selecting subject topic and pupil groups;
- considering materials and pupil support.

Approval and collaboration

Content and language integrated learning involves both subject knowledge and foreign language expertise. It is unlikely that this combination will be found in one person. Even if someone is a native speaker who has expertise in another subject, there may not be pedagogic knowledge relating to the relevant curriculum. So for example I might be a German teacher with history as my second subject but I might not be familiar with how history is taught in the UK. Thus in setting up a CLIL project there will be some need for collaboration with a subject teacher to ensure appropriate coverage of any topic.

As CLIL is also an unusual way of teaching and there may well be fears that subject coverage will be detrimentally affected, there will also need to be approval from relevant members of staff and parents of the pupils concerned.

Selection of subject, topic and group

Popular subjects for CLIL initiatives are history and geography because the genre language of these subjects is closer to general use than that of more technical subjects such as natural sciences. However, for a small-scale project, it may be easier to use a subject such as science, art or physical education, where understanding is helped by plenty of visual support. The choice of subject may also be affected by the interest and willingness of the subject teacher to co-operate. Some teachers may feel more territorial about their subject area than others.

Likewise the topic to be covered will need to be negotiated with the subject teacher. Likely aspects to be considered include:

- the appropriateness of a topic for the current stage of the curriculum;
- the amount of detail to be covered and length of the project;
- the development of subject skills (for example the analysis of evidence in history texts).

The question of the group to be taught is also important. It may be helpful to choose a non-examination group (not years 11 or 13); year seven may be more receptive to a different mode of teaching because the whole of the secondary curriculum is new for them. (This is the age group for the initiatives at Hasland Hall and Bolitho.) The question of ability may also be an issue to be considered. In CLIL initiatives in general there are mixed views as to who should take part. In Germany for example it is mostly grammar-school pupils (in *Gymnasien*) who are in *bilinguale Zügen*. In other initiatives pupils of all abilities take part. Again it will be helpful to collaborate with the subject teacher to find a suitable group.

Materials and pupil support

Pupils will be working hard in a CLIL project and will need maximum support. Pupils in Hockerill, for example, talk of the need for extra concentration (Ullmann, 1999). Suggested areas of support are:

- adapting materials;
- considering language needs;
- adding visuals;
- providing scaffolding.

Adapting materials

Materials will need to be found and adapted for a CLIL topic. There may be texts in the foreign language available but it is likely that these will need to be simplified. English texts may need to be translated.

Language needs

There will be a subject-specific or genre language for any topic, so key words will need to be identified in advance. It may well be useful to give these to pupils as a translated list. Using cognates can also be helpful, although it is important to verify that pupils know the relevant

English word! It can also be helpful to consider allowing the pupils to use their mother tongue as some kind of comfort zone. This seems to be agreed practice amongst teachers actually involved in CLIL teaching.

Visuals

Adding visual information (graphics, photographs, diagrams) will help pupils decode and structure information and, as was noted earlier in Chapter 4, will already be part of good practice in MFL teaching.

Scaffolding

Wood, Bruner and Ross (1976) use the notion of scaffolding to suggest help offered (by the teacher), which is then gradually removed. Help from the teacher could take the form of breaking down a written text into different sections for the pupils (Clegg, 1999), providing structured tasks for pupils so that the content of a text becomes more accessible and providing pupils with models to work from (Clegg, 1999).

Task 11.3
Find a year seven geography text in the target language on a particular topic and consider how you would simplify it, and provide the necessary support.

Task 11.4
Discuss with a teacher in your MFL department how a CLIL project might be set up and what procedures would need to be put in place.

A final issue

One contentious issue for writers on CLIL initiatives is the question of teacher intervention. Some writers see tight teacher control as important whereas others consider development of self-awareness and development of pupils more crucial. This could be an interesting issue to consider if you are able to launch and run a CLIL initiative yourself.

Links to teaching standards

Under *subject knowledge and understanding* trainees are asked to demonstrate evidence of being 'aware of and know[ing] how to access recent ... classroom-relevant research evidence on teaching secondary pupils in their specialist subject and know[ing] how to use this to inform and improve their teaching'.

Under *planning* they are asked to 'plan their teaching to achieve progression in their pupils' learning through 'setting tasks ... which challenge pupils and ensure high levels of pupil interest'. Including a CLIL project in classroom teaching may help to contribute towards these standards.

12 Personal and professional development

The aim of this chapter is to focus on aspects of personal and professional development – in particular life after the PGCE and the real world of employment as a teacher. It contains two sections: the first section deals with the practicalities of applying for jobs and the second considers various aspects of continuing professional development for teachers in their posts.

Objectives

By the end of this chapter, the trainee should:

- have a knowledge of the procedure for applying for jobs;
- be familiar with the application process;
- be familiar with some interview strategies;
- have a knowledge of some possible interview questions;
- have a knowledge of a range of possible ways in which to develop professionally throughout the teaching career.

Applying for a post

As you approach the middle of your training year you will need to consider applying for your first job. The best place to look for educational jobs is in the *Times Educational Supplement*, which appears on Fridays. You may also look on the Web pages, especially www.jobs.ac.uk. Some local authorities produce bulletins that are then sent to university departments, or individual schools send specific advertisements.

Applications

Some jobs expect teachers to have the ability to teach a great number of subjects and the more strings to your bow you have, the better. Be sure that you read the advertisement carefully, however, to ensure that you meet the criteria. A distinction is usually made between essential and desirable qualifications/experience or qualities. For example, if an advertisement states that 'experience of teaching A-level is essential' and you do not possess such experience, it is not worth your while applying for the job. The legislation makes it quite clear that applicants shortlisted for jobs must possess all the essential qualifications/experience at the time of applying. If, on the other hand, it states that 'experience of teaching A-level is desirable' you may apply even if you do not meet the requirements.

If, on the basis of the applications received, the school decides to change the essential or desirable criteria, they would need to readvertise. If, as in the example above, the school cannot shortlist any candidates who have experience of teaching A-level and this has been one of the essential criteria, they would be obliged to readvertise the post and could not simply shortlist candidates who have no such experience. If, on the other hand, the criterion of A-level experience had been only desirable, it would have been possible to shortlist those without experience of A-level.

When you find a job for which you possess the necessary essential requirements, you have to check how to apply. Some schools or local authorities produce application forms, which should be completed in detail. Others require a letter and/or curriculum vitae. If the advertisement does not state otherwise, you can submit a short letter and detailed CV or, alternatively, a detailed letter and summary CV. If it asks for letters of application only, make sure you put as much detail in the letter as possible, highlighting aspects of your application that make you the most suitable person for that job.

If you are required to write a letter of application, it is important to note a few things. According to Neumark (1996), the letter should:

- be no longer than two A4 sheets;
- be specific to the job advertised and not simply general;
- be word-processed;
- contain no jokes;
- contain the correct spelling of the school name;
- contain short, snappy paragraphs;
- contain details of referees;
- refer to practical experience.

If possible before submitting the application, try to procure a copy of the school prospectus. This will give details of the main aspects of the school and it will also show you whether this is the kind of establishment in which you would be happy working. You will also receive a detailed job description.

A CV should contain the following elements, and several companies are able to advise and design CVs for a fee:

> **Curriculum vitae**
> Name
> Qualifications
> Relevant projects/dissertation topics
> Relevant experience
> Other experience
> Responsibilities
> Awards
> Memberships of professional organizations
> Interests/hobbies
> Publications

In your CV, present yourself in the most positive light. Anything that you have done, any awards you have received, any relevant experience you have should be listed. You need to think how to structure the information to portray yourself as the best candidate for this post. It might be by highlighting your sporting achievements if sport is given a high profile in the school prospectus. It might be useful mentioning the fact that you have done a third modern language at university level or that you have an additional qualification in another language or in another subject which would show that you had potential to bring something new to the department or school.

If you have to complete an application form, make sure that you fill in all the details required. You would be surprised at how many job applicants are not shortlisted because they fail to give all the relevant information. Be sure, too, that you mention somewhere in the job application the essential qualifications and/or experience set out in the advertisement and job description. If it states that a GCSE pass in mathematics is essential, or the ability to teach religious education, make sure you mention these facts somewhere in your application.

Usually application forms have a final blank page, or they invite applicants to provide additional information to enhance the quality of the application. In this section you should focus on aspects not dealt with in sufficient detail in previous sections. Do not rewrite what has been said elsewhere unless it is to complement the information given earlier – elaboration rather than repetition is good practice. You might mention aspects of your experience that would fit in with the school ethos. For example, if you are applying to a community school, you could write about your enthusiasm for community education as evidenced by your involvement with many youth groups which have been held in your local community centres. Try to make your application as clear as possible and tailor it to the school to which you are applying. Be specific and relevant.

Procedures

Once you have submitted an application, you may want to view the school, speak to the department and generally find out whether this is the type of establishment you would like to work in. Each school has set procedures, so that it is important to check what these are before you go any further. Some schools like to welcome applicants to the school, but only those who have been shortlisted for the post. You would not be invited to the school, therefore, until you have received a letter inviting you to interview. Some principals like to see candidates at some stage before the interview, others prefer to organize a group visit either on the day of the interview or at a prearranged time. Telephone the school secretary to find out which procedure is being followed. Do not demand an audience with the principal as this is not likely to enhance your prospects of appointment.

Pre-interview visits

At the pre-interview session, find out as much as you can about the school, the department, the type of student in the school, resources, accommodation and other specific policies, such as: pastoral care, provision for children with special educational needs, the role of the school in the community, extracurricular activities, extra-departmental activities and links with other departments. You could mention specific interests you have and ask about how these might be incorporated into the department or school. If you are fluent in another language, for example, you could ask about the possibility of taking small classes after school or as taster subjects in the upper school. You should show that you are enthusiastic, but do not come across as too proactive. Be observant but do not appear to be critical or finding fault with the school or department. Make positive comments, where appropriate, but do not come across as superficial or flippant. No school wants to employ someone who knows it all. At all times be pleasant and positive. If there is something you are unhappy about, such as the state of the accommodation or the lack of resources, make discreet inquiries about specific future developments.

If you are asked to talk to the head of department or to a language teacher in the target language, take this seriously. The impression you give of your conversational ability in the target language may be reported after the interview and may be the deciding factor at the appointment stage. It is not the intention to mislead you, but a head of department will want someone who is fluent and accurate in the target language and who will contribute to the general ethos of the department.

Interviews

Applications will be shortlisted first according to the essential criteria and then, if there are too many to interview at this stage, by the desirable criteria. If you get through these stages, and if you have read the advertisement closely and meet all the essential and desirable criteria, there is no reason to expect that you will not be shortlisted and called for interview.

Although researchers would point out that interviews are not the best predictor of future success in a job, they are the most widely used selection tool and they are the approach with which we are very familiar. If you have successfully got onto a PGCE course, you will have had recent experience of interview and will interview well. The difficulty is, however, that you will be competing with equally well-qualified, suitable candidates who also have interview experience. The most important thing to remember is that *you* are the best person for the job but the interview panel does not know this yet!

The interview panel will consist of from three people upwards – normally the principal of the school, the appropriate head of department, a representative/s of the Board of Governors, an external assessor and, in some schools, a member of the clergy or local council may also be present.

Be prepared for the interview. Read about the school and the local area, find out from the prospectus as much relevant information on the school as possible – roll numbers, examination boards used, particular sporting strengths, community involvement, links with other countries/schools, and specific projects. In short, make sure you know your prospective future employer well.

Be prepared in terms of your knowledge of your subject, the curricular issues related to your subject, general educational issues currently in the press, how you might contribute to the general life of the school and how you might enhance the learning of students in that school. Revise all your notes from the PGCE or equivalent course and talk to teachers about their areas of concern at the present time.

Dress appropriately. Interview panels expect some formality, smart dress and appropriate behaviour. Now is not the time to make statements – wait until you are appointed.

The interview will normally start with an introduction of the members of the panel and by a settling-in phase, during which the chairperson may make some general remarks about finding the school, the weather or some such meaningless topic. This is just to put you at your ease and you should not be fooled into thinking that you have the job already. In some circumstances you may be asked if you would accept the job, if offered. Again this should not be taken as an indication that you are the successful candidate; it is simply to allow you to withdraw from the interview if at this late stage you have decided that the school is not for you. If you say 'no' to this question, they will probably abandon the interview. Each interview is unique although it will generally involve one of the following:

- questions asked by members of the panel;
- prepared questions distributed to candidates in advance (about 15 minutes before the interview);
- a group interview;
- a presentation of a lesson.

Questions asked by the panel

It is a requirement that all candidates are asked the same questions, although supplementary questions following on from information given by specific candidates may be asked in addition. Usually the interview panel will have decided on the broad areas to be covered. These will be aimed at detecting whether candidates meet the criteria that have been set out in the job description. The main aspects that they will be looking for will be:

- knowledge of subject area;
- knowledge of school;
- knowledge of curriculum demands of subject;
- knowledge of recent curricular developments;
- knowledge of examination syllabuses (especially those for which school enters students);

- communication skills;
- intellectual attributes;
- interpersonal skills;
- flexibility;
- extra-curricular interests;
- interest in working with young people;
- appearance;
- suitability for particular school;
- additional factors.

Generally speaking, the interviewers will not have a list of the exact answers they require for specific questions, although they will have a view on the kind of answers they are likely to expect. It is up to you as an applicant to answer the questions in a relevant, clear, succinct manner and to be convincing. All experienced interviewers can detect learnt answers and answers that lack conviction. Even if you do not answer in the way a panel might expect, they will be impressed by your honesty and your beliefs. The secret is to learn and to integrate facts with your own value system, experience and the school's requirements.

The following list of questions has been compiled over a number of years from students seeking jobs in post-primary schools. Although not exhaustive, it gives the general flavour of the direction of the questions. Obviously there is a need to keep up to date with the issues specifically affecting the teaching and learning of modern languages, as interview panels are constantly updating their questions to take account of the most recent developments.

General questions

- What qualities would you bring to this post?
- Why did you apply for this particular post?
- Could you tell us a bit about yourself and say why you think you are the most suitable candidate for this post?
- What contribution would you make to the school in general?
- What, in your opinion, makes a good modern languages teacher?
- What are the most important lessons you have learnt from your PGCE year?
- How might you contribute to the extra-curricular life of the school?
- What is your weakest point? Are there any aspects of the post that might cause you concern?
- What is the role of the form teacher? How would you feel about having a pastoral role in the school?

Questions on the curriculum

- How would you explain the current state of the National Curriculum and the place of modern languages in it to a parent who has little knowledge of language teaching?
- What are your views on the most recent programme of study for modern languages in the National Curriculum?

- What was your reaction to the findings and recommendations of the Nuffield Languages Inquiry? How realistic do you think these recommendations are?
- How familiar are you with the latest changes in external examinations? What might be the main difficulties teaching the new syllabuses?
- What are your views on coursework?
- How would you integrate key skills into your planning?
- How real is the 'gap' between GCSE and A-level? How would you attempt to bridge it?
- Do you see a place for teaching vocational languages? Which courses would you be confident teaching?
- If a student came to you in year 11 asking for advice on the type of language course to follow post-16, what would you advise?
- How would you teach literature at A-level? If you had a choice of literary texts, which would you choose and why? How would you present them? Choose any text and say how you would teach it.

Questions on teaching methodology

- What do you consider are the main strengths and weaknesses of communicative language teaching?
- To what extent would you regard the communicative approach as 'eclectic'?
- How feasible is autonomous learning in language classes? How would you foster this approach?
- How would you describe your own teaching preferences?
- What are your views on the teaching of grammar? How would you introduce, for example, the perfect tense/prepositions/gender etc?
- How would you motivate a class of unmotivated students?
- Do you think that girls and boys learn languages differently?
- How would you attempt to make languages more accessible to boys?
- How would you respond to students' different learning styles in your lessons?
- How important is differentiation? How would you incorporate it in your classes?
- What are you views on teaching in the target language?
- How would you encourage the students to use more of the target language?
- What are your views on homework?
- What place does AT4 have at key stage three? How would you ensure that it is not a neglected skill?
- What extra reading material would you make available to your students? How would you encourage them to read more independently in the target language?
- What is the role of culture in the modern language syllabus? How would you incorporate the cultural dimension into your teaching?
- How important is ICT in the language classroom? How would you encourage students to use more ICT? How are your own ICT skills?
- What resources would you expect to find in a good modern language department?
- How would you define good classroom management?

TEACHING MODERN FOREIGN LANGUAGES

Questions in the TL

- Tell us about your year abroad.
- How will the time you have spent abroad be of use to your students?
- What do you think of school exchanges?
- What are your plans for the summer?
- Compare and contrast the educational systems of England and the target country.
- What are the strengths and weaknesses of each system?
- Which aspects of the culture of France/Germany would you regard as the most important for your lessons?
- What is the role of modern languages in delivering the key skills?
- How important are languages in this country?

Final questions

- Is there anything else you would like to say in support of your application?
- How would you contribute to the extra-curricular life of the school?
- Would you accept the post, if offered?
- Do you have any questions for us?

Answering the questions

It would probably not be very helpful to provide a list of possible answers, since every candidate who had read this book would present themselves with a rather stilted list of replies. Nevertheless, it would be useful if you were to look at the general areas and decide how you might tackle the questions. There are some important aspects to consider that would feature in any answer.

Be confident in your answer. Preface it with a statement where possible. This gives the impression that you are competent in the topic and it also gives you more time to think of what you are going to say. Use phrases such as: 'There are two aspects to this question that I would like to deal with ...,' 'This is an important area and one that affects not only modern languages ...,' 'I have been thinking about this aspect for some time ...,' 'I do not think that this is a case of a simple dichotomy ...,' 'I am not sure that my view would be the generally accepted view but ...,' 'I am convinced that this is the key to successful learning.'

Also be prepared to seek clarification if you are not quite sure what a particular interviewer/question is getting at. Do not launch into an answer unless you are sure what is being asked.

Have good eye contact. Focus on all members of the panel, without staring. Do not just focus on the person who has asked a particular question. Smile, if you can without appearing insincere or forced. Take your time in giving answers and pause for breath and to take stock of the response of the interviewers. Do not ramble on and 'talk yourself out of the job' – once you have answered the question, stop. The questioner might prompt you with a supplementary question and you can continue. It is not a good sign if the interviewer has to stop you.

Do not appear to have an axe to grind; that is to say do not hold so firmly to an opinion that the principal will think that you will be trouble in the school. By all means have firm views but appear prepared to modify them in order to fit in with the ethos of the school and with school policies.

Weaknesses

If you perceive that you are weak in any area try to present this positively, in that you are taking steps to remedy any areas requiring development. One weakness that candidates sometimes speak of is their tendency to work too hard! To say that you are difficult to get on with or that you find working in a team problematic is not advisable.

Prepared questions

Similar, if not identical, questions to those listed above may feature as part of the set questions distributed in advance. In your preparation make brief notes and write down a sketch of a structure to your answers, but do not write out answers verbatim. Above all be relevant. Since you will have had time to think about your answers, the panel will expect direct, focused answers. Be flexible in your answers, however, and be prepared for interruptions or supplementary questions from the interview panel. They will be interested in how quickly you can think and in your general ability to communicate.

Group interviews

In group interviews you have to find a way of presenting yourself as better than the other candidates in the group without appearing to be domineering, superior or condescending. Give others a chance to speak, acknowledge the contributions of others and involve quieter ones in the discussion. This will show you as a considerate team player who takes the initiative but also works well with others and values other people. Most schools are not looking for lone wolves but teachers who will work together with other colleagues in the department and in the school for the benefit of the students.

Presentations

More and more schools are asking candidates for interview to present 10-minute lessons or to take a lesson with a class or part of a class. If this is going to feature as part of the interview, you will have been sent the specification together with the invitation to attend for interview. Some examples of presentations might be the following:

- Prepare a lesson with a text that would lend itself to oral work with a top set of year 11 students. The presentation should last no more than 10 minutes. Questions will be asked about the lesson plan.
- Devise a lesson on a key stage three topic from the list of areas of experience contained in the programme of study. You should introduce the topic and teach it to the panel. The lesson should last no longer than 15 minutes and should involve variety of resources and activities.
- Be prepared to talk about how you would introduce and develop a topic for AS-level to a class that has just completed GCSE. The lesson should involve integrated skills teaching and should be 15 minutes maximum.

It is difficult to give a presentation because most of the panel will not be linguists. However, they will be able to see that good lessons contain variety, good resources and it will be clear if good planning and preparation have been done. As your lesson will more than likely be conducted for the most part in the target language, you should ensure that you use enough 'comprehensible input' and that your lesson is supported by visual resources, overhead projectors, videos and realia. As with any lesson, you should set achievable objectives within the time limit and ensure that you meet these objectives. Do not be too ambitious and make sure that the equipment you require will be made available to you. The panel will no doubt expect to be treated as the class and you should not be afraid to treat them as such, getting them to repeat words and phrases. They will want to see that you have taken the exercise seriously, that you have prepared the lesson well and that you have the confidence and the linguistic ability to conduct the lesson. The head of department or other language specialist will be there to comment on your spoken language and this will be a major influence on the decision of the panel. If you have to teach a lesson then your inventor might help you beforehand by providing opportunities to teach an unknown class.

Any questions?

At the end of any interview, you will be given the opportunity to ask questions of the panel. This is the stage in the interview when you can ask specific things that you really want to know. These questions should be directly relevant to the job for which you have applied and should not be too general in nature. The principal will not be too impressed if you ask him or her for views on the National Curriculum.

Questions related to relevant aspects of policy in the school, for example language diversification or induction for new staff, should be asked only if they have not been detailed in the school prospectus or handbook. Do not give the impression that you have not taken the time to read the school documentation. If you have had the opportunity to meet with the head of department or with another senior member of staff who has answered your queries, it is in order to say that all your questions have been answered during the informal meeting. It is also in order to ask when you are likely to hear whether or not you have been successful.

When you accept the job, informally, you will be asked to sign a contract and you are now on your way to becoming an NQT, or newly qualified teacher (BT – beginning teacher in Northern Ireland).

> **Task 12.1**
>
> Write a skeleton letter of application that you can alter to suit any job specification. Prepare answers to some of the questions suggested above.

Conclusion

This section has set out some aspects of applying for a job and attending an interview. In many cases there will be more applicants than there are jobs available in schools and interview panels will have to turn down some very good candidates. If you are 'pipped at the post' do not become too discouraged. View the application procedure and the experience of interview as formative and try again from a stronger position.

The first post

Having come through the training process the trainee will have some idea as to what to expect in the classroom. The experiences of the classroom received during school experience in partner schools on the PGCE course will have prepared you for some of the demands of the teaching job, but taking up full-time, or even part-time employment in a school context will bring with it some unexpected surprises.

According to the Teaching and Higher Education Act of 1998, you receive qualified teacher status on completion of the PGCE, but it will not be confirmed until one year of full-time service is completed. This year is referred to as the 'induction' year (Williams, 1999: 211), the arrangements for which are governed by DfEE Circular 90/00 (see also DfEE 1999). You are now, therefore, a qualified teacher with the privileges and the responsibilities which entails. You will be paid for the job you do at the qualified teacher rate, but you will also be more accountable for the teaching you do in the classroom and, more importantly, the learning in which the students in your care engage.

During the induction phase, the new teacher will continue to receive support and guidance from the school, either the head of department, the member of staff responsible for induction arrangements and/or from senior staff in the school. Teaching is a lifelong learning profession and you should not be disillusioned if you feel you do not have all the answers to the situations you encounter in your new post.

Professional development

There are aspects to personal and professional development that are important for the teacher as an individual and every opportunity should be seized to avail oneself of development possibilities. The choice of professional development route will depend on a number of factors, including the demands of the job you are doing, the priorities identified by the school, changes in curriculum and your own needs as a continuing learner. Nicholls (1999b) identifies five questions that should provide a focus when considering the areas to develop:

- What areas of development arise from my Career Entry Profile (CEP)?
- What other areas do I want to develop?
- What is my preferred style of learning?
- What personal areas do I want to develop to help my career path?
- What do I want from my appraisal in terms of specifying development needs?

By answering these questions, the new teacher should be in a position to select the areas on which work will be done.

For modern language teachers specifically, it is necessary to keep oneself involved in the subject and in the methodology of the subject.

Language skills

It is necessary for any language teacher to keep language and language learning skills alive. It is to be expected that the language of the target country will continue to change and aspects of cultural life in the country/countries will develop. It is essential, therefore, that you plan to visit the target country on a regular basis, both for enjoyment and linguistic and cultural enrichment but also to collect up-to-date information and resources. Barnes (1996) identified that linguistic competence was even a problem for some students at PGCE level.

If it is not possible to visit the country it would be advisable for you to attend some evening classes or to become a member of a language group or language circle. The *Institut français*, the *Alliance française*, the *Goethe Institut*, the various language embassies and cultural centres all provide language courses, as do universities and colleges of further and higher education.

Exchanges/courses

The Central Bureau runs a system of teacher exchanges. Teachers with some years' experience can apply to teach in another country for a period, during which a teacher from the host country works in the UK school. This must be done with the agreement of the school and the department.

For those for whom an extended exchange is impractical there exist courses of some weeks' duration. These can be built around cultural and/or linguistic themes. Details of these courses are available from the CILT or from the Central Bureau.

Funding is also available from Europe in the form of SOCRATES project funds for work to be done with other countries. Examples of this are Comenius and LINGUA, details of which can again be obtained from the Central Bureau.

Language organizations

When you leave your PGCE institution, you will have had contact with the most recent research findings and the most recent developments in the teaching of your subjects. Teaching methods, resources and research also change, however, and it is therefore important that you seek to keep abreast of developments in your subject area. There are various ways to do this. The Association for Language Learning (ALL) is a national association and is well worth joining. Many join as student members. For an annual fee members gain language-specific journals and have access to various conferences at national and local level. There is a network of local branches that organize events for local members and CILT, together with its satellites (Scottish CILT, and NICILT) and with its national network of 13 Comenius Centres in addition to the National Comenius Centre for Wales, organizes a nationwide programme of training events. In addition it has a mailing service (CILT Direct) that, for a fee, gives teachers access to detailed information about publications, research and conferences. In this way teachers can gain an insight into the latest developments and resources in language learning.

Conferences

Both CILT and ALL organize annual national conferences in specific languages areas. These deal with the most up-to-date issues, including developments on the latest assessment and examinations, teaching and learning, resources and research. The network of Comenius centres and the two other CILT agencies, Scottish CILT and NI CILT, also offer a wide range of opportunities for professional development. Conferences and seminars provide a good opportunity to meet other teachers from the subject area who may be experiencing similar difficulties and demands in their schools. This type of 'networking' is essential for the sharing of ideas and examples of good practice.

Books and journals

Another source of up-to-date resources and information is journals. The Pathfinder series, published by CILT on various practical topics for the language teacher, is a valuable resource for busy teachers. Mary Glasgow publications also produce numerous materials on relevant topics. Professional journals such as the *Language Learning Journal, Francophonie, Deutsch Lehren und Lernen, Vida Hispanica, Tutti Italia*, all published by ALL, are useful in giving teachers new ideas for teaching and the findings from research in the classroom. The publisher Multilingual Matters also has a range of books on practical and theoretical topics linked to language.

For teachers interested in research on language learning the relatively new journal, *Language Teaching Research*, and the abstracting journal *Language Teaching* are good starting points.

Professional courses

When teachers have gained some years' experience they may want to embark on further study. Many universities offer courses on language-specific work, such as masters courses in language and literature. Education departments offer MAs or MEds in language in education. In many modular courses it is possible to combine some further language-specific courses with other areas of expertise, such as management, primary or special needs. For those teachers who are interested in developing their own research expertise there are numerous courses at MPhil, PhD or EdD level.

Contacting other teachers

Fora have been set up on the Internet to encourage teachers to share experiences and resources. One excellent example of this is the multilingual virtual resources centre, called lingu@net.europa, run by CILT in the UK, the Web address for which is: www.linguanet-europa.org. In Northern Ireland, the NINE Web site has facilities for teachers to exchange views and materials (www.nine.gov.uk).

Research

Whether you decide to register on an award-bearing course or not, it is still recommended that in the interests of personal and professional development you engage in some research, not least to improve your own working environment and, by definition, the learning environment of your students. Green (1996) recommends collaborative research as a means of successfully continuing professional development. From time to time the *Times Educational Supplement* advertises small-scale grants that are available (for example the TTA offers grants to teachers who wish to engage in research in their own schools).

Some specific guidelines on conducting action research for language teachers is provided by Freeman and Richards (1996), Wallace (1998) and Burns (1999).

Getting published

If you produce work as part of a higher degree or if you conduct small-scale action research projects, the results will be of interest to the wider teaching community. In collaboration with your tutor at university, you may decide to try and publish your work in a professional journal, such as the *Language Learning Journal* or one of the language-specific journals. You may want to target a more research-focused journal such as *Language Teaching Research* or a more general journal such as *Research in Education, Educational Research* or *Research Papers in Education*. Each journal contains guidelines for contributors that state the number of words, the format the article should take and details of submission criteria. Normally, submitted articles are sent out to referees who review them. Sometimes you will receive an article returned with comments from referees, which should be addressed before resubmitting.

PERSONAL AND PROFESSIONAL DEVELOPMENT

This is sometimes a painful process but it is ultimately worth revising the article in light of the comments.

For larger works, such as dissertations or theses, CORE publishes in a microfiche format. Some publishers, such as CILT or Multilingual Matters, produce series on classroom-related issues and they are interested in receiving high quality manuscripts from practitioners.

Although there appears to be a plethora of materials for teaching available, things change and there is always a niche in the market for new materials that meet new examination guidelines or that are geared at specific audiences. Individual teachers or groups of teachers might be encouraged to investigate areas where they could have an impact. There is a great need for additional materials for Irish in Northern Ireland schools, for example, and for Scottish Gaelic.

What teachers have to say is extremely valuable to other teachers: there is always a need for the reflective practitioner to contribute to language teaching throughout the country. You only need to take the first step of writing the first article or report.

Task 12.2

From the above list of possibilities, draw up a plan of action for your own professional development for the first two years of teaching.

Conclusion

Teaching is a profession that requires constant professional development from the teacher. Changes in curriculum, in methodology, within a school, findings from research and personal motivation all have an impact on the types of development engaged in. The most important fact is, however, that the teacher continues to be a reflective learner.

Links to teaching standards

Under *other professional requirements* trainees are asked to demonstrate that they 'understand the need to take responsibility for their own professional development and to keep up-to-date with research and developments in pedagogy and in the subjects they teach'. Considering aspects of personal and professional development, as we have outlined in this chapter, should help trainees to achieve this standard.

References

Alsop, S and Luth, R (1999) Special needs in the 'mainstream' in ed G Nicholls, *Learning to Teach*, Kogan Page, London

Anderson, J R (1985) *Cognitive Psychology and its Implications*, 2nd edn, Freeman, New York

AQA (1999) *General Certificate of Education 2001/2 German Advanced Subsidiary, Advanced Specifications*, AQA, Guildford

ARG (Assessment Reform Group) (1999) *Assessment for Learning: Beyond the black box*, University of Cambridge, Cambridge

Argondizzo, C (1992) *Children in Action: A resource book for language teachers of young learners*, Prentice Hall, New York

Atkinson, D (1993) Teaching in the target language: a problem in the current orthodoxy, *Language Learning Journal*, **8**, pp 2–5

Atkinson, T (1998) *www: The Internet, Info Tech 3*, CILT, London

Banner, G and Rayner, S (2000) Learning language and learning style: principles, process and practice, *Language Learning Journal*, **21**, pp 37–44

Barbour, S (2000) Discovering literature through the target language, in ed G Shaw, *Aiming High: Straight As*, CILT, London

Barnes, A (1996) Maintaining language skills in the initial training of foreign language teachers, *Language Learning Journal*, **14**, pp 58–64

Barnes, A (2000) Developing advanced reading skills, in ed G Shaw, *Aiming High 2: Straight As*, CILT, London

Biriotti, L (1999) *Grammar is Fun*, CILT, London

Black, P and Wiliam, D (1998) *Inside the Black Box: Raising standards through classroom assessment*, University of Cambridge, Cambridge

Blondin, C, Candelier, C, Edelenbos, P, Johnstone, R, Kubanet-German, A and Taeschner, T (1998) *Foreign Languages in Primary and Pre-School Education: A review of recent research within the European Union*, CILT, London

Blunkett, D (1999) Curriculum for all seasons, *Times Educational Supplement*, 26 March

Breen, M and Candlin, C (1987) Which materials? A consumer's guide and designer's guide, in *ELT Textbooks and Materials: Problems in evaluation and development, ELT Document 126* ed L Sheldon, London, Modern English Publications in association with the British Council

British Council, Goethe Institut and ENS Credif (eds) (1994) *Subject Learning and Teaching in a Foreign Language*, Triangle 13, Didier Erudition, Paris

Brown, H D (1994) *Principles of Language Learning and Teaching*, 2nd edn, Prentice-Hall Regents, Englewood Cliffs, NJ

Brown, K and Brown, M (1996) *New Contexts for Modern Language Learning: Cross-curricular approaches*, CILT, London

REFERENCES

Brown, M (2000) *Comparing Standards Internationally*, Oxford

Brumfit, C J (1983) Some problems with Krashen's concepts 'acquisition' and 'learning' *Nottingham Linguistic Circular*, **12** (2), pp 95–105

Bruner, J (1974) *Beyond the Information Given: Studies in the psychology of knowing*, introduction by J Anglin, George Allen & Unwin, London

Buckby, M (1985) The use of English in the foreign language classroom, in *York Papers in Language Teaching*, ed PS Green, University of York, York

Buckby, M, Jones, B and Berwick G (1992) *Learning Strategies: Teachers' manual*, Collins Educational, London

Buckland, D and Short, M (1993) *Nightshift: Ideas and strategies for homework*, CILT, London

Burns, A (1999) *Collaborative Action Research for English Language Teachers*, Cambridge University Press, Cambridge

Burstall, C, Jamieson, M, Cohen, S and Hargreaves, M (1974) *Primary French in the Balance*, NFER, Slough

Byram, M (1997) 'Cultural awareness' as vocabulary learning, *Language Learning Journal*, **16**, pp 51–57

Byram, M and Morgan, C (1994) *Teaching-and-Learning Language-and-Culture*, Multilingual Matters, Clevedon

Cajkler, W and Thornton, B (1999) Language learner perceptions of strategy use in secondary schools, *Language Learning Journal*, **20**, pp 45–50

Caldwell, E (1999a) TES Online, Languages, *Times Educational Supplement*, 16 April

Caldwell, E (1999b) Words that roll off the tongue, *Times Educational Supplement*, 8 January

Caldwell, E (2000) DVD setting the pace, *Times Educational Supplement*, 12 May

Callaghan, M (1998) An investigation into the causes of boys' underachievement in French, *Language Learning Journal*, **17**, pp 2–7

Calvert, M (1989) *Towards Diversification: Activities and notes for INSET leaders and teachers*, University of York Language Teaching Centre, York

Canale, M (1983) From communicative competence to communicative language pedagogy, in eds J C Richards and R W Schmidt, *Language and Communication*, Longman, London and New York

Canale, M and Swain, M (1980) Theoretical bases of communicative approaches to second language teaching and testing, *Applied Linguistics*, **1** (1), pp 1–47

Cassidy, S (2000a) Brightest will skip GCSEs, *Times Educational Supplement*, 19 May

Cassidy, S (2000b) Internet offers a Latin revival, *Times Educational Supplement*, 7 July

Cassidy, S (2000c) Primary language barriers, *Times Educational Supplement*, 7 July

Cassidy, S (2000d) Games staff must teach spelling, *Times Educational Supplement*, 25 August

Cassidy, S (2000e) Alarm at second literacy strategy, *Times Educational Supplement*, 6 October

Central Bureau (1997), *News*, 7

Central Bureau (1999), *News*, 12

Central Bureau (2000) *Central Bureau News*, Spring 2000

Central Bureau (2000) *Central Bureau News*, Autumn 2000

Chambers, F (1991) Promoting the use of the target language in the classroom, *Language Learning Journal*, **4**, pp 27–31

Chambers, G (1992) Teaching in the target language, *Language Learning Journal*, **6**, pp 66–67

Chambers, G (1995) Diversification: a curate's egg? *Education Today*, **45** (2), pp 43–52

Chambers, G (1997) The exchange vs the media: the struggle for cultural awareness, *Language Learning Journal*, **16**, pp 58–65

Chamot, A U (1987) The learning strategies of ESL students, in eds A Wenden and J Rubin, *Learner Strategies in Language Learning*, Prentice-Hall International, London

Cheater, C and Farren, A (in press) *The Literacy Link*, CILT, London

Chomsky, N (1957) *Syntactic Structures*, Mouton, The Hague

Christ, I (1998) European language portfolio, *Language Teaching*, **31** (4), pp 214–17

REFERENCES

CILT (Centre for Information on Language Teaching and Resources) (1985) *What is Meant by a 'Communicative' Approach to Modern Language Teaching?* Information Sheet 12, CILT, London
CILT (2000) *Early Language Learning Bulletin,* **4**
CILT (1997) *Primary Languages Bulletin,* **2**
CILT (1998) *Primary Languages Bulletin,* **3**
CILT DIRECT (1998) *CILT DIRECT 1999 Languages Yearbook,* CILT, London
Clark, A (1998) *Gender on the Agenda: Factors motivating boys and girls in MFLs,* CILT, London
Clark, A and Trafford, J (1996) Return to gender: boys and girls, attitudes and achievements, *Language Learning Journal,* **14**, pp 40–49
Clark, G (1989) Diversification and the National Curriculum: policy and provision, in ed D Phillips, *Which Language,* Hodder & Stoughton, London
Clarke, J (1994) Losing sight of the target, *Times Educational Supplement,* 24 June
Clegg, J (1999) Task design in the bilingual secondary classroom, in ed J Masih, *Learning through a Foreign Language: Models, methods and outcomes,* CILT, London
Cohen, A (1984) Studying second language learning strategies: how do we get the information? *Applied Linguistics,* **5**(2), pp 101–11
Collie, J and Slater, S (1987) *Literature in the Language Classroom: A resource book of ideas and activities,* Cambridge University Press, Cambridge
Collins, P (1993) The moving target, *Languages Forum,* **1** (1), pp 16–18
Coste, D, North, B, Sheils, J and Trim, J (1998) *Language Teaching,* **31**(3), pp 136–51
Council of Europe, Council for Cultural Co-operation (1998), *Modern Languages: Learning, teaching, assessment a common European framework of reference,* Council of Europe, Strasbourg
Coyle, D (1999) The next stage? Is there a future for the present? The legacy of the 'communicative' approach, *Francophonie,* **19**, pp 13–16
Cummins, J (1984) *Bilingualism and Special Education Issues in Assessment and Pedagogy,* Multilingual Matters, Clevedon
Dam, L (1995) *Learner Autonomy 3: From theory to classroom practice,* Authentik, Dublin
Danks, P (1997) Music to youthful ears, *Times Educational Supplement,* 14 November
Das, B K (ed) (1985) *Communicative Language Teaching,* Selected Papers from RELC Seminar Singapore 23–27 April 1984
Dean, C (1998) Private schools extend their own lead, *Times Educational Supplement,* 11 September
Deane, M (1992) Teaching modern languages to pupils with special educational needs? With pleasure! *Language Learning Journal,* **6**, pp 43–47
DENI (Department of Education for Northern Ireland) (1992) *The Northern Ireland Curriculum: Modern languages programme of study and attainment targets,* DENI, Bangor
DENI (1998) *The Teacher Education Handbook,* DENI, Bangor
DENI (1999) *Northern Ireland Strategy for Education Technology,* DENI, Bangor
DES (1990) *Modern Foreign Languages for ages 11 to 16: Proposals of the Secretary of State for Education and Science and the Secretary of State for Wales,* HMSO, London
DES (1991) *Modern Languages in the National Curriculum,* London, HMSO
DFE (1995) *Modern Foreign Languages in the National Curriculum,* London, HMSO
DfEE (1994) *SEN Code of Practice,* DfEE, London
DfEE (1998) *The National Literacy Strategy,* DfEE, London
DfEE (1999) *The Induction of Newly Qualified Teachers,* Circular 5/99, DfEE, London
DfEE (2000) *Disapplication of the National Curriculum,* Circular 84/2000, DfEE, London
DfEE/QCA (1999) *Modern Foreign Languages: The National Curriculum for England,* QCA, London
Dickson, P (1996) *Using the Target Language: A view from the classroom,* NFER, London
Dickson, P and Lee, B (1990) *Diversification of Foreign Languages in Schools: The ESG pilot programme,* NFER, Slough

REFERENCES

Dobson, A (1998) *MFL Inspected: Reflections on inspection findings*, CILT, London

Door, V (1999) *Contrasting Approaches to the Teaching of Foreign Languages in Germany and England with Particular Reference to Selected Textbooks*, unpublished MPhil Thesis, University of Newcastle

Downes, P (2000) *Boys' Performance in Modern Foreign Languages*, paper presented at British Educational Research Association Conference, University of Cardiff, September 2000

Downes, PJ (1978) Graded examinations for elementary language learners: the Oxfordshire project, *Modern Languages*, **54** (3), pp 153–56

Driscoll, P (1999a) Modern foreign languages in the primary school: a fresh start, in eds P Driscoll and D Frost, *The Teaching of Modern Foreign Languages in the Primary School*, Routledge, London

Driscoll, P (1999b) Teacher expertise in the primary modern foreign languages classroom, in eds P Driscoll and D Frost, *The Teaching of Modern Foreign Languages in the Primary School*, Routledge, London

Driscoll, P and Frost, D (1999) Introduction, in eds P Driscoll and D Frost, *The Teaching of Modern Foreign Languages in the Primary School*, Routledge, London

Edelenbos, P and Johnstone, R (eds) (1996) *Researching Languages at Primary School: Some European perspectives*, CILT, London

Edexcel (2000), *Advanced Subsidiary GCE in Modern Foreign Languages Specifications; Advanced GCE in Modern Foreign Languages Specifications*, Edexcel Foundation, Nottingham

Elwood, J and Gipps, C (1999) *Review of Recent Research on the Achievement of Girls in Single-sex Schools*, Institute of Education, London

Evans, M (1999) European school links as a vehicle for promoting languages in the UK, in eds P Driscoll and D Frost, *The Teaching of Modern Foreign Languages in the Primary School*, Routledge, London

Fawkes, S (1999) ICT training, *What's on-line for Languages*, **2**, p 1

Filmer-Sankey, C (1989) *A Study of First-year Pupils' Attitudes towards French, German and Spanish*, OXPROD Occasional Paper 3, University of Oxford Department of Educational Studies, Oxford

Filmer-Sankey, C (1991) *A Study of Second-year Pupils' Attitudes towards French, German and Spanish*, OXPROD Occasional Paper 5, University of Oxford Department of Educational Studies, Oxford

Filmer-Sankey, C (1993) OXPROD: a summative account, *Language Learning Journal*, **7**, pp 5–8

Fleming, F and Walls, G (1998) What pupils do: the role of strategic planning in modern foreign language learning, *Language Learning Journal*, **18**, pp 14–21

Franklin, C E M (1990a) Teaching in the target language: problems and prospects, *Language Learning Journal*, **2**, pp 20–24

Franklin, C E M (1990b) *The Use of the Target Language in the French Language Classroom: Co-operative teaching as an aid to implementation*, unpublished PhD, University of Edinburgh, Edinburgh

Freeman, D and Richards J C (1996) *Teaching Learning in Language Teaching*, Cambridge University Press, Cambridge

Frost, D (1999) Developing primary MFL: a teacher-led, community-focused approach, in eds P Driscoll and D Frost, *The Teaching of Modern Foreign Languages in the Primary School*, Routledge, London

Gerngross, G and Puchta, H (1992) *Pictures in Action*, Prentice Hall International, Hemel Hempstead

Giles-Jones, M (1994) Teaching subjects through the medium of a second or foreign language in England and Wales, in eds British Council, ENS-Crédif and Goethe Institut, *Subject Learning in Foreign Language*, Triangle 13, Didier-Erudition, Paris

Gill, C (2000), Review of the literacy MFL links working group, Bedfordshire, *Early Language Learning Bulletin*, **4**, p 8

Graham, S (1997) *Effective Language Learning*, Multilingual Matters, Clevedon

Gray, C (1996) Will your NVQ use IT ? *Language Learning Journal*, **13**, pp 58–61

Green, P S (ed) (1975) *The Language Laboratory in School: Performance and prediction: The York Study*, Oliver & Boyd, Edinburgh

REFERENCES

Green, S (1996) The professional development of modern language teachers, *Language Learning Journal*, **14**, pp 75–79

Gregg, K R (1984) Krashen's monitor and Occam's razor, *Applied Linguistics*, **5** (2), pp 79–100

Gregg, K R (1986) Review of Krashen: the input hypothesis, *TESOL Quarterly*, **20** (1), pp 116–22

Grenfell, M and Harris, V (1998) Learner strategies and the advanced language learner: problems and processes, *Language Learning Journal*, **17**, pp 23–28

Grittner, F M (ed) (1977) *Teaching Foreign Languages*, 2nd edn, Harper & Row, New York

Guthrie, E M L (1987) Six cases in classroom communication: a study of teacher discourse in the FL classroom, in eds J P Lantolf and A Labarca, *Research in Second Language Learning: Focus on the classroom*, Delaware Symposium 6, Ablex, Norwood NJ

Halliwell, S (1991) *Yes, But Will They Behave? Managing an interactive classroom*, CILT, London

Halliwell, S (1992) *Teaching English in the Primary Classroom*, Longman, London

Halliwell, S and Jones, B (1991) *On Target*, CILT, London

Harbord, J (1992) The use of the mother tongue in the classroom, *English Language Teaching Journal*, **46** (4), pp 350–55

Harris, V (1997) *Teaching Learners How to Learn: Strategy training in the modern languages classroom*, CILT, London

Hartmann, V (1996) Kreativ schreiben – ein E-mail Projekt des Goethe-Instituts London, *German Teaching* **13**, pp 19–20

Hawkins, E (1987) *Modern Languages in the Curriculum*, (rev edn, Cambridge University Press, Cambridge

Hawkins, E (1996) Language teaching in perspective, in ed E Hawkins, *Thirty Years of Language Learning*, CILT, London

Hewer, S (1997) *Text Manipulation: Computer-based activities to improve knowledge and use of the target language, InfoTech*, **2** CILT, London

Hill, B (1991) *Making the Most of Satellites and Interactive Video*, CILT, London

Holec, H (1981) *Autonomy in Foreign Language Learning*, Pergamon, Oxford

Holmes, B (1994a) *Keeping on Target*, CILT, London

Holmes, B (1994b) Learners in difficulty, in ed P McLagan, *Modern Languages for Students with Special Educational Needs*, CILT, NCET, London

Horner, S (2000) Use of language requirement, *Times Educational Supplement*, 26 May

Hurrell, A (1999) The four language skills: the whole works, in eds P Driscoll and D Frost, *The Teaching of Modern Foreign Languages* Routledge, London

Hymes, D (1972) On communicative competence, *Sociolinguistics: Selected readings*, in eds J B Pride and J Holmes, Penguin Education, Harmondsworth

Johnston, C (1998) Language learning evolution, *Times Educational Supplement*, 29 May

Johnston, C (1999a) Jeux sans frontières, *Times Educational Supplement*, 16 April

Johnston, C (1999b) New boys' network, *Times Educational Supplement*, 8 October

Johnston, C (2000) Surge in bills for Internet use, *Times Educational Supplement*, 3 November

Johnston, C A (1996) *Unlocking the Will to Learn*, Corwin Press, Thousand Oaks CA

Johnstone, R (1988) Communicative methodology: second generation, in ed PJ Kingston, *Language Breaking Barriers*, selected proceedings from the Joint Council of Language Associations' Annual Conference at University of Warwick, March, JCLA, Rugby

Johnstone, R (1994a) Grammar: acquisition and use, in eds L King and P Boaks, *Grammar! A conference report*, CILT, London

Johnstone, R (1994b) *Teaching Modern Languages at Primary School: Approaches and Implications*, SCRE, Edinburgh

Johnstone, R (1995) *The Role of Structure in the Development of Communicative Competence*, discussion paper for Scottish CILT Conference on Communicative Language Teaching, 11 March 1995, University of Stirling, Stirling

REFERENCES

Johnstone, R (2000) Research on language teaching and learning (1999), *Language Teaching*, **33** (3), pp 141–62

Jones, B (1992) *Being Creative*, CILT, London

Jones, B (1995) *Exploring Otherness: An approach to cultural awareness*, CILT, London

Jones, C (1996) Organising a French exchange, *Francophonie*, **14**, pp 5–8

Jones, S (1998) Modern languages and international co-operation in education, *Links* **18**, p 3

Kay, S (1996), Methodological issues in textbook composition, *Language Learning Journal*, **13**, pp 32–35

Kenning, M (1992) The joint languages diversification model: aspects of a case study, *Language Learning Journal*, **5**, pp 2–5

Kenning, M (1994) Language preference and time allocation in the joint languages diversification model, *Language Learning Journal*, **9**, pp 19–21

Kilmartin, J (2000) Time for a reality check, *Times Educational Supplement*, 6 October

King, L (1998) Director's introduction: 1998 – languages in the news *CILT DIRECT 1999 Languages Yearbook*, CILT, London

König, M (1998) Language learning with the Internet, *Central Bureau News*, **10**, p 4

Krashen, S D (1982) *Principles and Practice in Second Language Acquisition*, Pergamon, Oxford

Kress, G and van Leeuwen, T (1996) *Reading Images: The grammar of visual design*, Routledge, London

Lamb, T and Fisher, J (1999) Making connections: football, the Internet and reluctant language learners, *Language Learning Journal*, **20**, pp 32–36

Lee, B (1991) *Extending Opportunities: Modern foreign languages for pupils with special educational needs*, NFER, Slough

Lee, J, Buckland, D and Shaw, G (1998) *The Invisible Child: The responses and attitudes to the learning of modern foreign languages shown by year 9 pupils of average ability*, CILT, London

Leman, G (1999) Coursework: the parents' paper, *Deutsch: Lehren und Lernen*, **19**, pp 4–5

Littlewood, WT (1981) *Communicative Language Teaching*, Cambridge University Press, Cambridge

Lonsdale, T (2000) Study skills for A-level language learner, in ed G Shaw, *Aiming High 2: Straight As*, CILT, London

Low, L (1999) Policy issues for primary modern languages, in eds P Driscoll and D Frost, *The Teaching of Modern Foreign Languages in the Primary School*, Routledge, London

Marshall, J G (1988) *Mapping Foreign Language Provision in Schools: An instrument for surveying existing classroom provision, available teacher resources and for costing planned requirements*, CILT, London

Marshall, K (2000) Why do they do it? An investigation into rates of participation and learner motivation in modern languages after GCSE and A-level, in ed G Shaw, *Aiming High 2: Straight As*, CILT, London

Martin, C (1995) *Games and Fun Activities*, CILT, London

Martin, C and Cheater, C (1998) *Let's Join In: Rhymes, poems and songs*, CILT, London

Masih, J (ed) (1999) *Learning through a Foreign Language: Models, methods and outcomes*, CILT, London

Maynard, C (2000) New GCSE subject criteria, *Times Educational Supplement*, 20 October

McCrory, D (1990) Diversification: What does it mean? *Language Learning Journal*, **2**, pp 77–78

McDevitt, B (2000) Forewarned is not necessarily forearmed: A language learning experience, *Language Learning Journal*, **21**, pp 45–49

McDonald, C (1994) *Using the Target Language*, Mary Glasgow Publications, Cheltenham

McKenna, NS and McKenna, P (2000) Perception and reality: bridging the Internet gap, *Language Learning Journal*, **21**, pp 8–12

McLachlan, A (2000) Brushing up oral skills, in ed G Shaw, *Aiming High 2: Straight As*, CILT, London

McLagan, P (1996) *Modern Languages Survey of Secondary Schools: An outline of the preliminary findings*, CILT, London

McLaughlin, B (1987) *Theories of Second Language Learning*, Edward Arnold, London

McPake, J, Johnstone, R, Low, L and Lyall, L (1999) *Foreign Languages in the Upper Secondary School: A study of the causes of decline*, SCRE, Stirling

REFERENCES

Meiring, L and Norman, N (1999) Planning an integrated topic, in ed N Pachler, *Teaching Modern Foreign Languages at Advanced Level*, Routledge, London
Miller, A (1995) *Creativity*, Mary Glasgow Publications, Cheltenham
Milton, J and Meara, P (1998) Are the British really bad at learning foreign languages? *Language Learning Journal*, 18, pp 68–76
Mireylees, J (2000) Primary French and the essential art of storytelling, *Francophonie*, 21, pp 12–15
Mitchell, R and Myles, F (1998) *Second Language Learning Theories*, Arnold, London
Mohr, P (1997) German satellite TV as a source of teaching and learning materials, *German Teaching* 15, 12–16
Morgan, C (1995) Cultural awareness and the National Curriculum, *Language Learning Journal* 12, pp 9–12
Morgan, C (1996) Creative writing in foreign language learning, in ed L Thompson, *The Teaching of Poetry: European perspectives*, Cassell, London
Morgan, C (1998) Foreign language learning with a difference, *Language Learning Journal*, 18, pp 30–36
Morgan, C (1999) The process of transfer from primary to secondary in a bilingual schooling context, *International Journal of Bilingual Education and Bilingualism*, 2 (4), pp 233–51
Morgan, C and Cain, A (2000) *Foreign Language and Culture Learning from a Dialogic Perspective*, Multilingual Matters, Clevedon
Morgan, C and Freedman, E (1999) *Provision and Take-up of Modern Foreign Languages: Final Report*, University of Bath, QCA
Muir, J (1999) Classroom connections, in eds P Driscoll and D Frost, *The Teaching of Modern Foreign Languages in the Primary School*, Routledge, London
Naiman, N, Fröhlich, M , Stern, H H and Todesco, A (1978) *The Good Language Learner*, Ontario Institute for Studies in Education, Toronto
Naysmith, J (1999) Primary modern foreign language teaching: a picture of one county, *Language Learning Journal*, 20, pp 15–19
NCC (National Curriculum Council) (1993) *Target Practice*, NCC, York
Neather, E, Woods, C, Rodrigues, I, Davis, M and Dunne, E (1995) *Target Language Testing in Modern Foreign Languages: A report of a project on the testing of reading and listening without the use of English*, SCAA, London
Neil, P S (1993) Diversification in Scotland, *Language Learning Journal*, 8, pp 58–60
Neil, P, and Mallon, R (1998) *Diversification of Foreign Language Provision in Schools in the UK: A review of the literature*, Department of Education for Northern Ireland (DENI), Bangor
Neil, P S, Phipps, W and Mallon, R (1999) *Diversification of the First Modern Language in Northern Ireland Schools*, Department of Education for Northern Ireland (DENI), Bangor
Neumark, V (1996) What makes you the perfect candidate? *Times Educational Supplement*, 12 January
Neumark, V (1997) Good morning France, Germany, Sweden, *Times Educational Supplement*, 12 September
Neumark, V (2000) Journey to Planet Naranja, *Times Educational Supplement*, 20 October
NICC (1992) *Guidance Materials: Modern Languages*, NICC, Belfast
Nicholls, G (1999a) Assessment, recording and reporting, in ed G Nicholls, *Learning to Teach*, Kogan Page, London
Nicholls, G (1999b) Continual professional development, in ed G Nicholls, *Learning to Teach*, Kogan Page, London
Nuffield Foundation (2000) *Languages: The Next Generation. The final report and recommendations of the Nuffield Languages Inquiry*, Nuffield Foundation, London
Nunan, D (1992) *Research Methods in Language Learning*, Cambridge University Press, Cambridge
O'Malley, B (1996a) Drive on languages runs out of steam, *Times Educational Supplement*, 2 February
O'Malley, B (1996b) Students in need of a placement, *Times Educational Supplement*, 2 February

REFERENCES

O'Malley, B (1996c) Independents play a long game, *Times Educational Supplement*, 22 March

O'Malley, JM and Chamot AU (1990) *Learning Strategies in Second Language Acquisition*, Cambridge University Press, Cambridge

O'Malley, J, Chamot, AU, Stewner-Manzanares, G, Küpper, L and Russo, R (1985) Learning strategies used by beginning and intermediate ESL students, *Language Learning*, 35, pp 21–46

O'Shea, L (1999) The mercredi bunch, *Times Educational Supplement*, 5 February

O'Sullivan (1991) Foreign language course book: Ask your pupils!, *Language Learning Journal*, 3, pp 10–13

OCR (1999) *Advanced Subsidiary GCE, Advanced GCE, French, German, Spanish Approved Specifications*, 2nd edn, OCR, Cambridge

Oxford, R (1990) *Language Learning Strategies: What every teacher should know*, Newbury House, New York

Oxford, R (1993) Research on second language learning strategies, *Annual Review of Applied Linguistics*, 13, pp 175–87

Page, B (1993) Target language and examinations, *Language Learning Journal*, 8, pp 6–7

Passmore, B (1995) Why Spain is plainly not main choice, *Times Educational Supplement*, 26 May

Phillips, D (1987) Diversification of FL1 teaching: a new research project, *Modern Languages*, 68 (1), pp 29–31

Phillips, D (ed) (1989) *Which Language? Diversification and the National Curriculum*, Hodder & Stoughton, London

Phillips, D and Filmer-Sankey, C (1989) Vive la différence? Some problems in investigating diversification of first foreign language provision in schools, *British Educational Research Journal*, 15 (3), pp 317–29

Phin, D (1992) German in the primary, *German Teaching*, 6, pp 2–6

Phipps, W (1999) *Pairwork: Interaction in the modern languages classroom*, CILT, London

Poole, B and Roberts, T (1995) Primary school foreign language teaching: some unanswered questions, *Languages Forum*, 1 (4), pp 2–5

Purcell, S (1994) A holiday brochure as teaching aid, *Francophonie*, 9, pp 18–19

QCA (1997) *Keeping the Curriculum Under Review*, QCA, London

QCA (1998) *KS4 Curriculum in Action: A discussion document*, QCA, London

QCA/DfEE (2000) *Modern Foreign Languages: A scheme of work for key stage 3*, DfEE, London

Richards, JC and Rodgers, TS (1986) *Approaches and Methods in Teaching: A description and analysis*, Cambridge University Press, Cambridge

Rixon, S (1999) Resources for the teaching of modern foreign languages in the primary school, in eds P Driscoll and D Frost, *The Teaching of Modern Foreign Languages in the Primary School*, Routledge, London

Rowles, D, Carty, M and McLachlan, A (1998) *Foreign Language Assistants: A guide to good practice*, CILT, London

Rowlinson, W (1994) The historical ball and chain, in ed A Swarbrick, *Teaching Modern Languages*, Routledge, London

Rubin, J (1981) The study of cognitive processes in second language learning, *Applied Linguistics*, 2 (2), pp 117–31

Rumley, G (1999) Games and songs for teaching modern foreign languages in the primary school, in eds P Driscoll and D Frost, *The Teaching of Modern Foreign Languages in the Primary School*, Routledge, London

Rumley, G and Sharpe, K (1993) Generalisable game activities in primary language teaching, *Language Learning Journal*, 8, pp 35–38

Salters, J, Neil, P and Jarman, R (1995) Why did French bakers spit in the dough? *Language Learning Journal*, 11, pp 26–29

REFERENCES

Salvadori, E (1997) Taking language beyond the classroom, in ed M Byram, *Face to Face: Learning language and culture through visits and exchanges*, CILT, London

Satchwell, P (1997) *Keep Talking: Teaching in the target language*, CILT, London

Satchwell, P and de Silva, J (1995) *Catching Them Young*, CILT, London

Seidler, K (1989) Old wine in new bottles? A video-letter exchange project as a means of organising cross cultural leaning, *British Journal of Language Teaching*, **27**, pp 30–35

Sharpe, K (1999) Modern foreign languages in the primary school in England: Some implications for teacher training, in eds P Driscoll and D Frost, *The Teaching of Modern Foreign Languages in the Primary School*, Routledge, London

Sheldon, L (1998) Evaluating ELT textbooks and materials, *ELT Journal*, **42** (4), pp 237–46

Skarbek, C (1998) *First Steps to Reading and Writing*, CILT, London

Skehan, P (1989) *Individual Differences in Language Learning*, Edward Arnold, London

Snow, D and Byram, M (1997) *Crossing Frontiers: The school study visit abroad*, CILT, London

SOED (1991) *Report of the Task Group on Modern European Languages*, HMSO, Edinburgh

Stables, A and Wikeley, F (1999) From bad to worse? Pupils' attitudes to modern foreign languages at ages 14 and 15, *Language Learning Journal* **20**, pp 27–31

Stadtschulrat für Wein (1997) *Primary Goes Europe*, Stadtschulrat für Wein, Vienna

Stadtschulrat für Wein (1998) *Primary Goes Europe 2: The Norfolk Challenge*, Stadtschulrat für Wein, Vienna

Stadtschulrat für Wein (1999) *Primary Goes Europe 3: Primary goes Europe in many different ways*, Stadtschulrat für Wein, Vienna

Steele, R and Suozzo, M (1994) *Teaching French Culture: Theory and Practice*, National Textbook Company, Illinois

Stempelski, S and Tomalin, B (1990) *Video in Action: Recipes for using video in language teaching*, Prentice Hall, Hemel Hempstead

Stern, HH (1992) *Issues and Options in Language Teaching*, Oxford University Press, London

Stork, D (2000) Video conferencing and modern foreign languages in the East Riding of Yorkshire, *Comenius News*, **19**, p 2

Thomas, A (1998) Sporting chance, *Times Educational Supplement*, 9 October

Thomas, G (1997) The European challenge: education for a plurilingual Europe, *Language Learning Journal* **15**, pp 74–80

Thornton, B and Cajkler W (1996) A study of Year 10 students' attitudes to German language and life, *Language Learning Journal*, **4**, pp 35–39

Thürmann, E (ed) (1995) *Bilingual Education in Secondary Schools; Learning and teaching non-language subjects through a foreign language. Second progress report on the research and development programme of Workshop 12A*, Strasbourg, Council of Europe

Tierney, D (1997) Modern languages in the primary school in France and Scotland, *Language Learning Journal*, **15**, pp7–11

Tierney, D and Dobson, P (1995) *Are you Sitting Comfortably? Telling stories to young language learners*, CILT, London

Tierney, D and Humphrey, F (1992) *Improve Your Image: The effective use of the OHP*, CILT, London

Times Educational Supplement (TES) (2000) Noticeboard: Web sites, *Times Educational Supplement*, 20 October

Tomalin, B and Stempelski, S (1993) *Cultural Awareness*, Oxford University Press, Oxford

Townshend, K (1997) *E-mail: Using electronic communications in foreign language teaching*, InfoTech 1, CILT, London

Trenchard-Morgan (1999) An account of how pupils describe ways in which they learn and/or tackle ordinary classroom or homework tasks, *Links*, **20**, pp 15–19

TTA (Teacher Training Agency) (1999) *Using Information and Communications Technology to meet Teaching Objectives in Modern Foreign Languages*, TTA, London

REFERENCES

TTA/DfEE/WOED/DENI (1999) *The Use of ICT in Subject Teaching: Expected Outcomes for Teachers in England, Wales and Northern Ireland*, TTA, London

Turner, K (1999) Working with literature, in ed N Pachler, *Teaching Modern Foreign Languages at Advanced Level*, Routledge, London

Ullmann, M (1999) History and Geography through French: CLIL in a UK secondary school, in ed J Masih, *Learning through a Foreign Language: Models, methods and outcomes*, CILT, London

Ur, P (1996) *A Course in Language Teaching: Practice and theory*, Cambridge, Cambridge University Press

Van Ek, J and Alexander, L (1975), *Threshold Level English in a European Unit/Credit System for Modern Language Learning by Adults*, Pergamon, Oxford

Walker, D (1999) The Tower of Babel available on your PC, *Times Educational Supplement*, 8 January

Wallace, M J (1998) *Action Research for Language Teachers*, Cambridge University Press, Cambridge

Warnock Report (1978) *Committee of Enquiry into the Education of Handicapped Children and Young People, Special Educational Needs*, HMSO, London

Wenden, A and Rubin, J (eds) (1987) *Learner Strategies in Language Learning*, MacMillan, New York

Wickstead, C (1993) Working with A-level literature texts: twenty-two ideas for target-language activities, *Language Learning Journal*, 7, pp 17–18

Wilkins, DA (1974a) Grammatical, situational and notional syllabuses, in eds C J Brumfit and K Johnson, *The Communicative Approach to Language Teaching*, (1979), Oxford University Press, Oxford

Wilkins, DA (1974b) Notional syllabuses and the concept of a minimum adequate grammar, in eds C J Brumfit and K Johnson *The Communicative Approach to Language Teaching*, (1979), Oxford University Press, Oxford

Wilkins, D A (1976) *Notional Syllabuses*, Oxford University Press, Oxford

Willcocks, J (1983) Pupils in transition, in eds M Galton and J Willcocks, *Moving from the Primary Classroom*, Routledge & Kegan Paul, London

Williams, J (1999) Induction for newly qualified teachers, in ed G Nicholls, *Learning to Teach*, Kogan Page, London

Williams, M and Burden, R (1997) *Psychology for Language Teachers: A social constructivist approach*, Cambridge University Press, Cambridge

Wilson, D (1999) In the classroom, *Deutsch Lehren und Lernen*, 19, pp 2–6

Wong - Fillmore, L (1985) When does teacher talk work as input?, in eds S M Gass and C G Madden, *Input in Second Language Acquisition*, Newbury House, Rowley MA

Wood, D, Bruner, J and Ross, G (1976) The role of tutoring in problem solving, *Journal of Child Psychology and Psychiatry*, 17, pp 89–100

Wright, A and Haleem, S (1991) *Visuals for the Learning Classroom*, Longman, London

Yalden, J (1983) *The Communicative Syllabus: Evolution, design and implementation*, Pergamon, New York

Index

A-level   17, 19, 36, 51, 81–83, 94, 103, 107, 119–25, 133, 186, 191, 194
Applying for a job   185–95
AS level   107,120–22
Assessment Reform Group   108–09
Association of Language Learning (ALL)   15, 65, 197
attainment targets (ATs)   25–27, 29, 34, 40, 44–45, 47–48, 51, 55, 57, 62, 110–12, 115, 134, 153–55, 161,177,191
audio   82, 89–91, 97, 100, 110, 129, 143, 170
authentic texts   7, 24, 28, 48, 66–67, 83, 87, 90–91, 97–98, 103, 123
autonomous learning   8, 24, 90, 97, 99, 111, 127, 191

boys and languages   18, 66, 86, 97, 132–35, 139–40, 191

Career Entry Profile (CEP)   14, 96
Centre for Information on Language Teaching and Research (CILT)   15, 65, 92, 95, 97, 104, 161–62, 197–99
Chomsky   4–5
classroom management   12–14, 37, 57–63, 69, 74, 80, 84, 105, 130, 138, 141, 191
computer assisted language learning (CALL)   85, 95–97
content and language integrated learning (CLIL) ix,   79, 179–84
Council of Europe framework ix,   173–79
creativity   22, 33–37, 61, 90, 120
cross-curricular links   27, 37, 45–46, 72, 160, 165, 167
cultural awareness   22, 24–25, 27–32, 34, 48, 65, 68, 73, 75, 77–81, 83, 87, 89–91, 93, 97, 103, 121–22, 129, 174–75, 191

dictionaries   31, 99, 113, 122, 129
differentiation   49, 54–55, 57, 62, 98–99, 110–11, 126, 140–41, 170, 191
disapplication   136
diversification   9–12, 17, 19–20, 22, 119, 161, 164, 194
drama   35–36, 92, 134

e-mail   76, 86–88, 93, 103–04, 143
equal opportunities viii,   131–35, 141
European Language Portfolio   177
examination boards   23, 27, 88, 107, 112–14, 116–20, 189
exchanges   16, 64, 74–80, 192, 196

flashcards   70–73, 139, 166
foreign language assistant   64, 80–84, 89, 143, 168

games   96, 134, 165–66
graded objectives movement (GOML)   6
grammar   viii, 2, 6, 7, 26, 38–40, 44, 48, 53, 66, 70, 73, 97, 99, 113, 119, 121–22, 132–35, 143, 152, 154, 157, 166, 191
groupwork   54–55, 58, 81, 99, 110–11, 134, 144, 170

homework   44–45, 49, 60, 97, 107, 110, 126–30, 133, 191

information and communication technology (ICT)   3, 13–14, 24–25, 37, 40, 45–46, 48, 56, 75–76, 85–106, 113, 115–16, 120, 134, 140, 143, 191
Internet   3, 66, 87–88, 95–98, 100–05, 126, 129

key skills,   22, 25, 37–38, 40–42, 86, 88, 105, 109, 116, 119–120, 172, 176, 191–92

INDEX

key stage 3   16–17, 19, 23, 25, 27, 29, 43–44, 48, 86–87, 107–112, 114, 135–36, 191, 194
key stage 4   16–18, 23, 25, 27, 29, 35, 39, 43–44, 48, 87, 107–08, 110, 112–19, 122–24, 132–33, 135–36, 158
Krashen   5–6, 67

language colleges   15, 17, 21, 93, 95, 104, 168, 180
Languages National Training Organisation (LNTO)   16, 21
learner strategies viii,   8, 99, 122, 134, 150–58
listening   2, 24, 26, 38, 48, 72, 78, 82, 88–89, 109–110, 120–22, 155–56, 166, 176
literacy   22, 37–42, 44, 132, 136–37, 160, 164, 169–70
literature   31, 119–21, 124

native speakers   16, 24, 28–31, 48, 75, 80, 87, 90, 103, 134, 142–43, 145, 181
Northern Ireland   10, 12–15, 23, 27, 45, 58, 65, 86, 113, 119, 161, 194, 197, 199
Nuffield Languages Inquiry   ix, 15–16, 19–21, 23, 38–39, 75, 94, 119, 132, 161, 163, 168, 172–73, 175, 180, 191

overhead transparency (OHT)   35, 71

pairwork   72, 52–53, 55, 72, 134, 144
planning   viii, 13, 25, 29, 32–33, 37, 42–43, 58–59, 62–63, 68, 70, 78, 80, 84, 86, 94, 97, 104–05, 107, 118, 130, 141, 152–53, 156, 167–68, 184, 191
primary level languages   vii, 10, 15, 23, 38–39, 159–71, 173
professional development   157, 164, 185, 195–99
programmes of study (PoS)   13, 23–27, 34, 42–45, 51, 56, 63, 87, 97, 99, 109–11, 114, 118, 140, 153, 158, 190, 194
publishing   198–99

Qualifications and Curriculum Authority (QCA)   15–17, 19, 39, 112, 121, 161

reading   2, 24, 26, 38, 48, 51, 72, 81, 87–89, 97, 102, 109–11, 120–23, 129, 138, 155–56, 175, 191

satellite television   87, 91–93, 95, 97–98, 155
scheme of work (SoW)   43–48, 81, 103
Scotland   12, 14–15, 23, 27, 65, 107, 113, 125–26, 160, 162–63, 167–69, 197, 199
SOCRATES   16, 170, 196
speaking   2, 24–26, 41, 48, 51–53, 72, 78, 81, 88–90, 110–11, 116, 121, 123–24, 129, 155–56, 166
special needs   22, 40, 44, 132, 135–41, 188
Subject Centre for Languages, Linguistics and Area Studies   16

target language   viii, 2, 7, 18, 25, 35, 41, 44–45, 48–49, 51, 56–57, 60–62, 66, 73, 75, 82, 87, 89, 110–13, 115, 133, 135, 142–49, 155, 157, 163, 165, 167, 169, 183, 188, 191–92
teaching standards   ix, 12–15, 21, 27, 32, 37, 41, 58, 63, 69, 74, 84, 105, 118, 124–25, 130, 141, 158, 171, 173, 179, 183–84, 199
textbooks   29–30, 45, 50, 64–70, 75, 78, 82, 89–92, 97, 132, 141, 144, 148, 171

video   3, 74, 89, 91–92, 97–98, 100, 129, 143, 155, 162
video camera   91, 94, 166
video conferencing   39, 76, 91, 93–94, 104, 134
visits   64, 74–80
visuals   66, 69–74, 139, 148, 166, 182–83

Wales   15–16, 23, 27, 65, 113, 119, 197
writing   2, 24–26, 38, 41, 48, 51, 61, 72, 79, 87–88, 99, 109, 111, 116, 120, 121–24, 126, 128–29, 156, 166